MARIO AND GRISI

MARIO AND GRISI

A Biography

by

ELIZABETH FORBES

LONDON
VICTOR GOLLANCZ LTD
1985

First published in Great Britain 1985
by Victor Gollancz Ltd
14 Henrietta Street, London w c2e 8qj

NOTE

The two drawings by Princess (later Queen) Victoria are copyright reserved. Reproduced by gracious permission of Her Majesty The Queen. The extracts from the Journals of Queen Victoria and Lady Geraldine Somerset are reproduced by gracious permission of Her Majesty The Queen.

British Library Cataloguing in Publication Data
Forbes, Elizabeth
    Mario and Grisi: a biography.
    1. Grisi, Giulia   2. Mario, Giovanni Matteo
    3. Singers—Italy—Biography
    I. Title
    782.1'092'2   ML420.G86/
    ISBN 0-575-03606-0

Photoset in Great Britain by
Rowland Phototypesetting Ltd, Bury St Edmunds, Suffolk
and printed by St Edmundsbury Press
Bury St Edmunds, Suffolk

Following page 50

Mario as Nemorino in *L'elisir d'amore* (*courtesy Richard Bonynge*)
Grisi as Ninetta in *La gazza ladra*
Grisi as Pamira in *L'assedio di Corinto*—drawing by Princess Victoria
  (*courtesy Royal Archives*)
Mario as Arturo in *I puritani*
Giulia Grisi—print from drawing by Lord Leighton
Grisi in the title role of *Norma*
Grisi and Mario in *Otello*—playbill

Following page 114

Mario, Grisi, Tamburini and Lablache in *Don Pasquale*
Mario as the Duke in *Rigoletto*
Grisi—marble bust by C. F. Fuller, 1858 (*courtesy Royal College of
  Music*)
Mario—marble bust by C. F. Fuller, 1857 (*courtesy Royal College of
  Music*)
Mario as Jean de Leyden in *Le Prophète*—drawing by Queen Victoria
  (*courtesy Royal Archives*)
Grisi and Mario in *Les Huguenots*

Following page 146

Mario and Viardot in *Le Prophète*
Mario as Lionel in *Martha*
Faure, Patti and Mario in *Faust*
Mario as Raoul in Les Huguenots (*courtesy Stuart-Liff Collection*)
Mario after his retirement (*courtesy Stuart-Liff Collection*)
Grisi and Mario from a photograph by Caldesi

All unacknowledged photographs are from the author's collection

Preface

THROUGHOUT THE FIRST half of the nineteenth century, Paris was regarded as the Eldorado to which all aspiring artists and musicians must make their way if they were to achieve fame and fortune. This was particularly true of singers, for the French capital, with several theatres presenting opera virtually all the year round, provided much more chance of stable employment than the leading cities of other European countries, where the seasons were shorter or, as in Italy, the political outlook was uncertain.

If many of the pilgrims who flocked across the Rhine or over the Alps were disappointed in their hopes, a few, especially among the Italian singers, did find the streets of Paris almost literally paved with gold. For many years the Théâtre-Italien, from the beginning of October to the end of March, put on an amazing series of performances with stellar casts of the popular Italian operas of the day. In the summer the whole circus moved to the King's Theatre in London, where fat fees were also to be earned, not only in the opera house but at the many private parties and receptions given by society hostesses during the season.

Another city where Italian opera flourished was Saint Petersburg, and a number of the singers wintered there, before returning to Paris or to Italy. Quite a few, mainly political exiles from the Austrian-occupied provinces of Northern Italy, the Papal States, or the Bourbon-ruled kingdom of the two Sicilies, were precluded from appearing in their native country, and made their homes in Paris, where they were certain to find relatives, friends or sympathisers. This is the story of two such singers who for totally different reasons escaped from Italy to Paris, continued to London and eventually constructed new lives together based on those cities and their opera houses.

Chapter 1

ONE EVENING IN December 1838, a feeling of unusual excitement permeated the Paris Opéra or, to give that institution its correct title, *l'Académie Royale de Musique*. The opera that night was Meyerbeer's *Robert le diable*, which had already been given over 200 times since its first performance seven years previously; despite the enormous popularity of *Robert*, that alone was not sufficient cause for the crammed house and the air of expectation shown by the audience. For several months rumours had circulated in Paris concerning a new tenor discovered by Monsieur Duponchel, director of the Opéra or, as some said, by Meyerbeer himself. The original Robert, Adolphe Nourrit, had been succeeded in most of his roles by Gilbert Duprez, but Duprez could not sing every night and it had become necessary to find another tenor to share the repertory.

Therefore, on that evening of 5 December, in the second scene of *Robert le diable*, a 28-year-old Italian tenor made his first appearance on any stage before the most critical and sophisticated audience in the world. In looks and bearing he was all that the newspaper stories had promised; such a handsome figure, with dark hair and beard, well-drawn profile and upright carriage, had rarely, if ever, been seen before at the Opéra. His voice, when he sang his opening phrase, 'Chevaliers, c'est à vous que je bois', was revealed as fresh, pure, velvety, 'like a nightingale singing in a thicket', as one member of the audience, Théophile Gautier, afterwards described it. Despite his inexperience, which showed particularly in the stiffness of his acting, and a slight Italian accent, the more noticeable for his splendid diction, the new tenor made an excellent impression. His name was Mario.

Mario, as everyone in the audience knew, was a stage-name hiding the identity of one of the younger sons of a noble family. A party of Italians in a stage-box at the Opéra that night was surprised to recognize in the new tenor the Cavaliere Giovanni de Candia, son of the Marchese de Candia, a General in the Sardinian army and himself an officer in that army until a few years previously. How did a young man from such a background come to be a professional singer on the

Paris stage? In other words, how did Giovanni de Candia become
Mario?

Giovanni Matteo de Candia was born on 17 October 1810 at Cagliari
in Sardinia, at that time united with Piedmont as the Kingdom of
Sardinia and ruled by the house of Savoy. Giovanni was the seventh
son of Don Stefano de Candia, who was then adjutant to Prince
Charles Felix, later to become King of Sardinia. His mother was
Donna Caterina Grixoni, who married Don Stefano at the age of
fourteen and bore him fourteen children. The De Candia family had
come to Sardinia from Naples, then Spanish territory, in 1720, when
Victor Amadeus II of Savoy received the island in exchange for Sicily.
Soon after the birth of Giovanni, his father was appointed Governor of
Nice, which belonged to the Kingdom of Sardinia.

Don Stefano, a typical product of his class and period, was rigidly
conservative in his opinions and devotedly loyal to his King. He
considered Napoleon as the arch-enemy of mankind and deplored the
liberal ideas released all over Europe by the French Revolution. He
could not conceive of any profession for his sons other than the Army
or the Church and in 1822, at the age of twelve, Giovanni was sent to
the Military College in Turin, where among his fellow pupils was
Cavour. Turin was still seething from an abortive revolution the
previous year, when King Victor Emanuel I had abdicated, to be
succeeded by his brother Charles Felix, who stamped out the insurrec-
tion with merciless severity.

A free, united Italy would have seemed an impossible dream to the
majority of Italians at that time, but there were already many of the
younger generation willing to devote their lives to the translation of
that dream into reality. Foremost among these patriots was Count
Camille Cavour, the practical architect of the Risorgimento and the
greatest influence on Giovanni de Candia's early life. Although
Cavour left the Turin Academy in 1826, when Giovanni was only
sixteen, the two men, born in the same year, remained friends until
Cavour's death.

Having graduated from the Academy in 1829, Giovanni joined his
regiment, the Cacciatori della Guardia, at Genoa. Here he met for the
first time another leading personality of the united Italy movement,
Giuseppe Mazzini, also destined to remain a lifelong friend. By 1831
Italy was in turmoil; there were insurrections and rebellions in Rome,
Parma, Modena and Tuscany. Cavour and Mazzini were both imprisoned and later exiled. Members of Mazzini's Young Italy party
were not only threatened with exile or even death, but those who
refused to betray their comrades were heavily fined and imprisoned

for two years. The sympathy for his two exiled friends openly expressed by Giovanni was not calculated to make him popular with his superior officers.

Life in the Army, however, had its more agreeable side. Giovanni who, in common with the rest of his family, had started to sing as soon as he could speak, was in great demand by his brother officers as an entertainer. Never happier than when he was singing, Giovanni obliged with songs from the operas currently popular in Italy— Bellini's *La straniera* and Donizetti's *Anna Bolena* were among recent successes. A love of music and facility in expressing it appears to have been transmitted to her children by Donna Caterina de Candia, herself the possessor of a fine contralto voice. In the dark, shuttered and barred De Candia palazzo at Cagliari, where women were kept in almost oriental seclusion, whatever there was of light and human warmth had emanated from Donna Caterina, to be crystallized in the music made by the children and their mother.

In 1832 the Duchesse de Berri, exiled from France, interrupted her wanderings to stay for some time in Genoa and Giovanni was appointed her aide-de-camp. The Duchess's Bourbon relatives— she was the daughter of Francis IV, King of Naples—flocked to the little court, as did many of the Sardinian nobles and their families. Giovanni, young, handsome, well-born, with a ravishing tenor voice, made many conquests among the ladies, one of whom was shortly to give practical demonstration of the strength of her affection for him.

Later the same year, Giovanni was transferred to Nice as aide-de-camp to his father, who had been appointed Governor of the city for the second time. Frequent disputes arose between father and son, as Giovanni openly proclaimed his sympathy for the Young Italy party, while Don Stefano took every opportunity to reprimand his aide-de-camp, threatening him with relegation to the ranks or a posting back to Sardinia. In the early autumn of 1835, one of Giovanni's brother-officers, who shared his political views, suddenly disappeared and it was rumoured that he had been imprisoned in Genoa. Giovanni expressed his indignation to Don Stefano, who lost his temper and ordered his son back to Genoa, where he would be given 'important despatches'. On his arrival in Genoa, Giovanni discovered that not only were these despatches to be taken to Cagliari, but that his friend was imprisoned there, not in Genoa. Obviously a similar fate awaited Giovanni himself if he obeyed orders and returned to Cagliari.

Giovanni sought advice from his uncle, a high official at the Sardinian court, but the latter could tell him only that he was bound to comply with his father's command. Next he was summoned to the

presence of the Governor, the Marchese Paolucci, a friend of Don
Stefano and also a fierce opponent of Mazzini and his party. The
Governor informed Giovanni that if he did not take the despatches as
ordered, he would have to consider himself as under arrest. In a final
attempt to avert the now imminent catastrophe, Giovanni begged an
audience with the King, which was granted him. But in spite of—or
perhaps because of—the liberal inclinations of his youth, Charles
Albert, who had succeeded his distant cousin Charles Felix to the
Sardinian throne, was not willing to help a rebel and only confirmed
the decision of Don Stefano and Marchese Paolucci: Giovanni was
either to take the despatches as ordered to Cagliari, where presumably
he would be arrested or he would be imprisoned immediately in
Genoa.

There was only one way out of the impasse and after several hours
of agonizing doubt and hesitation, Giovanni took it. After burning
any papers that might incriminate his friends, he removed his uniform
and sent in his resignation, aware that it would not be accepted and
that from then on he was a deserter, in grave danger of his life. At this
point, when all seemed lost, help was offered from a totally unexpected direction. One of the Queen of Sardinia's ladies-in-waiting,
whom Giovanni had met and danced with at the receptions and balls
given for the Duchess de Berri, hid him in her own apartments in the
Royal Palace for over a month, until the hue and cry of the search for
the missing officer had died down. Towards the end of October
Giovanni was able to reach the port and escape from Genoa in a small
fishing smack. The weather was very bad and the boat crammed
with refugees, but after seventeen days at sea they arrived safely in
Marseilles.

Giovanni was promptly arrested by the police, but released a few
hours later after his identity had been established. He had been
mistaken for Don Carlos of Spain, son of Carlos IV, who was
suspected of trying to enter France in disguise. Giovanni had at one
time thought of travelling on to Spain, but he was persuaded that he
would be safer in France. Through the Sardinian Consul in Marseilles,
Cavaliere Peppino Polgano, Giovanni learnt that King Charles Albert
was willing to pardon him if he would reveal the names of those who
had helped him to escape and that his father would also forgive him on
the same terms. Sending back an indignant refusal to betray his
friends, Giovanni requested his father to meet him at the frontier.

Meanwhile the De Candia family had sent an emissary in the person
of Don Francesco Roych, the husband of Giovanni's sister Teresa. He
arrived in Marseilles on Christmas Day and found Giovanni at

the opera, where Auber's *Gustave III* was being performed. Don Francesco brought a message from Giovanni's mother, begging him to meet her. The two men set out for the frontier in a snowstorm, which became so bad that they had to leave their coach and walk the last few miles. At Saint-Laurent, in the house of an Englishman named David, they met Donna Caterina, accompanied by Donna Teresa. Don Stefano had refused to see his son. Both ladies pleaded with Giovanni to return, but as the terms were quite unacceptable, no amount of tears could make him change his mind.

After the departure of his mother, sister and brother-in-law, Giovanni waited a few days at the frontier in case his father might still relent. But there was no further word from Don Stefano and Giovanni set off for Paris. He found the French capital full of Italian exiles, all quite delighted to welcome Giovanni de Candia to their circle. Foremost among these expatriates were the Prince and Princess Belgioioso who, after five years of married life, had decided that they were happier apart. They continued to share the same house, though they no longer co-habited. As one of the Princess's biographers wrote, 'music and political intrigue this ill-assorted couple enjoyed in common, but these constituted the only bonds which held them together. At their home all the great musicians of the day found an enthusiastic welcome and an appreciative audience.'

The Princess's salon was patronized not only by musicians such as Chopin, Thalberg, Liszt, Rossini and Bellini, but also by literary celebrities of the order of George Sand, Alfred de Musset, Balzac, Alessandro Manzoni and Heine, who was heard to remark that Italy had now produced at least three outstanding figures—Raphael, Rossini and the Princess Belgioioso. The Prince, an extremely kind and generous man, spent a great deal of his fortune in supporting the poorer Italian exiles. He offered to assist Giovanni with a loan, as the young man was now completely penniless. Giovanni was too proud to accept money that he saw no prospect of being able to repay and refused the offer.

Some source of income had, however, become necessary to a young man brought up in comparative luxury, with the expensive tastes of his age and social position, living, moreover, in a city where those tastes were easy to gratify, provided one had the means to pay for them. The former officer swallowed his pride and gave lessons in fencing and equitation, two accomplishments at which he excelled. He also began to sing, literally, for his supper. The possessor of a voice as beautiful as his could always find a welcome in any of the Parisian salons. Prince Belgioioso was also a gifted amateur singer and the two friends frequently sang duets together. But Giovanni was still very far from thinking of becoming a professional singer. The idea of appearing on the public stage was not one to occur to a gentleman.

In the summer of 1837 Giovanni went to London to see if he could find any suitable employment. Through an old family friend, Rear-Admiral Fielding, he approached the Duke of Wellington, hoping for a commission in the British Army, but the Duke, though affable, could not help. Meanwhile London was full of friends, such as Charles and Henry Greville, while every door was open, as in Paris, to a handsome young man who sang like an angel. But such an existence could not continue indefinitely; the season ended and the society hostesses departed to their country estates. Early in September Giovanni returned to Paris with Henry Greville, who was attached to the British Embassy there. A few weeks later Greville noted in his diary: 'I live a great deal with De Candia, with whom I formed a close acquaintance in London and whom I saw almost daily. Our acquaintance, from a similarity of tastes and perhaps from a great dissimilarity of opinions, and still more from the interest which his unfortunate position excited in me, had quickly ripened into friendship.'

Among the wealthier Italian exiles in Paris was the Marchese de Brême, later Duke of Sartirana, whose purse was always at the disposal of his poorer compatriots. One evening in October 1837, a few weeks after Giovanni's return from London, when he was seriously considering going to America to see if he could find employment there, the young man was asked by De Brême, as so often before, to sing to the guests after a supper party. When Giovanni and De Brême came to leave the party, they discovered that a large crowd had gathered in the street outside to listen to the tenor. De Brême suggested, only half seriously, that Giovanni should take up singing as a career. A few days later, at a musical soirée given by the Countess Merlin, the guests included, as well as Prince Belgioioso, De Brême and Giovanni, both Duponchel, director of the Opéra, and Meyerbeer.

The composer asked Giovanni to sing some of the music from his latest opera, *Les Huguenots*, which had first been produced, with huge success, some eighteen months previously. Giovanni complied and the whole company was enchanted, not least Meyerbeer, always on the lookout for suitable new interpreters of his music, and Duponchel, who needed another tenor. After that evening it appears to have been taken for granted that Giovanni de Candia should adopt the career of operatic singer. Though he himself was still very doubtful about the idea, all his friends were enthusiastic.

Henry Greville put the case in a nutshell: 'he has a great deal of talent and facility, particularly for music, having one of the finest voices I ever heard, and a good deal of imagination (of this, indeed, too much for his own welfare), and I think he is worthy of a better lot than that which has befallen upon him. As it is, it seems probable that, for want of other means of gaining for himself an independence, he will be obliged to resort to the stage as a profession, and I think it not improbable but that, with study and with his remarkable advantages of looks and voice, he may rise to great eminence in this very thorny career.'

Greville pointed out to the reluctant Giovanni that independence should be his first object and that despite 'the scruples which a man of birth and education may justly entertain against embracing a profession which is considered as more or less inferior to any other', there was nothing degrading in adopting the only career likely to ensure that independence. When Duponchel offered to pay him a year's salary while he studied and then engage him at the Opéra, Giovanni capitulated. He had no choice. Two singing teachers were provided, Louis Ponchard and Giulio Bordogni, both of them former tenors, while Michelot of the Comédie Française instructed him in stage deportment. Meyerbeer himself coached him in the part of Robert, chosen for his debut. Working harder than he had ever had to work in his life before, Giovanni had no time to ponder or regret his decision.

Through his highly efficient network of spies, King Charles Albert heard that a member of the De Candia family was about to appear on the public stage. A message was sent to Giovanni by way of the Sardinian Embassy in Paris, offering him a free pardon to return to Italy, still on the same condition that he divulge the names of the people who had helped him to escape. Giovanni again refused the offer, but in a letter to his mother he promised not to use the name of De Candia for the stage and also swore never to sing professionally in Italy—an oath he was always to keep.

There only remained the choice of a *nom-de-guerre*. At Meyerbeer's house one evening after dinner, while the composer played the piano and the other guests sat smoking and discussing possible names, Giovanni suddenly made up his mind. An ancestor of his, brother to Lucrezia Borgia and son of Pope Alexander VI, had rebelled against *his* father and was consequently assassinated on Monte Mario in Rome. His widow and two sons had fled to Spain and from one of those sons was descended the De Candia family. Furthermore, Caius Marius, Roman general and consul of the first century BC, had always been a great hero to Giovanni, who at two in the morning leapt to his feet in

Meyerbeer's music-room, crying: *'Je l'ai, oui! Mario sera mon nom.'* So Giovanni de Candia became Mario, and Mario he remained for the rest of his life.

Robert le diable, chosen for the new tenor's début, was Meyerbeer's first French opera. The German composer had arrived in Paris in 1826 to supervise the production there of his Italian opera *Il crociato in Egitto*, last and most successful of a series of such works. *Robert*, with a text by the prolific playwright and librettist Eugène Scribe, was finished and ready for production when the July revolution of 1830 broke out, closing the theatres. After the accession of King Louis-Philippe, the Opéra reopened under a new director, Dr Véron, who inaugurated, with the staging of *Robert de diable* in November 1833, a style of French grand opera that was to dominate the repertory for nearly 40 years. *Robert* and the three subsequent Scribe/Meyerbeer grand operas all followed the same pattern. They were in five acts; they had a highly dramatic plot, with many characters and a strong quasi-historical interest; an important part in the action was reserved for the chorus; above all, there was at least one opportunity for a really spectacular ballet—in *Robert* this was provided by the cloister scene, where the ghosts of nuns unfaithful to their vows rise from their tombs, led by the Abbess, who was danced at the first performance by Marie Taglioni.

On the evening of 5 December 1838, therefore, when every box was crammed, every seat taken well before the rise of the curtain and even King Louis-Philippe and Queen Amélie had taken their places, it was no easy trial that awaited Mario. The role of Robert was long and heavy for a débutant, while a large proportion of the audience had memories not only of Duprez but also of Nourrit with which to compare the new tenor. As he waited for his entrance, Mario must have felt a little like an early Christian about to face the lions in the Colosseum, aware that at any moment the spectators might turn down their thumbs.

No such disaster occurred, however, and the friendly applause that greeted Mario on his first entrance gave him the necessary confidence to attack his role successfully. Most revealing of the many descriptions of this performance is the one, already quoted, by Théophile Gautier. No orthodox music critic, Gautier used his painter's eye as well as his wonderfully facile pen to evoke a scene, a character, an emotion or even a voice. He could convey a very exact impression of an actor or a singer especially when, as in the case of Mario, the performer appealed to Gautier's highly sensitive appreciation of physical beauty, whether of form or of sound.

M. Mario has a voice that is fresh, pure, velvety, with an admirable and youthful timbre. It is like a nightingale that sings in a thicket. He excels in rendering tender thoughts of love and melancholy, regret for a lost country, and all the sweetest sentiments of the soul; not that he is incapable of energy and strength—on the contrary; but the character of his talent is essentially elegiac; there is something pastoral and bucolic about it that reminds one of a beautiful Greek shepherd, singing at the foot of a laurel to a fugitive nymph, in rhymed couplets, elegant and naïf at the same time.

Meyerbeer had expressly composed a song for Mario, a Prayer in which Robert invoked the spirit of his mother, and begged for her blessing. This number was much applauded, as was Robert's cavatina 'Ah! qu'elle est belle!' At the end of the performance the new tenor was called before the curtain together with the soprano Julie Dorus-Gras, who sang Alice, and the bass Nicolas Levasseur, who sang Bertram, both members of the original cast of *Robert le diable*. The consensus of opinion was that Mario had acquitted himself extremely well, despite a certain awkwardness that betrayed his lack of experience.

Robert was repeated on average three times a month for the rest of the season. Meanwhile Mario was studying a new part, the title role of Rossini's *Le Comte Ory*. He also appeared at a concert given in aid of the victims of an earthquake in Martinique, when he sang for the first time in public music from the regular Italian operatic repertory, including excerpts from Rossini's *L'Italiana in Algeri*, Bellini's *Beatrice di Tenda* and Donizetti's *Roberto Devereux*, which last work had only recently received its first Paris performance. Donizetti was apparently present at the concert. Mario was also made to sing some verses by Nourrit, written shortly before the death of the great French tenor, who had committed suicide in Naples during March 1839. According to Hector Berlioz, writing in *Le Journal des Débats*, 'this so-called swan-song was quite out of place in such a programme and general opinion agreed that it would have been much better to include an excerpt from the charming score of *Le Comte Ory*, in which Mario has just appeared so successfully.'

The revival of *Le Comte Ory* took place on 6 May 1839 when the cast again included Dorus-Gras and Levasseur, as well as Mario. Berlioz considered that Comte Ory, though not such a demanding role as Meyerbeer's Robert, 'nevertheless requires from actor and singer certain rather rare talents. It is therefore already high praise of Mario to report his success. He still appears ill at ease quite often; he does not know how to bring a character to life, he hesitates or stays motionless when the action requires decisive gesture; nor is his singing what it will become when he has worked to smooth certain rough and throaty notes that mar it; but his voice is open, natural, with an extended range, sonorous at the bottom, which is very unusual, and biting at the top . . . Above all the voice is perfectly in tune, which, although the first and most important attribute of all, none the less is conspicuous by its absence in many famous singers.'

Berlioz also commented on the handsome face and elegant bearing of the young singer, assets in any role but especially in a part such as Comte Ory. Rossini's comic opera was given four more performances during May, then at the end of the month Mario, who had been granted eight weeks leave of absence from the Opéra, left Paris for London, where he was engaged to sing in the Italian opera season at Her Majesty's Theatre. The English newspapers had announced Mario's engagement in London as early as the middle of April, but it was not until Thursday 6 June, 1839 that he made his first appearance at Her Majesty's, singing the part of Gennaro in Donizetti's *Lucrezia Borgia*, an opera new to London. Lucrezia, who is in fact Gennaro's mother, was sung by Giulia Grisi.

Though it seems almost impossible that Mario and Grisi should not have met before this, or at least seen each other on stage, apparently they had not. During the previous winter while Mario was appearing at the Opéra in Paris, Grisi was singing at the Théâtre-Italien in the same city, where she had sung for the last seven seasons. The Opéra played on Monday, Wednesday and Friday; the Italiens on Tuesday, Thursday and Saturday, with extra nights on Sunday. But during his earlier years in Paris Mario had had no money to spare for opera tickets while the months since he himself began to sing professionally had been too occupied to permit any visits to the theatre.

While in London during the early summer of 1837, Mario had queued up for the pit at the King's Theatre (as Her Majesty's was called before the accession of Queen Victoria on 20 June), in order to hear Grisi. In the queue beside him was a French gentleman with whom he got into conversation. But the opera was cancelled and Mario obtained nothing from the long wait apart from the acquaintance of the future Emperor Napoleon III.

When they finally came face to face at the rehearsals for *Lucrezia Borgia* in June 1839, Mario and Grisi therefore knew each other by repute alone. Mario saw a beautiful woman of his own age, with black hair and blue eyes, who had been singing for more than ten years. Grisi saw a good-looking young man whose career was only just beginning. That they felt an immediate sympathy for each other is certain.

But Grisi's affections were for the moment engaged elsewhere—
she was in fact pregnant—so her interest in the new tenor,
though proprietorial from the start, was limited to friendly patronage.
Neither Mario nor Grisi could have been aware that they would
spend the next 30 years together in a unique professional and
personal partnership.

Chapter 2

GIULIA GRISI WAS born on 22 May 1811 in Milan. Her father, Gaetano Grisi, was an engineer officer in the service of Napoleon. Although Italian by birth, Gaetano was educated from the age of twelve in Paris, where he lived through the Revolution and the Reign of Terror. Many years later he described to his grandchildren how he had stood in the crowd to watch Charlotte Corday pass by on the tumbril taking her to the guillotine for the murder of Marat. Gaetano Grisi did not die until 1871, when in his late nineties. Giulia's mother, Giovanna Grassini, died when comparatively young, having borne her husband six children of whom only two, Giulia and her elder sister Giuditta, also a singer, survived infancy.

Giovanna was sister to the renowned contralto Josephina Grassini, who so captivated Napoleon when he heard her sing at a gala performance in Milan after the battle of Marengo that he invited her to return to Paris with him: Giulia and Giuditta undoubtedly inherited musical talent from their mother's side of the family; but vocal ability also flourished in their paternal heritage. Gaetano's brother had two daughters, Ernesta, who had a successful if unspectacular career as a mezzo soprano, and Carlotta, the famous dancer, who also studied singing as a girl.

Giulia was educated at a convent in Gorizia, a small town between Trieste and Udine. She was taught the rudiments of music and to play the piano by the nuns, and displayed a talent for singing at a very early age. After leaving the convent at the age of fourteen, she made her home with her aunt Grassini in Milan, or with her sister Giuditta, who began her career in 1826 at Vienna in Rossini's *Bianca e Faliero*. Giulia studied in Bologna with Antonio Giacomelli and Giacomo Guglielmi, also taking lessons with Grassini and, probably, her sister.

In 1827 Giuditta was engaged at the Teatro alla Pergola in Florence. The following spring she sang at Parma, Turin and Lucca, before returning to Florence in the autumn. She was apparently instrumental in arranging, that same autumn of 1828, for her younger sister's début. The seventeen-year-old Giulia Grisi made her first appearance on any stage at the Teatro Comunale in Bologna, singing the small part of

Emma in Rossini's opera *Zelmira*. Her performance was successful and resulted in an engagement at the Comunale for the forthcoming Carnival season.

Meanwhile, in late November or early December, a young man arrived in Bologna on his way south to Sicily. This was the Irish composer Michael William Balfe who, under the name of Guglielmo Balfe, had a short but successful career as a baritone, before turning all his energies to composition. Balfe, only three years older than Giulia, had been singing Figaro in Rossini's *Il barbiere di Siviglia* at the Théâtre-Italien in Paris. He was about to fulfil an engagement at the Real Teatro Carolino in Palermo and broke his journey in Bologna to visit his patron, the Marchese Sampieri.

Giulia Grisi and Balfe met at a ball given in honour of the Princess Baciocchi. They were immediately attracted to each other. Soprano and baritone sang solos and duets, to their mutual satisfaction and to the great delight of the guests. Balfe stayed on in Bologna for some weeks. To celebrate the birthday of his patron he composed a cantata, in which the Marchese's friends sang as chorus. The soloists included Giulia Grisi and the tenor Francesco Pedrazzi, who had only recently made his début and who would, five years later, create the role of Gennaro in *Lucrezia Borgia* at La Scala, Milan. Balfe himself accompanied the singers. The young Irishman finally continued his journey to Palermo; his path was to cross Giulia's fairly frequently in later years.

During the Carnival season of 1829 at Bologna, Giulia sang in Rossini's *Torvaldo e Dorliska* and *Il barbiere*; she also appeared in *Lo sposo di provincia* by Giacomo Cordella, a Neapolitan composer whose operas achieved a certain popularity in the 1820s. Her success was such that she was approached by the impresario Alessandro Lanari, then managing the Pergola in Florence, who put her under contract for six years. This rash signing away of her independence was to have momentous consequences for the young singer, but for the moment Lanari's management was wholly beneficial to her career.

During her first season in Florence, Giulia added two more Rossini operas, *Tancredi* and *Riccardo e Zoraide*, to her repertory. She sang the part of Giulietta in Vaccai's *Giulietta e Romeo*, and on 26 December she appeared in a revival of *Ezio* by Filippo Celli, with whom she also studied for some months. Giuditta, meanwhile, was engaged at the Teatro La Fenice in Venice, where on 11 March 1830 she created the role of Romeo in Bellini's *I Capuleti e i Montecchi*.

In May 1830 Giulia, who was singing at Pisa, wrote an affectionate letter to Lanari, with whom she was still on the best of terms. The impresario had apparently suggested the transfer of his nineteen-year-old prima donna to Milan. 'Thank you for your kindness,' wrote Giulia, 'but have patience. I would not sing at La Scala this year for all the gold in the world. Later I would go if it were necessary.' The letter ended with various messages to her friends and colleagues in Florence. It also sent best wishes to Lanari from Marliani, introducing another musician destined to play a significant role in Giulia's life.

Count Marco Aurelio Marliani, born in 1805 and therefore six years older than Giulia, had just graduated in Philosophy at Siena University but was determined to become a composer. The son of a wealthy family, he was an ardent supporter of the movement for a free, united Italy and gave all his money to the Carbonari, the precursors of Mazzini's Young Italy party. While pursuing his own musical studies, Marliani earned a living as a singing teacher.

Giulia, who had sung Desdemona in Rossini's *Otello* and the title role of the same composer's *Semiramide* at Pisa, returned for a second season to the Pergola in Florence, where in February 1831 she appeared as Giulietta in Bellini's operatic version of the Shakespeare tragedy. Then Lanari transferred his increasingly valuable property to the Teatro alla Scala, Milan. Ironically, the soprano herself got none of the gold she had renounced the previous year, though the impresario undoubtedly earned a great deal from the transaction.

Giulia Grisi made her debut at the most prestigious theatre in Italy on 20 September 1831, in the first performance of *Ulla di Bassora* by Feliciano Strepponi (whose daughter Giuseppina later became Verdi's second wife). Her next appearance at La Scala, during November, was in Carlo Coccia's *Enrico di Montfort*, when she was joined by her sister Giuditta. A short break followed, then on 26 December 1831 the new season opened with the first performance of Bellini's *Norma*. The title role was sung by Giuditta Pasta, for over a decade the leading soprano in Paris and London; Domenico Donzelli took the heroic tenor part of Pollione; and Giulia Grisi sang Adalgisa.

Bellini's opera was coldly received by its first audience. According to the composer himself, there were various reasons for this: the cast was tired, having had to rehearse the second act on the morning of the première; then Donzelli did not yet know his part; and a small but vociferous section of the audience was prejudiced against Pasta, who was singing at La Scala for the first time, though she had just finished a highly successful season at the Teatro Carcano in Milan, during which she created the title roles of Bellini's *La sonnambula* and Donizetti's *Anna Bolena*. The second performance of *Norma* went much better and the opera's popularity grew with every repetition. There were more than 30 performances at La Scala that season alone.

The youthful Adalgisa gained her fair share of praise and applause, though Bellini considered her a trifle cold and the Russian composer Mikhail Glinka, who attended a performance of *Norma* in the spring of 1832, wrote in his *Memoirs* that Giulia Grisi 'sang in a sort of caterwauling manner, that is, wishing to soften or modify a given musical phrase, she more or less miaowed in her nose.' In between performances of *Norma*, Giulia also sang Gulnara in Pacini's *Il corsaro*, Jane Seymour in *Anna Bolena*, which was heard at La Scala for the first time on 25 February 1832, and Adelia in the première of another Donizetti opera, *Ugo, conte di Parigi*, on 13 March. In all, she sang 62 performances during the season, which ended in April.

Giulia's contract with Lanari, transferred to La Scala, still had at least three years to run. All attempts to break it, on the grounds that she had signed it without her father's consent, while still a minor, were unsuccessful. Meanwhile she was singing leading roles at a salary that had looked good to an inexperienced beginner but which now seemed totally inadequate. Also, Giulia would not have been human had she not cast longing eyes on the title roles of *Norma* and *Anna Bolena* as she sang in those operas beside Pasta. Giulia, by listening and watching, had learnt a great deal from the older singer, with whom she studied for a brief period as well. It seems probable that she also worked with Marliani, as it was to him that she turned for help in her determination to get out of the contract by the only way left to her: flight from Milan.

Giulia's aunt Grassini was living in Paris; her sister Giuditta, who that spring and summer was engaged to sing in London at the King's Theatre, had a contract with the Théâtre-Italien in Paris for the autumn and winter season. Paris was the capital of the musical world, the Mecca of all singers and musicians. Giulia resolved to escape to Paris and Marliani, determined to leave Italy because of the growing danger occasioned by his political opinions and also aware that he stood a better chance of realizing his musical ambitions in Paris than in Italy, agreed to accompany her.

The two fugitives left Milan some time during the summer. According to legend it was discovered, when they reached the Swiss border at Bellinzona, that they had forgotten their passports. Marliani returned to Milan for them but Giulia, fearing pursuit, borrowed her maid's passport to cross the border and instead of waiting for her escort in Switzerland as arranged, continued alone, travelling without pause until she reached Paris. As a result of her breach of contract, Giulia Grisi never sang professionally in Italy again.

The Théâtre-Italien, then managed by Édouard Robert and Carlo Severini, with Rossini acting as adviser, was urgently in need of a prima donna. Maria Malibran, elder daughter of the Spanish tenor Manuel Garcia, had had to cancel her engagement at the theatre in January 1832 as she was pregnant, a consequence of her tempestuous love affair with the Belgian violinist Charles de Bériot. Her child did not survive and Malibran was contracted to return to the Italiens in April. Instead, she went to Italy accompanied by Bériot. They, too, like Giulia and Marliani, had trouble at the Lombard frontier, though travelling in the opposite direction. Having no passports they had to wait until the necessary papers were obtained from Milan.

Rossini had heard Giulia sing in Bologna, so on her arrival in Paris she had no difficulty in getting an engagement at the Théâtre-Italien. She made her Paris début on 16 October 1832 in the title role of *Semiramide*. A month later Giuditta Grisi made her first appearance at the Italiens in Bellini's *La straniera*. Giulia also sang Desdemona, a role in which she had inevitably to stand comparison with both Pasta and Malibran. Then on 10 January 1833 the sisters appeared together as Romeo and Juliet in *I Capuleti e i Montecchi*. Giuditta Grisi was not much appreciated by the Parisian public, who considered her voice unduly harsh; but Giulia, though as yet unable to rival Pasta or Malibran as actress and interpreter, won all hearts with the freshness of her voice and the youthful beauty of her face and figure.

The six months during which the Théâtre-Italien was closed were spent by Giulia in study with Marliani, now established in Paris as teacher of singing as well as student of composition. When the Italiens reopened in October, Giulia fulfilled one of her ambitions: she took over the title role of *Anna Bolena*. She also sang Rosina in *Il barbiere* and, on 24 October, Ninetta in Rossini's *La gazza ladra*. During December she took the part of Zerlina in Mozart's *Don Giovanni* and in January 1834 that of Elena in yet another Rossini opera, *La donna del lago*.

Marliani's first opera, *Il bravo*, was performed at the Théâtre-Italien on 1 February, with Giulia Grisi as the heroine, Violetta Tiepolo, the tenor Giovanni Rubini in the title role and the bass Antonio Tamburini as the villainous Gradenigo, his rival for the affections of Violetta. Despite the acknowledged excellence of the performance, the opera was not a success, but at least it allowed Marliani to gain professional experience in the theatre.

After two seasons, Giulia was firmly established in Paris and ready to embark on the next stage in her career: the conquest of London. The company at the King's Theatre in 1834 included the tenors Nikolay

Ivanov and Alberico Curioni as well as Rubini and Tamburini. The new soprano was billed to make her first appearance on Tuesday 8 April, as Ninetta in *La gazza ladra*.

This performance, according to one member of the audience, the Reverend T. C. Cox, was to remain for ever in the records of the King's Theatre as a night 'marked with white chalk'. The overture was so well played that it had to be repeated, and the delay caused some impatience, manifested by a hum of conversation throughout the first scene, which passed 'all but in dumb show until the moment arrived for the entrée of Ninetta', when the house was immediately hushed to absolute quiet. 'When Grisi came down the bridge upon the stage,' continued Cox, 'there was on the instant such a burst of applause that made the house ring from end to end.' Hardly anyone in the audience knew anything about her abilities, 'but the personal beauty of that youthful Italian face, the slimness of her figure, and the modest confidence' of her demeanour roused even the most impassive spectator to wild excitement.

But Giulia did not win over the London audience by her charm and beauty alone, as Cox made clear: 'The peculiarity of her rich and full tone, the decision of her manner, and the undoubted signs of her proficiency, disarmed all criticism, and made her at once that favourite she never ceased to be so long as she remained in the full vigour of her powers.'

A week later, Giulia appeared in *Anna Bolena*, and won equal praise for her portrayal of Donizetti's unhappy heroine. According to the critic of *The Times*, 'her singing was exquisite throughout, far too good for the music, but it might be said to give it a new charm, so much did the workmanship excel the material.' Another critic, amateur but even at the age of fifteen well-informed and with decided opinions of her own, attended the performance of *Anna Bolena* on 19 April. This was the Princess Victoria. She considered Grisi 'a most beautiful singer and actress and is likewise very young and pretty.' The Princess particularly admired Anna's mad-scene at the end of the opera.

Grisi's next role was Desdemona, which she sang in a performance of *Otello* on 22 April. This time, memories of Malibran could not altogether be effaced by the new singer. Grisi's Donna Anna, on the other hand, first heard when *Don Giovanni* entered the repertory on Thursday 25 April, was considered the finest ever to have been seen or heard in London. The role was one that obviously suited Grisi much better than that of Zerlina, and she continued to sing Donna Anna for the rest of her career.

Two Rossini operas, *La donna del lago* on 27 May and *L'assedio di Corinto* on 5 June, were neither of them particularly successful despite the presence of Grisi, Rubini and Tamburini in the casts, but the same three singers in *Il barbiere* 'was indeed an event to be remembered', as Cox admitted, since the performance 'embraced a cast that since that time has not been surpassed'. This production was transferred to Covent Garden for one performance on 4 July, but Grisi had already appeared at that theatre the previous month, when she sang the finale of *Anna Bolena* at a benefit performance for the stage manager.

Grisi's last new part of the season was Amina in Bellini's *La sonnambula*, which she sang on 10 July. Here again the comparison with Malibran was unavoidable and not in favour of the younger singer. The previous year Malibran had sung *La sonnambula* in English at Drury Lane and later at Covent Garden, to enormous public and critical acclaim. Amina never became one of Grisi's favourite roles; she sang it infrequently and then usually outside London.

Whatever the critical reservations, Giulia Grisi's first London season had been a succession of public triumphs. The pattern of her professional life was set for the next few years: six months in Paris from October to March, the spring and summer in London, followed by a concert tour in the English provinces. Her colleagues on both sides of the Channel invariably included Rubini, Tamburini and, from 1835, Luigi Lablache, the great Neapolitan-born bass whose enormous size was equalled by his artistic stature.

Two operas were composed for this unrivalled quartet in 1835—Bellini's *I puritani* and Donizetti's *Marin Faliero*. The former had its première on 24 January at the Théâtre-Italien in Paris and was an instant success; the first London performance at the King's Theatre on 21 May was equally triumphant. The latter opera was coldly received, both in Paris (12 March) and London (14 May). 'On such occasions there is always a success and a failure,' wrote Henry Chorley, music critic of the *Athenaeum*. 'The public will not endure two favourites . . . *Marin Faliero* languished—in part from the want of interest in the female character—a fault fatal to an opera's popularity. On the other hand, from first to last note, *I puritani* was found enchanting.'

That summer, according to Chorley, 'London was steeped in the music of *I puritani*; organs ground it, adventurous amateurs dared it, the singers themselves sang it to such satiety as to lose all consciousness of what they were engaged in and, once launched, to go on mechanically. I must have heard Mlle. Grisi's Polacca that year alone, if once, one hundred times—to speak without exaggeration.'

Meanwhile on Monday 18 May, three days before the first performance of Bellini's opera at the King's Theatre, Princess Victoria was given a preview of the new work at an evening party in Kensington Palace. The concert began at half-past ten; the singers engaged were Grisi, Rubini, Tamburini and Lablache—the *Puritani* quartet as they had now been christened—plus Ivanov and, in the second half, Malibran. 'Grisi is *quite beautiful* off the stage', wrote Princess Victoria in her journal. 'She is not tall and rather pale; and she has such a lovely mild expression in her face . . . She has such beautiful dark eyes with fine long eyelashes, a fine nose, and very sweet mouth . . . Her beautiful dark hair was as usual quite flat in front with an amethyst bandeau round it, and a fine plait at the very back of her head. She is very quiet, ladylike and unaffected in her manners.'

The concert began with four numbers by Rossini, two from *L'assedio di Corinto*, one from *Guillaume Tell* and one, an aria for Grisi, from *La donna del lago*. Next came the first excerpt from *I puritani*, the duet for two basses (or baritone and bass, as we would say today) 'Il rival salvar tu dei', sung by Tamburini and Lablache. 'They sing beautifully together,' commented Princess Victoria, 'Lablache's voice is immensely powerful but not too much so (for my taste) *even* in a room. Tamburini's too is most splendid. He is even a more skilful and finished singer than Lablache.'

Rubini then sang an aria from *Marin Faliero* and the first half of the concert ended with a trio from *Guillaume Tell*. Just before the interval, when the guests went into the refreshment room, Malibran arrived. 'She was dressed in white satin with a scarlet hat and feathers,' recorded the Princess. 'She is shorter than Grisi and *not near so pretty*.' The second half began with another piece from *I puritani*, Elvira's Polacca 'Son vergin vezzosa,' which 'Grisi sang most exquisitely, accompanied by all the singers except Malibran.' A duet for Grisi and Tamburini from *L'assedio* followed and then Malibran sang an aria from *Irene* by Persiani. 'Her low notes are beautiful,' thought Princess Victoria, 'but her high notes are thick and not clear. *I* like Grisi by far *better* than her.'

The soprano/tenor duet from *I puritani* was followed by an aria for Ivanov by Pacini and a duet for Malibran and Lablache by Fioravanti. The concert ended with 'A te o cara', the quartet from *I puritani*. 'It was the *most delightful concert I ever heard,*' enthused Princess Victoria. 'It was Mamma's birthday present for me. [Victoria would be sixteen on 24 May.] I stayed up till 20 minutes past 1. I was MOST EXCEEDINGLY DELIGHTED.'

Later in the season Princess Victoria saw at least two actual performances of *I puritani* at the King's Theatre. By 14 July she was already calling the opera the *dear Puritani* and noticing that Grisi 'forgot to change her dress when she came on to sing the Polacca. In general she comes on to sing that as a bride, attired in a white satin dress with a wreath of white roses round her head; instead of which she remained in her first dress . . . of blue satin with a little sort of handkerchief at the back of her head.'

Princess Victoria also commented that Grisi, though in perfect voice, had grown thinner and showed 'her many fatigues in her face.' One of these fatigues was the realization of another of Grisi's ambitions—to sing the title role of *Norma*. This was on Thursday 25 June in a benefit performance for Curioni, who took the part of Pollione. Next day the critic of *The Times* expressed rather qualified approval of Grisi's first attempt at a role which was to become one of her finest interpretations. 'Strange to say there was more to criticize in her singing than in her acting. It was more an exhibition of pulmonary effort than tasteful singing. Perhaps this was occasioned by too great an eagerness to give force to the expression of the dramatic part, in order to suffer as little as possible by any comparison with Madame Pasta's able manner of sustaining the character.'

It was to be expected that Grisi's first Norma should be considered as inferior to Pasta's. Later that summer Giulia appeared on the same stage as her other rival, Malibran, at a concert given by conductor Julius Benedict in the King's Theatre on 15 July. Grisi and Malibran sang a duet from *La gazza ladra*, which 'left an impression so strong that it can never be obliterated' from the memory of the Rev. T. C. Cox. Each of the two singers was incited to do her utmost, 'not to rival, but to keep pace with her companion.' Grisi was always stimulated by competition to give of her best, and the sustained displays of passion and brilliant execution recalled by Cox were no doubt directly inspired by the presence of Malibran.

In September the Italian singers took part in the York Festival, which lasted a week and was attended by Princess Victoria. *Messiah* was sung in York Minster on 9 September, but the Princess found the work heavy and boring, with the exception of some of the choruses. She also enjoyed 'Rejoice greatly', sung by Grisi. 'She pronounces the English so *very well* and sang the whole in such excellent style . . . But I am not at all fond of Handel's music,' remarked the Princess, 'I like the present Italian school such as Rossini, Bellini, Donizetti, *much better* . . .'

Two days later, Grisi sang Mozart's *Laudate Dominum* accompanied by Dr Matthew Camidge, organist at the Minster. Luncheon was taken at the Deanery, both by the audience and the singers, enabling

Princess Victoria to give another of her acute pen-portraits of Giulia Grisi: 'She is extremely handsome, near-by, by daylight. Her features are not small, but extremely fine, and her eyes are beautiful as are also her teeth. She has such a sweet amiable expression when she smiles, and has pleasing quiet manners.'

The Princess did not, however, approve of Grisi's dress, an ugly dingy foulard with a large muslin collar, nor of her hat, 'a frightful little pink bonnet.'

Grisi introduced her Norma to Paris at the Italiens on 8 December, repeating it in London the following spring—and indeed every season that she sang in London until the end of her career. It was a role that she made peculiarly her own, though Chorley thought that 'her Norma was modelled on that of Madame Pasta—perhaps, in some points was an improvement on the model, because there was more of animal passion in it; and this . . . could be driven to extremity without it becoming repulsive, owing to the absence of the slightest coarseness in her personal beauty. There was in it the wild ferocity of the tigress, but a certain charm therewith . . . which possibly belongs to the true reading of the character of the Druid Priestess, unfaithful to her vows.'

Charm notwithstanding, Grisi's 'wild ferocity' as Norma was apt to disconcert the tenor singing opposite her as Pollione, an unpopular role in any case. In years to come not even Mario appreciated the fury with which this Norma turned on her former lover, particularly at the end of the first act.

A new opera by Mercadante, *I briganti* (adapted, like Verdi's *I masnadieri* eleven years later, from Schiller's drama *Die Räuber*), was given its first performance at the Théâtre-Italien on 22 March 1836. Despite the presence of the entire *Puritani* quartet in the cast, the opera was not a success, while its music was considered too classical in style for the melodramatic plot. In London, where *I briganti* was transferred later in the spring, the verdict was much the same; Lablache could not be taken seriously as the famine-starved old Moor (a role he also played in Verdi's version) and even Grisi was unable to breathe life into Amelia. 'There was a mediocre respectability in the music not to be endured,' wrote Chorley, 'and accordingly the opera died.'

Meanwhile, on Sunday 24 April, after singing in *La gazza ladra* at the King's Theatre the previous evening, Giulia Grisi was married to the Vicomte Gérard de Melcy, an impoverished young man of twenty with nothing to offer his bride but his name. The marriage was, from Grisi's point of view, an unmitigated disaster. By now she was earning enormous sums of money. According to Arthur Pougin she received 125,000 francs a season in London and 80,000 francs in

Paris. This fortune, all of which now belonged legally to her husband, combined with her personal attractions and growing fame, must have made her an irresistible catch to de Melcy. Before two years were out, Grisi was to regret her hasty decision; the full extent of the tragedy would not be apparent until 1841.

For the moment, her career kept her too busy for reflection or regret. Two days after her marriage, Grisi was back at the King's Theatre in *Norma*. On 28 April she appeared in *I puritani*. She also sang in innumerable concerts, public and private. The Duchess of Kent gave an evening reception at Kensington Palace on Monday 16 May at which Malibran, as well as the Italian Opera singers took part. Grisi sang an aria from *I briganti* and, together with Malibran, a duet from an earlier Mercadante opera, *Andronico*. The programme also included popular numbers by Rossini, Bellini and Donizetti.

The performance of *I puritani* on Friday 20 May was attended by Princess Victoria and her cousin, Prince Albert of Saxe-Coburg-Gotha, who, together with his father and elder brother Ernest, was making his first visit to England. *I puritani* was not the first opera that Albert, not yet quite seventeen, heard in London: two evenings previously, on the day of his arrival in London, he had visited Drury Lane to hear Malibran in Beethoven's *Fidelio* (sung in English); but Bellini's opera was the first that he and his future wife heard together, one more reason why Victoria remained so fond of the 'dear *Puritani*' all her life.

The King's Theatre did not normally perform on a Friday— Tuesday, Thursday and Saturday were the regular opera nights—but the following day, 21 May, was Whit Saturday and Ole Bull, the Norwegian violinist, gave a concert of sacred music at the King's Theatre. It was Bull's first London appearance. Grisi was announced to sing two items, but did not appear, nor, according to *The Times*, did she send any apology. Yet another performance of *I puritani*, the following Thursday, was attended by Queen Adelaide, wife of William IV.

The King was notoriously unappreciative of music, but Queen Adelaide, a great patroness of the opera and concert hall, undoubtedly loved it almost as much as her niece Victoria. The Queen gave two evening concerts that week at St James's Palace; the first, on Friday 27 May, consisted chiefly of music by 'the modern Italian school' with, as usual, the singers from the King's Theatre and Malibran; the second, the following night, was of English music. Prince Albert, having recovered from a bilious attack which had caused his early retirement from the State Ball given in honour of Princess Victoria's seventeenth birthday three days previously, attended the 'beautiful concert' given by the Italian singers on the Friday, which went on till two o'clock the following morning. He also went to the English concert.

After singing in *La gazza ladra* on Tuesday 31 May, Grisi participated, the next day, in Ole Bull's second concert. *Il barbiere di Siviglia* was performed at the King's on Thursday 2 June. Grisi sang Rosina and interpolated variations on *La donna del lago* into the Lesson scene.

Two of the cast of *Il barbiere*, Grisi and Lablache, sang at a concert in Lansdowne House later the same night. This was probably the occasion mentioned by Gronow in his *Reminiscences and Recollections*, when 'a rather ludicrous scene took place at L——House.' Grisi and Malibran were to sing a duet, but the latter artist, who was appearing in Balfe's hugely successful opera *The Maid of Artois* at Drury Lane, did not arrive and 'the noble and courteous host supplied her place by an inferior artist [Mrs Alfred Shaw, presumably, the only other female singer in the concert] and Grisi had all the honours of the evening. In the midst of her triumph, who should march in but the Diva herself, flushed with anger . . . Lord L—— with the scrupulous urbanity which always distinguished him, advanced towards Malibran and made her a thousand apologies for having begun the concert without her.' But Malibran was not to be appeased and, catching sight of 'the beautiful face of her rival wreathed in triumphant smiles, saluted the astonished Marquis with a volley of abuse; to which he kept bowing politely till she had exhausted her vocabulary (a pretty large one) and had darted frantically out of the room.'

A busy week ended on Saturday 4 June with the first performance that season of *L'assedio di Corinto*. Grisi, who sang Pamira, was in her best voice and, according to *The Times*, 'in the long and trying scene in the tent of Mahomet . . . and in the subsequent long duet with Mahomet (Tamburini) fully sustained her great reputation.' The following Thursday, at Charles de Bériot's Morning Concert at the King's Theatre, Grisi and Malibran (who was now married to the violinist) repeated the duet from *Andronico* that they had sung at the Duchess of Kent's reception. 'As a vocal performance it would be impossible to express the merits of both Malibran and Grisi.'

The same evening, 9 June, *Marin Faliero* was revived for the benefit of Lablache, who sang the title role. 'Grisi in the character of Elena distinguished herself as usual throughout the piece.' This performance was attended by Princess Victoria and her cousins, Ernest and Albert, who left England the following day.

During the season Grisi also sang in *Anna Bolena*, *Otello* and *Don Giovanni*. Concerts, too, continued right through into July. There was

a particularly grand reception at Stafford House (now Lancaster
House) on Wednesday 13 July, when 'the splendid mansion of the
Duke and Duchess of Sutherland was thrown open to the fashionable
world . . . and upwards of one thousand of the Nobility and Gentry
were present.' All four members of the *Puritani* quartet sang at this
concert, with Michael Costa, conductor of the Italian Opera, at the
piano. The programme consisted of selections from 'the most admired
works of Rossini, Bellini, Pacini and Balfe.' Two nights later Queen
Adelaide gave her last concert of the season at St James's Palace and
again the Italian singers all took part.

   The importance attached to these concerts by the singers, whose
earnings they considerably augmented, is illustrated by Alfred Bunn,
then manager of both Covent Garden and Drury Lane Theatres. The
previous summer, wishing to repeat the 1834 success of *Il barbiere* at
Covent Garden, he had presented a performance of *La gazza ladra*,
with Grisi and most of the usual cast from the King's, at Drury Lane.
Two days later, for a Whit Saturday performance of Haydn's oratorio
The Seasons, Bunn engaged three of the singers, Grisi, Ivanov and
Tamburini. They, apparently, were in a hurry to finish their contribu-
tions and leave: '*The Seasons* was therefore interrupted by the sudden
appearance of Grisi, who in addition to her own airs favoured the
audience with two Italian ones and then bolted out of the theatre; and
as soon as Tamburini and Ivanov had followed her example, they
followed her to—a PRIVATE CONCERT!'

   A proposed second performance of *La gazza ladra* at Drury Lane
was cancelled. Laporte, the manager of the King's Theatre, wrote to
Bunn to apologize for the behaviour of his flock of exotic and
temperamental songbirds, admitting that he had little control over
them outside his own theatre. Bunn ran into further trouble, as the
patent under which he managed Drury Lane did not allow the
performance of Italian opera.

Chapter 3

TWO NEW OPERAS, both dealing with the Crusades or the exploits of Crusaders, had their first performances in Paris during the early months of 1837. In Costa's *Malek Adhel*, produced at the Théâtre-Italien on 14 January, Grisi sang the part of Matilda, sister to King Richard Lionheart, who falls in love with the Turkish commander, Malek Adhel, sung by Rubini. Though Costa was a fine musician and, by common consent, an outstanding conductor, he never succeeded in writing a successful opera. *Malek Adhel*, 'a thoroughly conscientious work', according to Chorley, contained several numbers that achieved at least fleeting popularity. These included a grand *scena* for Matilda, which Grisi sang consummately, and a tenor aria with which Rubini used to make a tremendous impression, rising at the climax to an E flat.

The other opera, Marliani's *Il degonda*, was first given at the Italiens on 17 March. Grisi sang the title role and again had an effective scene in which she could display both her dramatic and vocal strength: *Il degonda* rouses the people of Milan to help her save the Crusading Knight Riccardo from the stake. Grisi's marriage had made no difference to her excellent professional relationship with Marliani. She continued to sing the display aria 'Stanca di piu combattere', which he had composed specially for her, on her first entrance as Desdemona in *Otello*, while 'Ah! si fugga' from *Il degonda* became one of her favourite concert pieces.

She sang it at Buckingham Palace on 28 July 1837, at Queen Victoria's first concert since her accession to the throne five weeks previously. King William IV had died very early in the morning of 20 June. The King's Theatre had become Her Majesty's. That summer Giuditta Pasta was singing again in London. Apart from a single disastrous appearance a dozen years later, this was her last London season. Her voice was not in a good state, but her dramatic power, especially in the title role of Mayr's *Medea*, was as potent as ever. She, too, sang at the young Queen's first concert, the last recorded occasion when Pasta and Grisi, the original Norma and Adalgisa, appeared together.

Grisi sang at two other Buckingham Palace concerts during August, but Pasta's name was not on the programmes. As Maria Malibran had died in Manchester the previous September, after a miscarriage or stillbirth caused by a fall from her horse several weeks earlier, Giulia Grisi was now without rival.

In Paris winds of change were also blowing. On the night of 14/15 January 1838, after a performance of *Don Giovanni*, the Salle Favart, home of the Théâtre-Italien, was destroyed by fire. One of the directors, Carlo Severini, was killed when he jumped from a window and, landing on a pile of stones, broke his spine. The other director, Édouard Robert, was quite severely burned. Rossini, though in Italy at the time, lost a large collection of music. Robert transferred his company to the Salle Ventadour with a repertory of four operas, including the immensely successful production of Donizetti's *Lucia di Lammermoor*, first given at the Italiens the previous December, with Fanny Tacchinardi-Persiani in the title role, which she had created two years previously in Naples.

The first new production at the Salle Ventadour was another Donizetti opera, *Parisina*, performed on 24 February with Grisi in the title role. 'What great and dramatic sighs trouble that marble bosom,' wrote Théophile Gautier. 'What noble and modest blushes pass across that pure, Greek forehead, and what superb cries of indignation issue from those divinely modelled lips.'

Gautier, ever susceptible to physical beauty, as he would again demonstrate later that same year in his notice of Mario's début, carried on a triple love affair with the Grisi cousins. He passionately admired Giulia for her voice and appearance, as the dedication of his novel *Mademoiselle de Maupin* amply proves; he fell romantically in love with Carlotta, though the dancer did not reciprocate his feelings; and he lived for twenty years with Ernesta, who bore him two daughters, one of whom at least, Judith Gautier, inherited the Grisi family good looks.

'Mlle. Grisi is marvellously beautiful!' declared Gautier in his review of *Parisina*. 'Her shoulders, her neck, her arms are as perfect as the most famous statue of antiquity. No sculpture is more exquisitely formed, nor of a pallor more smooth and white. A crown would certainly become those bands of black hair and that amber brow. If beauty alone deserved a sceptre, Mlle. Grisi would long ago have become Sovereign; after Malibran, Grisi, the Queen is dead, long live the Queen! Perhaps she does not sing quite so well, but she has the most beautiful blue eyes in the world, a profile like Niobe and hands as fine and transparent as any royalty.'

Gautier thought that Grisi sang admirably and acted like a first-class tragedienne in *Parisina*, even if she still lacked the dedicated artistry of Malibran. *Parisina* was not much liked when Donizetti's opera was given its first London performance at Her Majesty's on Friday 1 June—the subject, taken from a poem by Lord Byron, was considered rather distasteful—but the performance, with Grisi, Rubini and Tamburini repeating their Paris roles, received the highest praise.

In London the Coronation season of 1838 was an especially brilliant one. Her Majesty's had reopened after Easter with *La sonnambula*, in which Fanny Persiani made her London début. Persiani introduced *Lucia di Lammermoor* to a wildly enthusiastic audience at Her Majesty's on Thursday 5 April, while Grisi made her first appearance of the season as Desdemona in *Otello* on Saturday 21 April. There was no rivalry between the two sopranos. Persiani was a very different kind of singer from Grisi; technically immensely proficient, she had a voice that was pure-toned but completely lacking in the warmth that characterized Grisi's lustrous timbre. At a concert given by the Queen at Buckingham Palace on 18 May, Persiani as the Countess and Grisi as Susanna sang the Letter Duet from Mozart's *Le nozze di Figaro*, foretaste of a revival of the opera at Her Majesty's later in the season.

Persiani replaced Malibran at the private concert given by Lord and Lady Lansdowne on Wednesday 6 June, when the *Puritani* quartet was also present in full force. The following night, Thursday, Rossini's *Matilda di Shabran* was revived at Her Majesty's for Persiani's benefit, followed by the final scene from *Anna Bolena*, sung by Grisi, and the second act of *La Sylphide*, danced by Marie Taglioni. On Friday the Italian singers all took part in Julius Benedict's concert—Grisi sang Marliani's 'Stanca di piu combattere', and, with Rubini and Lablache, a trio from Costa's *Malek Adhel*—and the week ended with a performance of *Parisina*, attended by the Queen.

The following week was Ascot Race Week and the Queen took up residence at Windsor Castle. On Monday Grisi sang in the Society Armonica's sixth concert of the season. Later that evening there was a private concert, given by the Countess of Manvers at her house in Portman Square, which ended at two the following morning with 'A te o cara' from *I puritani* sung by the original quartet.

Tuesday 12 June, *Matilda di Shabran* was performed again at Her Majesty's. Either that day or the next, a letter for Giulia Grisi was delivered at her lodgings and intercepted by her husband, Gérard de Melcy. The letter was from Viscount Castlereagh, a young man to be seen every night at the Opera when Grisi sang; its contents were such as to make the Vicomte de Melcy go immediately to Castlereagh's house in Chapel Street, to demand satisfaction.

Castlereagh was not at home—he was in fact at Ascot—and on Thursday when de Melcy called again, he was still away. That evening Cimarosa's comic opera *Il matrimonio segreto*, with Persiani and Lablache, followed by the last act of *Otello*, with Grisi and Rubini, were given at Her Majesty's for the benefit of the ballet-master Paolo Taglioni, whose sister Marie danced the final item of the long programme, the ballet *Miranda*.

Castlereagh returned to London from Ascot on Friday 15 June and de Melcy was finally able to deliver his challenge. This was accepted by Castlereagh, who named a Mr Bentinck as his second; M. de Cottreau answered for de Melcy. The duel was arranged to take place at 4.30 the following morning, at Wormwood Scrubs; pistols were the chosen weapons and the distance twelve paces.

Both principals arrived on time at Wormwood Scrubs next morning, but their seconds had meanwhile decided that the pistols used should not be the contestants' own, which might give an unfair advantage to one party or the other, but that two pairs should be bought at random from a gunsmith. By the time this was done, it was already ten o'clock.

When Castlereagh and de Melcy had chosen their pistols, 'they were placed at the distance agreed upon and instructed that the words to be given were "Gentlemen, are you ready? Fire!" accompanied by the dropping of a handkerchief.'

Before the signal was given, Lord Castlereagh, according to J. G. Millingen in *The History of Duelling*, 'caused his second to deliver into the hands of M. Cottreau a paper signed by him, declaring that Madame Grisi had not, in the slightest manner, encouraged his attentions, and that he had never corresponded with her before. The word was given and the signal dropped. They fired at the same time. M. de Melcy's ball passed through his antagonist's right arm, near the wrist. His Lordship discharged his pistol in the air.'

Mr Bentinck, seeing that his principal was wounded, declared that the affair should be carried no further. While the surgeon in attendance dressed Castlereagh's arm, de Melcy read the letter delivered to his second and, considering that his honour was satisfied, agreed to end the duel.

Il matrimonio segreto had been announced for that evening at Her Majesty's but the opera had been changed to *Matilda di Shabran*, at the express wish of the Queen. A very large and fashionable audience arrived at a most unfashionable hour, as the duel was already known about to everyone and formed the sole topic of conversation. It was rumoured that Lord Castlereagh had been badly wounded and all eyes were fixed on the Marchioness of Londonderry's box as, in the words of the *Morning Post*, 'it was supposed that her presence would indicate that Lord Castlereagh [her stepson] was not mortally wounded. Her Ladyship did not arrive until the opera was nearly over, but even then she was welcomed by every person who felt an interest in her young and noble relative.'

By 1838 duels were officially frowned upon in England and consequently had become rare events worthy of wide press coverage, especially when one of the participants was a member of the aristocracy. On Monday there was a full column's description of the duel in the *Morning Post*, including the contents of Castlereagh's letter exonerating Grisi of all blame. The *Standard* had an article beginning that 'it seems there is a singing woman named Grisi, a foreigner at some of the theatres . . .' and going on to imply that de Melcy had no right to defend his wife's honour, as he and Grisi were not legally married.

This allegation was answered next day by several letters, all of which defended the behaviour of both de Melcy and Grisi. One letter mentioned 'the legal process instituted in France to confirm their marriage, which had taken place in England [and] must be fresh in the recollection of even readers of newspapers.'

Parisina was given again on Tuesday 19 June. The theatre was crowded even before the rise of the curtain. When Grisi appeared, for the first time since the 'late fracas' the applause was so prolonged and the singer so much affected by it, that it was several minutes before the performance could be continued. Queen Victoria, attending Donizetti's opera for the second time, noted in her Journal that 'we came in just after Grisi had appeared & before she sang. I never saw Grisi so splendid, or sing so well. The scene with Tamburini is really the finest scene I ever saw. Both acted so beautifully.' This scene, in which Parisina is unjustly accused of adultery by her husband Azzo, was particularly apt. Parisina's dream, 'Sogno talor', was encored, but Queen Victoria thought the applause 'abominably cold'. At the end Grisi was called out, 'looking rather nervous I thought, & much applauded'.

The next day, Wednesday, Handel's *Acis and Galatea*, given for the benefit of Mr and Mrs Seguin at Drury Lane, was followed by a Grand Concert with, among the singers, Grisi, Tamburini and Lablache. The revival of *Le nozze di Figaro* at Her Majesty's took place on Thursday 21 June, for the benefit of the manager, Laporte. Susanna was not considered one of Grisi's best roles, but her singing of the Letter Duet with Persiani's Countess was again much appreciated. The Italian singers all participated in a concert at Buckingham Palace on Friday night.

There was no performance at Her Majesty's on Thursday 28 June—Coronation Day—as it was feared that the press of traffic might prevent the audience from reaching the theatre; but a special performance of *I puritani* was given on Friday, followed by *Le nozze di Figaro* on Saturday. Westminster Abbey, with the Coronation decorations still in place, was used for a concert of sacred music, in which all the Italian singers took part, on Monday 2 July.

The last new opera of the season, Michael Balfe's *Falstaff*, was performed at Her Majesty's on Thursday 19 July, with Grisi as Mistress Ford, Rubini as Fenton, Tamburini as Master Ford and Lablache as Falstaff. Not even 'such a protagonist as would have made Shakespeare's heart leap for joy to look upon' could ensure lasting popularity for Balfe's opera. Chorley dismissed the music as eclectic— 'Here we meet an Italian rhythm, there a French interval, anon a German harmony, sometimes a strain of artless Irish melody'—and criticized the orchestration as too often thin. A trio for the two Merry Wives and Anne Page scored some success and appeared in concert programmes for a year or two.

By October the Italian singers were back in Paris, giving much admired performances of *Otello*, with Lablache thundering out a father's curse on Desdemona-Grisi, who moved all hearts as she begged for forgiveness. Donizetti's *Roberto Devereux*, first heard at the Italiens in December, had Rubini in the title role of the Earl of Essex, 'loved at the same time by Elizabeth, Queen of England, and Sarah, Duchess of Nottingham: this is to say, by Mlle. Grisi and by Mme. Albertazzi. Lucky man!' commented Gautier.

In his cavatina, Rubini achieved 'a miraculous G in alt, which made the audience explode in cries of admiration and frantic applause . . . Mlle. Grisi, from beginning to end, was beautiful, pathetic, with dark flashes of tragic inspiration and the transports of a lioness in love. The passionate cries of the music of our time seem to issue from the marble lips of an antique muse.'

Meanwhile Mario had made his début at the Opéra earlier that December and the two singers, still unknown to each other except, presumably, by repute, continued to appear in the same city, though at different theatres, for the next four months. The season at the Théâtre-Italien ended on 31 March with a performance of *I puritani* and the whole circus moved to London, where Her Majesty's reopened on 4 April with Persiani in *La sonnambula*. Two months later, on 6 June

1839, as has already been related, Donizetti's *Lucrezia Borgia*, an opera new to London, was produced for Grisi's benefit, with Mario, singing for the first time at Her Majesty's, in the part of Gennaro.

The opera was heartily disliked by the critics, Chorley in the *Athenaeum* writing that 'Grisi did her best to make her new part tell—looking in the second act more striking than we ever remember to have seen her, having put on for the character such a malicious and fascinating beauty as befits a sorceress . . . but the music baffled her exertions.' Despite this critical coolness the opera rapidly became popular and Lucrezia remained one of Grisi's finest and favourite roles.

As for Mario, Chorley complimented 'the new Romeo of the Italian stage upon possessing a handsome presence and a delicious voice, rather than commend him for using either as an artist should do, that is zealously and to good effect . . . M. Mario's success was complete, but he must work hard to make it lasting.'

Queen Victoria attended performances of *Lucrezia Borgia* on both 8 and 11 June and enjoyed them very much. 'Grisi, Mario & Tamburini sang beautifully; the 2 finest things are a Trio in the 1st Act . . . between Lucrezia, Gennaro and Il Duco [Alfonso d'Este, Lucrezia's husband]; & the part which the dying Gennaro sings: "Madre, so ognor lontano", & which Mario sings most touchingly; the last Scene is dreadful, and was beautifully acted by Grisi; her despair at her son's death was very touching; it is,' concluded the Queen, 'a beautiful opera.' She also admired Mario's appearance, 'tall, quite young and handsome'.

Mario's only other roles during his first London season were Pollione in *Norma*, where he was exposed to the full force of Grisi's scorn and derision; and Nemorino in Donizetti's *L'elisir d'amore*, when the cast included Persiani, Tamburini and Lablache. On this occasion, unstinted praise was showered on all four singers. 'Signor Mario with his exquisitely musical tones and prepossessing face and figure, neither of which have been trained so as to *tell* upon the stage in more heroic parts, is because of that very simplicity and slight awkwardness so exact a representative of the innocent peasant Nemorino that we found ourselves constantly forgetting the stage lights and shabby old trees of the back scene.'

Another singer making her London début—indeed, her first appearance on any stage—during the summer of 1839 was Pauline Garcia, younger sister of Malibran. Braving comparisons not merely with Grisi, but with still vivid memories of Malibran, Garcia chose Desdemona as her début role. Though her performance, deeply committed, musically sensitive but naturally in some ways tentative, was not at all what the habitués of Her Majesty's were accustomed to, she displayed enough of the Garcia genius and artistry to conquer her audience.

Mario had to be back at the Paris Opéra by the beginning of August, when his leave of absence was up. His last performance in London was as Pollione on Tuesday 30 July. One admirer, at least, was extremely sad to see him go: 'It was again *Norma*,' wrote the Queen in her Journal, 'and oh! more splendid than before. Grisi was perfection; it really is quite a treat to see and hear her; Mario too so delightful; alas! his and *Norma*'s last night, for he went away last night to Paris, and this charming opera can't be performed any more.'

When Mario left London there was no reason to suppose that any emotion stronger than the friendship of a professional colleague bound him to Giulia Grisi. And there was every reason to believe that Grisi had no deeper interest in the young tenor. She had left de Melcy after the duel and, while Castlereagh's assertion of her innocence was probably justified at the time he made it, she became his mistress shortly afterwards. When she first met Mario, Grisi was carrying Castlereagh's child.

She did not sing at the Théâtre-Italien during the autumn of 1839 and gave birth to a boy in November. Castlereagh acknowledged his son, who went under the name of George Frederick Ormsby (Castlereagh's own Christian names were Frederick William Robert), and was responsible for the boy's upbringing and education.

Grisi saw her son fairly regularly, as a letter from Mario to Michael Costa dated, according to internal evidence, about 1849 proves: 'Dear Costa, Giulia asks to be excused from the rehearsal today as it is the first time her little boy is visiting her since he arrived in London, and she asks you to forgive her and set another time that suits you . . .'

Castlereagh, though he married a few years later, had no other children. In 1854 he succeeded his father to become fourth Marquess of Londonderry. The following December, when Frederick Ormsby was sixteen, he was gazetted Cornet in the 7th (The Queen's Own) Regiment of Light Dragoons.

Mario reappeared at the Opéra on 7 August 1839 in *Robert le diable* and a week later sang in *Le Comte Ory*. He continued to sing in these two operas throughout the autumn, but meanwhile he was in communication with Louis Viardot, who had taken over the directorship of the Théâtre-Italien from Robert. Viardot had gone to London during the summer to hear Pauline Garcia, and had engaged her for his Paris theatre. He had also entered into negotiations with Mario who, soon after his return to Paris, wrote to Viardot to enquire about the date of his engagement.

The Théâtre-Italien opened on 3 October with Persiani in *Lucia di Lammermoor*; five days later Pauline Garcia made her Paris début as Desdemona; and on 22 October Mario made his first appearance at the Italiens as Nemorino in *L'elisir d'amore*, with the same cast as at Her Majesty's.

It was at once decided that the young tenor had found his true place, and that he was destined to succeed Rubini, not Duprez. The style as well as the language of Italian opera came more naturally to him; 'Una furtiva lagrima', ravishingly sung, was encored although the proximity of Tamburini and Persiani showed up the deficiencies in his technique.

'Mario's voice is naturally flexible,' wrote E. E. Délécluze in the *Journal des Débats*, 'but it lacks practice. This interesting young singer should find new difficulties to conquer daily, so that instead of his voice carrying him away, as sometimes happens, it becomes the slave of his will.' The time would shortly come when 'new difficulties' would be thrust on Mario, but for the moment he had enough to do, alternating at the two theatres all through November and December.

In January 1840 Mario was given a role to create at the Opéra, in Halévy's *Le Drapier*. The work itself, which mixed burlesque and tragic elements in a manner not congenial to French taste, was not popular, but Mario had at least two effective numbers to sing and received praise for his performance. Even so severe a critic as Hector Berlioz allowed that the tenor had made progress in the art of managing his voice, if not in the art of singing itself. Berlioz considered the costumes in *Le Drapier* particularly hideous and presumed that Mario could only have consented to wear his out of pity for all the beautiful ladies dying for love of the handsome tenor: they would at once be cured if they saw him in *Le Drapier*.

Two days before the première of Halévy's opera, Grisi made a triumphant return to the Théâtre-Italien as Norma. She was in very fine voice and looked more beautiful than ever. Grisi also sang in *La donna del lago*, *Don Giovanni* and *Le nozze di Figaro* before the season ended on 31 March with *I puritani*, sung as usual by the original quartet.

When Bellini's opera was given its first performance of the season at Her Majesty's, on Saturday 25 April, one member of the quartet was missing. Laporte, manager of the theatre, felt that the singers, as he had admitted to Alfred Bunn some years previously, wielded far too much power in his establishment. This applied particularly to the *vieille garde*, the nucleus of which was the *Puritani* quartet, and Laporte decided to assert his authority by not engaging one of them. As he could hardly dispense with his leading soprano or leading tenor, and Lablache was far too popular to be left out of the company, Laporte chose Tamburini as his victim.

Tamburini's replacement, the baritone Filippo Coletti, made his appearance that Saturday as Riccardo, causing the most violent theatrical disturbances witnessed in London 'since the days of the OP riots or the Catalani contest.' As the *Morning Post* reported, 'the moment Coletti stepped on the stage, and before he could utter his first words, some very violent, but not very numerous, hisses were heard, accompanied with cries of "Tamburini!" which were mingled with a few calls for Laporte.'

A counter-demonstration in favour of Coletti was then launched, and as those who wished the performance to continue greatly out-numbered those who did not—'the better part of the audience seeming to keep neutral in the contention'—*I puritani* was allowed to resume in peace.

The arrival of the Queen and Prince Albert, married for not quite three months, may have had something to do with the subsidence of the demonstration.

When *I puritani* was given again, five days later, the demonstrations began immediately after the opera was over. There were cries of 'Tamburini' and 'Laporte' and when after a long delay, the manager appeared, a furious explosion of hostility broke out. Laporte began to make excuses, but his voice was drowned by shouts from the audience of 'engage Tamburini!' and he had to leave the stage. After a further long interval, Laporte returned, to be greeted by renewed signs of displeasure and more cries of 'engage Tamburini!'. The tumult con-tinued until one in the morning and the ballet had to be cancelled.

Two nights later the opera was *La sonnambula* and the demonstra-tions began as soon as Costa raised his baton. The row continued for twenty minutes until Laporte came on stage to announce that he was already in communication with Tamburini. Three nights after that, on Tuesday 5 May, Tamburini duly appeared, to sing Iago in *Otello* with Grisi, Rubini and Lablache also in their accustomed roles. The first round of the battle had been won by the *vieille garde*. Benjamin Lumley, at that time legal adviser to Laporte, whom he succeeded as manager of Her Majesty's the following year, put the whole blame for the planning and execution of the Tamburini riots on Lord Castlereagh. Lumley, when he wrote in *Reminiscences of the Opera* some years later, was deeply prejudiced—and not without some cause—against Grisi and the other members of the *vieille garde*, but his theory is none the less interesting.

'Madame Grisi, at that time in the zenith of her beauty and her artistic fame, held in allegiance beneath her fair sort and sceptre a whole string of young fashionables of the day, over whom she had acquired an extraordinary influence. At the head of this group was a noble Viscount, whose duel with her husband, M. de Melcy, had furnished one of the notable scandals of the town, and whose partizanship in the battle about to be fought she scorned to deny. These then were the skirmishers, ready to aid the campaign of a commander who could direct the manoeuvres, although unable to appear openly in the field. For this purpose no better Lieutenant could be desired than the noble lord already referred to . . . Thus Madame Grisi, "like another Helen, fired another Troy".'

Lumley accused Castlereagh of drawing up the plan of attack in the House of Commons, of which Castlereagh at the time was a member.

During April and May, while the Tamburini riots were taking place, Mario was still in Paris, singing at the Opéra. He arrived in London about the middle of June and made his first appearance on Thursday 18 June, when the second act of *L'elisir d'amore* and one act of Bellini's *Il pirata* were given for Taglioni's benefit. 'Una furtiva lagrima' was, as usual, encored. A complete performance of *L'elisir* followed two nights later, while Mario also sang with Grisi in *Lucrezia Borgia* and *La donna del lago*, taking on the part of Rodrigo in the latter opera.

During the season it was announced that Mario had resigned from the *Académie Royale de Musique* (where his place as second tenor was to be filled by Marié), and would henceforth devote himself exclusively to the Italian stage. Mario's name does not figure on the programme of a concert given by the Queen on 29 June, but he sang at a concert given by the Duke and Duchess of Beaufort on 3 July, and also at Buckingham Palace, together with the *Puritani* quartet and Persiani, on 10 August, when his contribution included Schubert's Serenade, sung in French.

Queen Victoria's taste, under the influence of her beloved Albert, was beginning to change. A few years ago she had confided in her journal that she found Handel dry and boring, while she had greatly startled Lord Melbourne by declaring that the music of Mozart was old-fashioned. Now songs by Schubert and Beethoven began creeping into the programmes of the concerts given by the Italian singers. Mario's repertory included, as well as several Schubert songs, Beethoven's 'Adelaïde' and 'Busslied' ('La Pénitence').

Chapter 4

MARIO'S CAREER, AS well as Grisi's, was now set in the pattern it would follow for most of the next decade. The Théâtre-Italien reopened on 1 October 1840 with Persiani and Rubini in *Lucia di Lammermoor*. Grisi made her first appearance on 6 October as Norma. Pollione was sung by the tenor Mirate who, ten days later, was replaced by Mario. Neither Pollione pleased the Italiens audiences and it was not until the end of the month, when *Lucrezia Borgia* was given its first Paris performance, that Mario found favour with the critics.

'After his failure as Pollione,' wrote Gautier, 'Mario, who took the role of Gennaro, recovered completely and, apart from a few over-guttural notes, sang with a great deal of charm and expression.' In the first scene, where Gennaro lies on a bench and goes to sleep, Gautier advised Mario to choose a more comfortable position, 'one more conducive to slumber, not to meditation;' and also to find a quieter corner as, 'to sleep in the midst of the noise of a party requires a more mysterious hiding-place.'

Gautier also counselled Grisi to be less affected when she kissed the sleeping Gennaro: 'the tender, noble kiss that a goddess would let fall from her chaste lips on the forehead of an Endymion' was infinitely preferable. But, continued Gautier, 'Grisi acted sublimely in the scene where Maffio tears off her mask; it is impossible to imagine anything more beautiful than that pale, marble visage, as terrifying, despite its beauty, as the head of Medusa, flashing poisonous glances from her basilisk eyes; after such a look, vengeance is assured; people thus regarded are already dead.'

A somewhat belated benefit performance was given for Mario at the Opéra on 19 January 1841, though apparently he never touched any of the receipts and this caused a final rupture between the tenor and Pillet, the director of the Opéra. The programme, however, was of particular interest, comprising the third and fourth acts of Meyerbeer's *Les Huguenots*, an act from Rossini's *Guillaume Tell*, a scene from Donizetti's *Torquato Tasso* (sung by the baritone Paul Barroilhet) and the ballet *Les Noces de Gamache*. This last piece had not been performed since the night of the assassination outside the Opéra of the Duc de Berri; it must have aroused memories of Genoa and the Duchesse de Berri in the mind of Mario.

Gautier thought that Mario surpassed all expectations in *Les Huguenots* as Raoul, a part in which no tenor, even Duprez, could entirely efface the memory of Nourrit. The piece from *Torquato Tasso* was dismissed as a deplorable omelette or soufflé of notes, but in *Guillaume Tell* 'Mario, inspired by this divine music, excelled himself; he was touching, passionate, full of enthusiasm and pain, while keeping that freshness, that ingenuousness, that naïf sensibility which is the particular character of his talent; his voice, young, facile, charming, expressive without effort or clamour of such ardent yet respectful passion, caused a frisson of pleasure to run through the theatre and thunderclaps of applause for the composer and the singer exploded in all parts of the house.'

Bellini's *Beatrice di Tenda* was given at the Théâtre-Italien in February for Persiani's benefit and Mario sang the part of Orombello for the first time. For her benefit on 23 February Grisi chose *Semiramide* and she sang Desdemona in the performance of *Otello* given for Rubini's benefit on 15 March. The season ended on 31 March with *I puritani*, the last performance in Paris with the original quartet and Rubini's final appearance at the Italiens.

Meanwhile, in London Her Majesty's had opened on 11 March with Pauline Garcia, now married to Louis Viardot, and Mario in Cimarosa's *Gli Orazi e i Curiazi*. Viardot, in the highly dramatic part of Horatia, was much admired. Her crowning achievement, according to the *Morning Post* critic, was 'the last scene with Mario, in which arduous part of the opera her execution displayed extraordinary brilliancy. Mario, as Publicus Horatius, proved worthy of sharing in the applause bestowed upon Horatia. In him also we could perceive notable improvements which his removal from the French Opéra to his own native stage must have promoted. His voice has acquired more firmness, while his acting has cast off almost all the gaucherie natural to one who was neither born nor brought up to the dramatic art.'

Both the second and third performances, on 13 and 16 March, were attended by the Queen and Prince Albert, who liked the music and the singers. Then Mario was recalled to Paris because of the indisposition of Rubini and did not return to London for a fortnight.

Her Majesty's reopened after the Easter closure on Saturday 17 April with a double bill comprising *Norma*, with Grisi, Mario and Lablache, followed by *Lucia*, with Persiani, Rubini and Tamburini;

even if both works were substantially cut, the subscribers certainly got their money's worth that evening.

At the third performance of *Norma*, a week later, which was followed by a shortened version of *La sonnambula*, the audience was particularly large and distinguished; it included Lord Castlereagh who, although his affair with Grisi was now over, continued to admire and support her as a singer. The following Thursday, in contrast, *Otello* was played 'to about the thinnest and coldest house we have seen at this period of the season. Perhaps,' continued the *Morning Post*, 'some contention between the prime donne may have like-wise contributed to the triste aspect of the house. *Otello* had been announced for Tuesday, and Grisi (if we mistake not) was to have been Desdemona, whereas it was Madame Viardot who was in possession of the part last night.'

This brought a reply, in Saturday's *Morning Post*, as follows:

Sir, as the public might be led to infer, from the article in your journal of this day Friday 30 April, with reference to the Italian Opera, that some contention between the Prime Donne may have contributed to the triste aspect of the house, there having been some dispute as to the part of Desdemona, I have to assure you that I have not had any misunderstanding or dispute with either Madame Viardot or the management, M. Laporte having informed me at Paris previous to my engagement that I was not expected to appear in the opera of *Otello*. I am sure, Sir, that having inflicted an unjust censure, you will repair the mistake by inserting this letter and oblige, Your obedient servant, Giulia Grisi.

The malicious gossip, which was to foment so much bad feeling between Viardot and Grisi, had already begun. The situation was not helped by comments such as that made by her friend and ardent supporter George Sand in a letter to Pauline Viardot. Viardot had written to Madame Sand declaring that she had no intention of flattering the bad taste of the London audiences—as, she asserted, Grisi did—just to win their applause. Sand wrote back: 'I hope you will wring the neck of that fat goose who competes *beside* you, I don't say *with* you, that would do her too much honour.'

Whether or not it showed their bad taste, most London opera-goers continued to prefer Grisi to Viardot. After a performance of *Semiramide*, in which both singers took part, Queen Victoria noted in her diary that 'Grisi sang beautifully, so did Tamburini. Pauline

Viardot sang very well, but her voice was so small, one could hardly hear it at times.'

Mario's next new role was Arturo in Bellini's *La straniera*, which was given for Tamburini's benefit on Thursday 13 May, with a new soprano, Sophie Loewe, making her London début. Neither the lady nor the opera was much liked, but Mario was encored in the last act, when he sang an interpolated romanza by Schira, the maestro who coached him in his roles and also the composer of several successful songs. *La straniera* was followed by two acts of *Le nozze di Figaro*, with Grisi, Persiani and Lablache.

By now the season was in full swing, with concerts, sometimes two or three the same evening, on those days that the Italian Opera did not play. At Julius Benedict's Matinée Concert on Monday 17 May, there was a performance of the Prayer from Rossini's *Mosé* in which one of the most staggering collection of artists ever assembled took part. The singers included Grisi, Persiani, Loewe, Viardot, Ernesta Grisi and Julie Dorus-Gras (the Belgian soprano who had created Alice in *Robert le diable*) among the ladies; Rubini, Mario, Lablache, his son Frederick Lablache and Parry (replacing Tamburini, who was indisposed) among the gentlemen. The accompaniment was provided by Franz Liszt and Julius Benedict, pianos; Dorus, flute; Vieuxtemps, violin; Puzzi, horn and Mlle. Bertucat, harp.

The same evening the Queen gave a Grand Concert at Buckingham Palace at which all the Italian singers performed.

At Her Majesty's, two Donizetti operas new to London were produced: *Fausta*, with Grisi, Mario and Tamburini; and *Roberto Devereux*, with Grisi, Rubini and Tamburini. Neither opera had much of a success, though the performance of *Fausta*, according to Chorley in the *Athenaeum*, 'left nothing to be desired. Mario,' he continued, 'is rapidly justifying all our prognostics in his favour, and will become ere long, we are disposed to hope, one of the very first tenors of modern Italy.'

A revival of *Marin Faliero*, despite the magnificent performance by Lablache in the title role, was scarcely more popular. Mario sang the off-stage Gondolier's Barcarolle, a piece which became one of his favourite concert items.

The great success of the season was *Il barbiere di Siviglia*, revived on Saturday 17 July. The comic acting of Tamburini (Figaro) and Lablache (Dr Bartolo) was much appreciated, while Grisi, in the opinion of Chorley, 'is unquestionably the best Rosina we have ever seen: rioting in the grace and gay spirit of her music, as if she enjoyed her deliverance from the grim tragedy of Donizetti's diluted *opere serie* as much as we did.' Mario sang Almaviva, a part he was to repeat over a hundred times in London alone during the next 30 years.

That summer, when they sang together two or three times a week at Her Majesty's and almost every night at concerts, public or private, the growing attraction between Mario and Grisi became obvious. Free at last from her liaison with Castlereagh, Grisi was properly aware of 'her' tenor as a man, not just a stage partner, for the first time since their meeting two years previously. She began to exhibit signs of possessiveness and even jealousy, indicating that she already considered him as her private property. Mario, too, conducted his wooing in public. The sudden improvement in his acting, particularly the greatly increased ardour he displayed in love scenes with Grisi, proved that the sentiments he expressed so mellifluously on stage were mirrored by the emotions in his own heart.

It is possible that Mario and Grisi became lovers while still in London, but more likely that this happened in Dublin, where a party of singers consisting of Giulia Grisi, her cousin Ernesta Grisi, Mario, Luigi and Frederick Lablache, arrived at the end of August. Together with Michael Costa, the conductor, and Frederick Beale, manager of the touring party and a director of the music publishers Cramer and Beale, they were staying at Morrisson's Hotel.

The short season at the Theatre Royal opened on Monday 30 August with *I puritani*. It was the first time that Mario had tackled the part of Arturo, written for Rubini and tailored exactly to fit the characteristics of the older tenor's voice. The next night *Norma* was given and, on Thursday 2 September, *La sonnambula*, with Mario as Elvino, another first performance for him.

'Last night the house, from its foundation to its rooftree—pit, boxes, dress and undress circles, lattices, galleries, etc, etc—was literally as full as the moon,' wrote the Dublin *Evening Mail* critic next day. 'Not merely the dress circle presented a blaze of rank and wealth, fine persons and elegant costumes, but that, and every part of the theatre dazzled the admiring eye of the individual spectator with an array of female beauty, which in loveliness and number surpassed anything we ever witnessed before . . . But we must not dwell on the charms of four fair countrywomen, when a stranger, lovely in person and accomplishment in art, awaits our award.'

After praising the charm and beauty of Grisi's voice and appearance, the *Evening Mail* critic continued: 'To say that she delights and astonishes, captivates and overpowers her auditory is strong but inadequate language, and unhappily give no idea of the means of her fascination. One might as well attempt to define the perfume of the

Mario as Nemorino in *L'elisir d'amore*

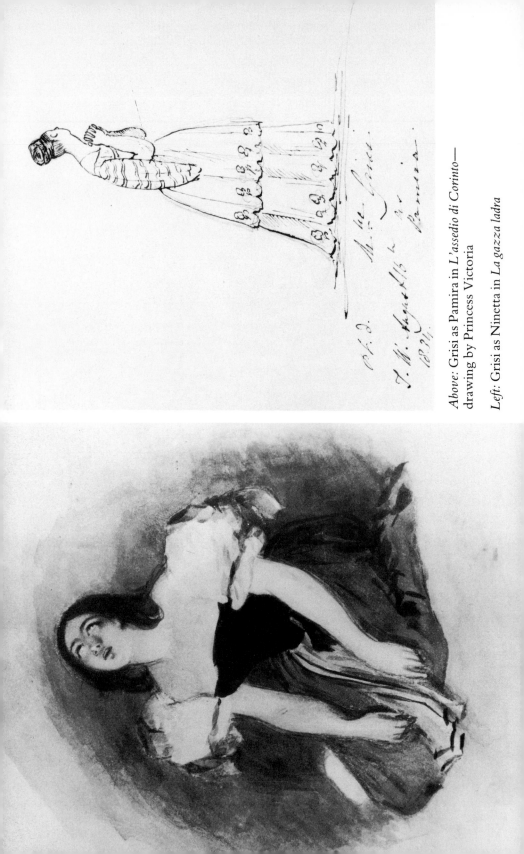

Above: Grisi as Pamira in *L'assedio di Corinto*— drawing by Princess Victoria

Left: Grisi as Ninetta in *La gazza ladra*

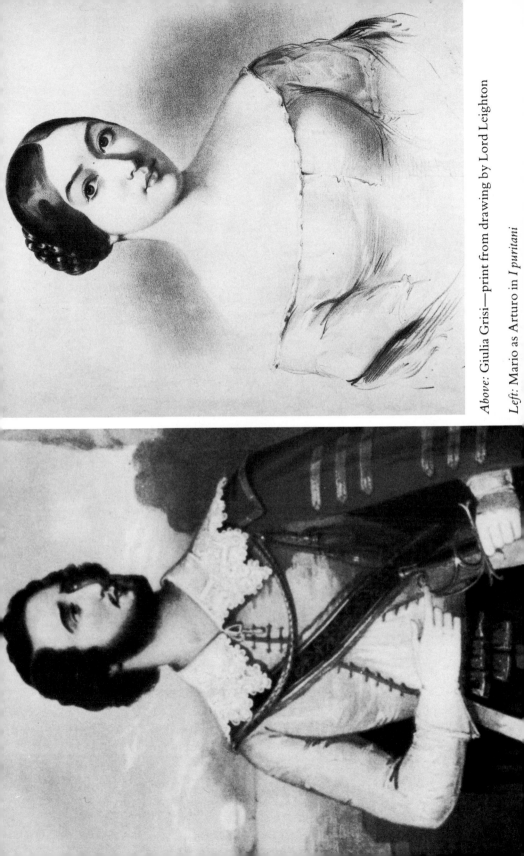

Above: Giulia Grisi—print from drawing by Lord Leighton

Left: Mario as Arturo in *I puritani*

Above: Grisi in the
title role of *Norma*

Right: Grisi and Mario
in *Otello*—playbill

violet, or render colours intelligible to a blind man by sounds, as to describe the combination of qualities which in this unrivalled canta-trice take the senses by suprice and "lap them in Elysium".'

Mario's Elvino was also highly praised; 'it is an exquisite perform-ance. His fine tenor is capable of the richest inflexions; and in passion-ate expression, whether of love, jealousy or anger, we have never heard it surpassed.' The duet with Amina, 'Prendi l'anel ti dono' and Elvino's recitative and aria 'Tutto è sciolto' were encored, as was Grisi's final rondo 'Ah non giunge', and when at the end of the opera she and Mario came before the curtain, they were showered with garlands and bouquets, 'the feeble but enthusiastic offering of many fair hands and sensitive hearts.'

In one of the bouquets thrown to Mario was a billet-doux from some unknown admirer. Though he immediately destroyed the note, Grisi had already noticed it and, jumping to the wildest conclusions, burst into a fit of jealous rage. She refused to be pacified by Mario's protestations of innocence and instead of joining the rest of the party for supper at the hotel as usual, retired to her room.

At midnight the lights in the hotel, apart from those in the touring party's sitting room, were all extinguished and guests had only dim wax candles to light them on their way to bed. 'We had risen from table,' wrote Frederick Beale, 'and were preparing to find our re-spective apartments when, to our astonishment, Grisi burst into the room in a most abject state of terror. "Save me! save me!" she cried, rushing into Lablache's arms. "I may have killed him."

'"Whatever is the matter?" we all asked eagerly in chorus.

'"I have been waiting at my door for Mario—I thought I heard him coming along the corridor—I went out and seized him by the arm—he dropped the candle—we were in the dark—I shook him—he screamed—and then I found that it was someone else—I believe I have frightened him to death."'

The stranger whom Grisi had mistaken for Mario was not dead, only surprised and alarmed. The situation was explained to him and Grisi, whose fits of jealousy, however violent, never lasted long, was reconciled with Mario. The story became one that she loved to tell whenever she was in Dublin at Morrisson's Hotel, pointing out the door of the room where she had waited—a room that no doubt had other, more sentimental memories for her as well.

I puritani was repeated on Saturday and *Norma* on Monday 6 September. The *Evening Mail* critic was rapidly running out of superlatives: 'Every succeeding performance seems to give Grisi the power of touching new chords of sympathy, and of opening new springs of delight in the breasts of her hearers. The enthusiasm goes on like her own voice, in a crescendo passage, mounting, soaring, cumulating, till the pitch of rapture is complete, and the power of enjoyment seems strained to the utmost, yet a new sweetness attends the next strain, and a new and corresponding capacity of delight develops itself as fast as the enchantress calls for it.'

The other singers also received their share of praise: 'We can add nothing to Lablache's fame; but if our warm commendations can aid in the least in increasing the reputation of Signor Mario, he has them most heartily.'

Another performance of *La sonnambula* was followed by a concert in the Round Room of the Rotunda. The programme began with the Prayer from *Mosé* and if the chorus of voices was not quite so illustrious as in London during May, the combination of the Grisi cousins, Mario and the two Lablaches must still have been extremely impressive.

The final opera to be presented in Dublin was *Il barbiere di Siviglia* given on Friday 10 September for the benefit of Lablache, who sang Bartolo and 'was excused in desiring for himself a being as lively and so charming in every action and movement' as the Rosina of Grisi. She sang the Variations on an Air by Rode in the Lesson scene, 'giving her an opportunity of displaying the peculiar brilliancy of her mode of execution.'

Mario's Almaviva was also much admired and it was remarked that he courted his Rosina with particular fervour and intensity. '*The source of his emotion appears to be derived from nature* [my italics] and if the current at times runs too rapidly and breaks its legitimate channels, no surprise ought to be entertained, for talent is always intolerant of control, however it may ultimately obey its influence.'

After a final performance of *I puritani* on Saturday 11 September, the fortnight's season in Dublin ended; the singers made a short tour of the English provinces before returning to Paris. Touring, in the days before the railway network had spread across the country, was no light undertaking. Frederick Beale's son Willert, who as a child accompanied his father on several such tours, described some of the hazards confronting the singers: 'Private carriages were provided for the vocalists, who frequently made it a condition in their contracts that they were not to travel by stage-coach. Grisi and Mario, Lablache and Tamburini, during one of the early tours, were lost for a day and night in the Derbyshire hills, the postilions having missed their way owing to a dense fog. The singers suffered serious privations and were greatly alarmed. They were travelling from Buxton to Sheffield and did not reach the latter place until some time after the audience that had assembled to listen to them had been dismissed, and messengers had been sent in all directions to search for them.'

The Théâtre-Italien re-opened in a newly furbished and decorated Salle Ventadour on Saturday 2 October 1841 with *Semiramide*. Grisi, in the title role, evoked the splendour of Babylon by 'the superb brilliance of her gaze, the majesty of her regal deportment and that sovereign manner which she derives from the knowledge of her own perfect beauty.'

Mario made his first appearance a week later in a familiar part, that of Nemorino in *L'elisir d'amore*. The event for which the regulars of the Italiens were waiting with particular interest, took place on Tuesday 11 October, when *I puritani* was given with the new quartet of Grisi, Mario, Tamburini and Lablache.

'The public is slowly getting accustomed to the absence of Rubini,' wrote Gautier. 'After all, we bet the ladies genuinely prefer a noble and handsome young man like Mario to the tea-strainer face and thick figure of the King of tenors.'

It was not for his appearance alone that Mario won applause that night. 'The young tenor obtained a real and well-merited success in the role of Arturo,' wrote Délécluze in the *Journal des Débats*. 'In the quartet of the first act and the finale of the last, where the tenor has such an important part and which we have always heard sung with such perfection, Mario was listened to with the liveliest attention and was greatly applauded. The finale, in particular, was sung with so much purity and expression, that the audience insisted on hearing it a second time.'

Quite apart from the beauty of his voice and the marked improvement of his technique, Mario showed, in the opinion of Délécluze, both modesty and good taste in the manner in which he sang the role of Arturo. 'He had at the same time to follow the tradition, in many ways sacred, laid down by his predecessor, and also to avoid any servile imitation. Powerfully aided by the admirably fresh, young timbre of his voice, Mario was himself, his singing simple, expressive and refined. At the beginning his emotion was intense and naturally it would be so; but his good reception by the public gradually gave him confidence and by the end of the opera the young singer was in full possession of his powers and demonstrating them in the most brilliant way.'

The first and in many ways most severe hurdle successfully overcome, Mario had next to tackle the roles of Elvino in *La sonnambula* and of Edgardo in *Lucia di Lammermoor*, both with Persiani as his partner. Grisi appeared in *Norma*, winning her customary success, and at the end of November there were some particularly high-spirited performances of *Il barbiere di Siviglia*, with Grisi, Mario and the two Lablaches—the same cast as in Dublin. Mario was considered to have made excellent progress since taking on so many new and important roles, and to have worked hard at increasing the flexibility of his voice.

After a revival of *Lucrezia Borgia* at the beginning of December, there followed Mercadante's *La Vestale* on 23 December. This opera, much admired in Italy, was not greatly liked by the Théâtre-Italien audiences, according to Gautier, perhaps because it contained many choral passages and gave little opportunity for display by the soloists. When the cast contained Grisi, Mario and Tamburini, this was felt to be a waste of talent.

Nevertheless, 'Mlle. Grisi, whose beautiful face is marvellously suited by the antique fillet, has in the part of Emilia moments of tragic inspiration which recall her Norma and which produce a great effect. The scene of her execution in the third act was played with admirable pathos, truth and poetry. Mario wears a superb golden armour and looks like the god Mars in person.'

If Mercadante's opera received respectful rather than enthusiastic notices and only six performances, the next 'new' work to be heard at the Italiens was given a very different reception. This was Rossini's revised and completed *Stabat Mater*, first performed in public on 7 January 1842. Rossini had written no major work since *Guillaume Tell*, more than a dozen years previously and in default of a new opera, the audience was perfectly willing to take the *Stabat Mater* to its heart, especially when sung by Grisi, Albertazzi, Mario and Tamburini. The work was in ten sections, comprising the original six plus four new numbers.

The opening section, *Stabat Mater*, for solo quartet, full chorus and orchestra, evoked thunderous applause. *Cujus animam*, for tenor, was superbly sung by Mario, whose silvery, elegiac tones perfectly suited the slow, melancholy music; this was followed by *Quis est homo*, a duet for the two female voices. *Pro peccatis*, sung by Tamburini, was encored, and followed by *Eia, Mater*, also for the bass. *Sancta Mater*, which in this performance began the second part, consisted of a quartet that Gautier found a little too theatrical, though very beautiful. Albertazzi sang *Fac ut portem* for mezzo-soprano, and then Grisi brought the entire audience to its feet, cheering wildly, with her magnificent rendering of the *Inflammatus*. *Quando corpus morietur*, for unaccompanied vocal quartet, and *Amen* in a four-part fugal setting, brought the *Stabat Mater* to a close.

Towards the end of January a concert was held in the Salle des Maréchaux at the Royal Palace of the Tuileries. It was attended by King Louis-Philippe, Queen Marie Amélie, Queen Cristina of Spain and the royal Dukes and Duchesses of Orléans, Nemours, Aumale and Montpensier. The orchestra was under the direction of Auber and the singers included Grisi, Persiani, Albertazzi, Mario, Tamburini and Lablache. The programme for the first half consisted of music by Grétry, Donizetti and Mercadante, while in the second part Grisi and Persiani sang the Letter Duet from *Le nozze di Figaro*; Balfe and his wife, the Hungarian-born Lina Rosa, sang a duet from Donizetti's *Pia de' Tolomei*; Persiani, Albertazzi and Mario gave the trio from *Beatrice di Tenda*; Tamburini and Lablache sang a duet from Balfe's *Falstaff* and the concert ended with the finale of *Norma*.

Balfe and his wife had come to Paris the previous autumn, after the failure of his attempt to establish English Opera at the Lyceum in London with his own *Keolanthe*, in which Mrs Balfe sang the leading role. According to a paragraph in *La France Musicale*, Balfe, 'the Auber of England' had come to Paris to prepare the production of a three-act opera, *Elfrida*, for the Théâtre-Italien. The principal parts were to be sung by Grisi, Mario and Tamburini. *Elfrida* never materialized, neither in Paris nor anywhere else. Balfe, as one of his biographers later wrote, 'was suddenly and pressingly summoned to an audience with the fair and fascinating prima donna, at whose instigation and under whose auspices the work had been begun and almost completed, and the ultimate destinies whereof were inextricably bound up with her sovereign will or whim.'

The truth behind Charles Lamb Kenney's heavily ironic insinuations is simple enough: Grisi was pregnant. Her child had probably been conceived the previous September, either in Dublin or during the subsequent tour of the English provinces. By the last night of the Théâtre-Italien season, 30 March, when *Lucrezia Borgia* was given for Mario's benefit, she was over six months pregnant. During the final scene she became ill and had to leave the stage. What followed was described in the *Morning Post* of a few days later:

'The other night in Paris when Grisi was suddenly taken ill in the middle of a roulade and was led off the stage in a fainting state, the audience screamed and yelled and hooted at the manager when he came forward to request their indulgence; nor would the barbarians cease their clamour, until the unfortunate "singing woman" (*Standard* loquitur) [a reference to the duel between de Melcy and Castlereagh] screwed up her almost exhausted energies and finished the opera.'

Grisi did not, of course, sing that summer at Her Majesty's Theatre.

Lumley, who was now manager, soon found himself in trouble. The contingent of Italian singers from Paris, including Persiani, Mario and Lablache, did not arrive in London until the second week in April. After some performances of *Lucia*, on Saturday 16 April *L'elisir d'amore* was presented, with Persiani, Mario, Lablache and, in Tamburini's usual role of Sergeant Belcore, the baritone Giorgio Ronconi.

Creator of many Donizetti roles and, the previous month, of the title role of Verdi's *Nabucco* at La Scala, Ronconi was not greatly liked on this, his first engagement in London. It was as difficult for him to follow Tamburini, probably the most technically perfect of all the *vieille garde* singers, as it was for Mario to replace Rubini. Queen Victoria, who was at the performance of *L'elisir* on 16 April, summed up the general opinions of her opera-loving subjects: 'Ronconi I cannot very much admire. He has a powerful, but a harsh voice, and does not act well.'

When Ronconi returned to London a few years later, he quickly became popular; his voice remained harsh, but his dramatic ability was recognized as outstanding.

L'elisir was popular with the public, despite the absence of Tamburini, but Persiani became indisposed and *Norma* was announced, with a Madame Moltini in the title role. As Carlo Guasco, the second tenor, was also ill, Lumley asked Mario to sing Pollione. Mario refused, giving as excuse a sore throat and producing two doctors' certificates to prove it. Lumley then wrote to Mario imploring him, if he could not sing, at least to appear in *Norma*. Mario replied that he was engaged to sing, not to appear. Lumley finally managed to find another tenor and suspended Mario on the grounds that he had violated the articles of his engagement.

Lumley's account of the incident is prejudiced, but basically not far from the truth. Mario nearly always did refuse to sing Pollione with any Norma other than Grisi. As soon as he was in a position to do so, he gave up the part in London altogether, only consenting to sing it occasionally on tour.

Mario remained in London throughout the summer, singing in concerts and at private parties. At the Earl of Westmorland's Concert of Ancient Music, patronized by the Queen and Prince Albert, the programme included the quartet from Mozart's *Idomeneo*, a trio from *Così fan tutte* and an aria from Paisiello's version of *Il barbiere di Siviglia*, sung by Mario, 'the very Lindoro of the opera—sweet, sentimental and Spanish-looking.'

There were concerts at Buckingham Palace on 20 May, when Mario sang Raoul's romance, 'Plus blanche que la blanche hermine' from *Les*

Huguenots; and on 1 June, when the Queen noted in her journal that Mario sang more beautifully than ever. At the end of June he took part in an evening of *Tableaux vivants* at Gloucester House with a largely amateur—and aristocratic—cast.

Rossini's *Stabat Mater* was given at the Princes Theatre on 1 July, when Mario again took the tenor part. The work itself was not so ecstatically received as in Paris, but the performance was highly praised, with Mario and Joseph Staudigl, the Austrian bass, earning special commendation. At a concert on Saturday 9 July given by the Duke and Duchess of Cambridge, the male-voice quartet from the second act of *Le Comte Ory* was sung by Rubini, Mario, Ronconi and Lablache, almost certainly the last occasion when the two tenors sang together. Rubini did not sing in London after the summer of 1842, though he continued to appear in Russia.

Meanwhile, at the beginning of June, Grisi's and Mario's first child was born. Later accounts mostly refer to the baby as Giulia, but on her burial certificate at Père Lachaise cemetery in Paris, where she was buried on 24 January 1844, two days after her death aged eighteen months, her names are given as Marie-Jeanne-Catherine.

By the end of August 1842 Grisi was sufficiently recovered to join a touring party, again managed by Frederick Beale, with Mario and the two Lablaches. The company opened in Dublin on Monday 5 September with *I puritani*. Grisi was suffering from a cold and there was no performance the following night. *Norma* was announced for Wednesday, but had to be cancelled as Grisi was still indisposed, and a concert substituted. There were further concerts on Thursday, Friday and Saturday; *Norma* was finally given on Monday 12 September, with Grisi back in her best voice and Mario making no objections to singing Pollione. At a performance of *Anna Bolena* on 14 September Mario sang the role of Percy for the first time; he was encored in 'Vivi tu' as Rubini always had been. The season ended on Monday 19 September with *La sonnambula*.

Chapter 5

HAD HIS CAREER allowed him the time, or had he had the inclination for such retrospective indulgence, Mario could have been justifiably proud of his achievements to date. In less than four years he had risen from the status of gifted amateur to the position of undisputed *primo tenore* in both Paris and London. He had won the love of a beautiful woman, herself established at the top of their profession even more securely than he was, and who had borne him a child.

Only two shadows marred the brilliance of their joint future: one was Mario's continuing exile from the country of his birth; the other was Grisi's now bitterly regretted marriage to de Melcy. Divorce for Catholics was at that time out of the question; presumably there were no grounds for an annulment such as that obtained by Malibran, whose first marriage had been contracted in America when she was a minor. The only loosening of the marriage tie that Grisi was ever able to obtain from her husband was a legal separation that allowed her to keep at least part of her huge earnings. A percentage still had to be paid to de Melcy, who outlived his wife by many years. Meanwhile both singers were at their peak and could command enormous salaries; a lack of money was the least of their worries.

The Théâtre-Italien reopened on Saturday 1 October 1842 with Persiani and Mario in *Lucia di Lammermoor*, which was followed a week later by the same singers in *La sonnambula*. Grisi made her first appearance since the painful scenes of *Lucrezia Borgia* the previous spring in *Semiramide*, with Viardot in the role of Arsace. To begin with the house was a little cold and unresponsive. Viardot was understandably nervous, but soon recovered her confidence. Grisi, 'in the full brilliance of her beauty and with all the power of her prodigious talents', rose as always to the challenge of an artistic rival. The scenes for Semiramide and Arsace were wildly applauded and several numbers encored, while at the end the stage was covered in bouquets.

The first opera of the season new to Paris was Donizetti's *Linda di Chamounix*, presented on Thursday 17 November with Persiani, Mario, Tamburini, the two Lablaches and, in the role of the boy Pierotto, which she had created in Vienna the previous May, the contralto Marietta Brambilla. The opera was quite well received and the singers were all praised, especially Mario and Persiani, whose duet in the third act was considered absolutely ravishing.

Six weeks later another Donizetti opera, this time a work specially written for the Théâtre-Italien, received its first performance. After rehearsals supervised by the composer that had continued all through December, *Don Pasquale* began its triumphant career on 3 January 1843, launched with such a flood of praise as very few operas can ever have enjoyed.

'Of all the Italian operas written expressly for Paris,' wrote Délécluze in the *Journal des Débats*, 'none since *I puritani* has obtained more favour with the public for which it was composed. *Don Pasquale*, written for Mme. Grisi, Mario, Tamburini and Lablache, gained a complete success on the third of this month. Several pieces were encored, and at the end of the second act the composer was led before the curtain by Lablache and received an ovation.'

Grisi's Norina, Mario's Ernesto and Tamburini's Doctor Malatesta were all lauded to the skies, but the greatest number of superlatives was heaped on Lablache in the title role. In *La Presse* Gautier described the old man, dressed up to meet, as he thinks, his modest young bride: 'He wears a superb mahogany-coloured wig, so tightly curled it rises of its own accord, a green tail coat with carved gold buttons, which does not meet across his enormous paunch, giving him the aspect of some monstrous beetle that tries to open its wings and fly away, without success.'

Gautier also included another of his romantic evocations of Mario's voice. 'In the last scene,' he wrote, 'it is a beautiful Italian night, a clear April night, with the moonlight partly azure, partly silver. The ashes and poplars in the garden tremble under the stars like spangles on a dancer's dress. A voice, sweet and melancholy, rises in the silence like a golden rocket, singing a delicious serenade, to which he gives the innocent charm of a dream.'

After praising the overture for the freshness of its themes and the cleverness of the orchestration, Gautier singled out the chorus for maids, modistes and menservants, which he found original and effective, while 'the serenade at the rendez-vous is colourful and will quickly become popular.'

The story, related by Charles de Boigne in *Petits Mémoires de l'Opéra*, that Donizetti produced this serenade, 'Com' è gentil', from among the papers in his apartment after the dress rehearsal, which had fallen completely flat, and sent it round to Mario to learn immediately, is a little difficult to believe. The tune is quoted in the overture and

Ernesto specifically mentions a serenade in his letter of assignation to Norina, so presumably Donizetti must always have intended something to be sung at that point. On the other hand, *Don Pasquale* was composed in a great hurry (although no faster than many other of Donizetti's operas), and many alterations to text and music were made during the rehearsal period.

Whatever the truth of the matter, Gautier was indubitably right in his prediction that 'Com' è gentil' would rapidly become popular. Mario himself sang it with great frequency in concert halls and drawing rooms, while in stage performances of the opera it was always encored.

Don Pasquale was given fifteen times that season, the most successful that Donizetti ever achieved at the Théâtre-Italien; there were nearly 40 performances of five of his operas.

At the beginning of March, in a performance for Grisi's benefit, Mario attempted yet another part long associated with Rubini—the title role of Rossini's *Otello*. 'The evening offered a double attraction,' wrote Gautier. 'Mdlle. Grisi has not appeared in the part of Desdemona for a long time, having ceded it to Mme. Pauline Garcia-Viardot, and we know how beautiful, pathetic and sublime Mdlle. Grisi can be in this character, which Rossini and Shakespeare have made the living incarnation of grace and tragedy; then it is the first time that Mario has tackled the role of the Moor of Venice.'

The fanatical admirers of Rubini who cried sacrilege and profanation at the idea of another tenor taking over their idol's finest roles received little sympathy from Gautier. 'To regret the past and despise the present is an eccentricity common to old men and theatre-goers. "Ah! if you had heard Garcia! if you had heard Donzelli as Otello!" these same enthusiasts used to exclaim in the time of Rubini, as they now use the name and memory of Rubini as weapons against Mario. Perhaps we who are young today will say in our turn, in later years, "Ah! if you had heard Mario sing the Moor of Venice!" We do not share this admiration for the past in any way. Let the dead sleep under their marble slabs or mounds of grass.'

Gautier may have firmly stated his conviction that the present was as good as, or even better than the past, but not all the critics agreed with him. Mario was condemned by several newspapers with an exaggerated love of tradition, for making his first appearance dressed as a Venetian general of the sixteenth century, 'in brassards and gauntlets of gold, coat of mail with surcoat of patterned damask, as painted by Veronese or Giorgione.'

Gautier found this change perfectly logical. 'Naturally Otello, when in the service of Venice, wears the costume of his rank. At home he can put on his caftans and embroidered coats, together with his eastern habits, nothing is easier. Mario showed good taste.'

Opinions were also divided over the way in which Mario sang the role of Otello. He was criticized for phrasing the first-act cavatina with too much mildness and elegance, but again Gautier sprang to his defence. 'The indolence and luxuriousness can well be indicated in this way, to form a happy contrast with the ranting and roaring of the catastrophe. Nothing is gentler than a Moor when he is not engaged in cutting your throat or strangling you. Such tigers in repose have a smooth, coaxing, languorous air about them, so they are mistaken for the gentlest animals in the world. It is not necessary, therefore, that Otello should act like a wild beast from the very beginning.'

Mario showed much spirit and energy in the very dramatic second-act duet with Iago and 'displayed unexpected strength, both in feeling and voice, in all the savage parts of the role . . . As for Madame Grisi, her beauty, her acting and her singing left nothing to be desired—a magnificent trinity, so rarely found in the same person. At the end of the opera, with an avalanche of camellias and a flood of bouquets, there was a new and appropriate idea; from one of the boxes a little white dove was launched, carrying a coronet, but instead of alighting mythologically at the feet of the diva, the bird, frightened by the shouting and noise, settled on the head of a gentleman in the stalls.'

Less than a week after the closure of the Théâtre-Italien at the end of March, Mario reappeared on 6 April at Her Majesty's Theatre as Elvino in *La sonnambula*, the first time that he had sung the role in London. In the words of Lumley, 'to Mario the past had been forgiven. He was universally declared to have gained sensibly in finish and style; and from his reappearance may be dated the commencement of that confirmed and undisputed popularity which he afterwards enjoyed.'

Twelve days later, when Grisi sang in *Norma*, the second prodigal was welcomed home with equal warmth and enthusiasm. At the beginning of May, both singers appeared in *Il barbiere di Siviglia*, with the Lablaches and, replacing Tamburini in the title role, Luciano Fornasari. Chorley, who had noted somewhat sourly earlier in the season that 'the delicious bloom of [Mario's] voice is gone; the tone may be steadier than formerly, but in its general delivery it is certainly coarser', now made amends by his more gracious praise of the tenor: 'Signor Mario was a very graceful Lindoro, almost the best in our recollection, singing with greater refinement and flexibility than he has done this season.'

Queen Victoria was present at a later performance of *Il barbiere* in
June. She thought that 'Grisi (whom I had not seen for two years) sang
most beautifully; she has grown older and much fatter, but she is still
very handsome, and I would prefer to hear a few notes of hers, to a
whole scene of Persiani's. Mario, as Count Almaviva, sang and acted
delightfully, and was beautifully "costumé" in four different old
Spanish costumes.' The Queen praised Lablache (Bartolo) and young
Lablache (Don Basilio) but did not mention Fornasari, who suffered
the fate of all Tamburini replacements and was treated at first with
total indifference, if not downright disapproval. *La gazza ladra* was
revived on 11 May, with Grisi in her old part of Ninetta and Mario
singing Gianetto for the first time in London. He appeared in eight
roles new to London that summer, some, like Lindoro in Rossini's
L'italiana in Algeri, never to be repeated, some, like Don Ottavio in
Don Giovanni, destined to become favourites.

'What predecessor in the part of Ottavio,' enquired *The Illustrated
London News*, 'ever sang the music of Mozart with the sound, the
purity, the love-breathing quality of voice of Mario? We fearlessly
answer our own question and say—none! Not even the great Rubini
himself. We never heard "Il mio tesoro" sung by anyone before
Mario's time with the chasteness and tenderness which he infuses into
it, with his deep feeling for the author's meaning, and the young
freshness of intonation that breathes from his voice without exertion,
"like the unforced aroma of a flower".'

Linda di Chamounix was produced on 1 June for Persiani's benefit,
with the same cast as in Paris, apart from the substitution of Fornasari
for Tamburini. As in Paris the opera was politely if coolly received.
The London public was reserving for *Don Pasquale* the warmth and
enthusiasm it could display when a new opera genuinely pleased and
caught its fancy.

Don Pasquale was not performed complete until 29 June, but
meanwhile, as in the case of *I puritani* eight years previously, tantaliz-
ing fragments were heard at concerts earlier in the month. At Mme.
Dulckens' benefit, for instance, which was 'one of those luxurious
entertainments in which every dish is a delicacy . . . the chief novelty
was a pretty buffo duet from *Don Pasquale*, inimitably sung by Grisi
and Lablache.' A week later, the programme for Mr Benedict's
Concert, which 'exceeded all former exceedings, both as to extent and
novelty in the music selected and multitude of executants', included
Ernesto's Serenade, sung by Mario, with chorus, and encored.
Chorley considered that this Serenade 'surpasses in elegance (if that
can be) the Barcarolle in *Marin Faliero*, and is one of the most

fascinating of those modern tunes which, having crept into the ear, are not to be dislodged thence.'

Finally *Don Pasquale* reached the stage of Her Majesty's, at a benefit performance for Lablache, and scored the same overwhelming popular success as in Paris, despite the absence of Tamburini in the role of Malatesta. Lablache rightly came in for the lion's share of compliments, but Grisi and Mario also received much praise and the Serenade was, as always, encored.

When *I puritani* was revived on 15 July with only two members of the original quartet, the English critics were less willing than their French colleagues to accept the replacements. 'Grisi and Lablache remain,' wrote Chorley, 'the one a fount of melody, the other a tower of strength—and both in this opera, apparently, stronger than Time; since not even in the first season of "Son vergin" and "Suoni la tromba" was the one more brilliant the other more impressive, than on Saturday; but Mario vice Rubini is cold, half-finished and, as far as falsetto goes, incompetent.'

This last deficiency caused no regret to Chorley. He thought that 'with Rubini ought to retire all those altissimo tenor parts which are in fact the property of the contralto, and, however amazing from the lips of the person whose peculiar powers they were meant to exhibit, are intrinsically unnatural and offensive.'

Chorley there pinpoints one of the chief difficulties that Mario had to surmount when he took over Rubini's repertory. The public did not at all share the critic's view that use of the falsetto was 'unnatural and offensive.' The tenor singing Arturo, or Elvino or Percy, was expected to be able to sing the four or five extra notes up to the high F or even G, that Rubini used to attain and which formed, in the later part of his career, the strongest register of his voice. Mario quite soon taught himself to use the falsetto with comparative ease, but at this stage in his career it seems that he was unable to join it to the rest of his voice without a break.

For his final new part of the season he attempted Don Ramiro in Rossini's *La Cenerentola*, a role he sang three times, then never returned to again. Grisi took the title role, with Fornasari as Dandini and Lablache as Don Magnifico. Once more Chorley found fault with the cast, apart from Lablache: 'Mme. Grisi leaves nothing to wish for, as far as brilliant execution goes—but so buxom and prosperous a lady is not our Cinderella . . . the innocence, pathos and elegance of the part, in short, are wanting.' The *Times* critic also praised Grisi's singing, especially in the final rondo, and found her touching and expressive in the ballad 'Una volta c'era un rè', but he, too, felt that 'Grisi neither looks nor acts the meek, oppressed Cinderella.'

Mario was similarly taken to task. 'Signor Mario makes a beautifully dressed walking Prince,' wrote Chorley, 'but will he always remain *near* singing well and never accomplish the feat? or does he wait, like Rubini, till his voice begins to leave him, to call in the aid of art?'

On 19 August Lumley sent Grisi a letter renewing her contract for the following three seasons, 1844, 1845 and 1846, 'which will begin for you at the re-opening of the Theatre after Easter, though you will never be asked to sing before 10 April and your engagement will terminate regularly on 20 August each year.'

Lumley offered his prima donna £3,200 for each season, payable in three equal instalments on 1 June, 1 July and 3 August. The other clauses of the contract, such as that concerning the roles she should sing, were to be the same as in the preceding engagements. In his final paragraph Lumley added: 'I count, Madame, on the renewal of the promise you gave me last year relative to clause seven of your previous contract, which limits the number of your performances each week.'

Grisi, having crossed out two words, initialled the contract and returned it to Lumley, making no reference to the promise mentioned by the manager in his last paragraph. Officially, Grisi was obliged to give only two performances a week, but the management frequently tried to make her increase that number to three and on occasion she had agreed to waive the strict application of clause seven. During the 1844 season, as will be seen, there were frequent disputes on this—and other—subjects between Lumley and all the singers of the *vieille garde*.

Meanwhile the Théâtre-Italien reopened as usual early in October 1843. The first two novelties of the season, *Belisario*, given on 24 October with Grisi and Fornasari, and *Maria di Rohan*, on 14 November, with Grisi, Brambilla and Ronconi, were both by Donizetti. Neither opera was received with more than polite enthusiasm, though Grisi was much admired in the title role of the latter work. Gautier, however, did not approve of her hair style in *Maria di Rohan*: 'Grisi is always Grisi, even though her hair is done in ringlets as the costume demands. The antique style suits her better, with a head that would not look out of place on the shoulders of the Venus de Milo. A curly-headed goddess is not the less beautiful; but she appears a little strange at first. Marble statues are not usually seen in curlers.'

The third new opera of the Italiens season was *Il fantasma*, composed by Giuseppe Persiani for his wife Fanny Tacchinardi-Persiani and first performed on 14 December with a cast that included Mario, Fornasari and Ronconi as well as Persiani. Despite some spectacular music for the soprano and tenor, both of whom were much applauded, and a sleep-walking scene for the bass, *Il fantasma* on the whole failed to please and was given only four times.

The same fate was suffered by Federico Ricci's *Corrado d'Alta-mura*, presented at the Théâtre-Italien on 15 March 1844. Not even the participation of Grisi, Mario and Ronconi could save this opera. The best received number, a cavatina for soprano, 'Oh! cara tu sei', made an effective concert piece for Grisi, who had already sung it in London the previous summer, at Sir William Abdy's private concert.

Revivals during the season included *Norma*, *Semiramide*, *Anna Bolena*, *Il barbiere* and *Don Pasquale*. *Otello* had been announced for Grisi's benefit on 22 January, but little Marie-Jeanne-Catherine died on that day, and the performance was cancelled. The child was buried two days later in Père Lachaise cemetery. Grisi and Mario did not openly live together until about a year later, when she finally obtained her separation from de Melcy. But the two singers must have been deeply upset at the death of their first child. Nevertheless, Mario appeared in *Il barbiere* on 28 January and Grisi sang in *Maria di Rohan* two nights later. *Otello* received several performances during February and March, and the season ended on 31 March with *I puritani*.

The same opera, nine days afterwards, brought back Grisi and Mario to Her Majesty's in London. The lady, at least, was given a rapturous welcome by Chorley: 'Never was Grisi more welcome to our ears than on Tuesday evening (9 April), when she made her entry for the season in *I puritani*. Never indeed was her voice more lustrous and brilliant or more perfectly under command; she is thinner than she was last year, but this is to the advantage of her appearance.'

The tenor was greeted with rather more cautious words of praise: 'Mario sang the elegant "A te o cara" very well, and we hoped to find progress in him also; but he would disenchant us in his third act; which was generally dispatched with indifference . . . There is too much of the *enfant gâté* in his singing; and it is a pity, for his voice is delicious.'

Less than a month after the triumphant return of his prima donna, Lumley was once more fighting a rearguard action against a frigidly polite but implacable opponent. He had apparently asked Grisi to sing the role of Elisetta, the plainer of the two sisters in Cimarosa's *Il matrimonio segreto*, as she had done on a memorable occasion three years previously. Grisi replied to this suggestion on Sunday 6 May in a letter of unconcealed outrage.

I believe my letter will cause you some annoyance, but you will understand without difficulty that my reason for refusing your request are not caused by ill will. From the way you spoke to me, I understand that you are determined to make me accept the role of Elisetta in *Il matrimonio segreto*, a role I sang in the past only for the benefit of Monsieur Laporte.

Last winter I absolutely refused to sing this role in Paris, because it is far too *secondary* and has always been filled by the *seconda donna*. As my repertory is sufficiently tiring, I think it unnecessary to add to it a role that is beneath me, and which Mme. Bellini could quite well sing, without doing the work the slightest harm. Also, the part of Carolina has always been my role, until I ceded it to Mme. Persiani, and it would be most unsuitable for me to give it up for a *secondary* role.

I am always happy, Monsieur, to be of help to you, but I cannot descend to being a seconda donna, almost a *member of the chorus,* when I have so much else to do.

Lumley must have returned to the attack, for Grisi wrote him another letter a few days later, expressing in even stronger terms her belief that to sing such a secondary role as Elisetta would harm her reputation.

The only operas new to London provided by Lumley that summer were *Corrado d'Altamura*, which was received as coldly as in Paris, and Costa's *Don Carlos*. Like Verdi's version some twenty years later, Costa's opera was based on the tragedy by Schiller. Despite a magnificent cast, which included Grisi as the Queen, Mario as Don Carlos, Fornasari as the Marquis of Posa and Lablache as King Philip, the work did not become popular. At the first performance, on Thursday 20 June, Mario was hoarse and had to omit his principal aria. Nevertheless, the audience applauded both composer and singers with some enthusiasm. Chorley blamed the ultimate lack of success of Costa's *Don Carlos* on the gloomy and painful subject of the opera—a criticism also advanced against Verdi's *Don Carlos* on its first production.

Otello was performed on 4 July for Grisi's benefit, when Mario sang the title role for the first time in London. He did not please the critic of the *Athenaeum*: 'The hero's part is the noblest in the Italian singer's repertory,' wrote Chorley, 'it is not however in Signor Mario's reach . . . His voice is essentially a sentimental rather than a passionate or a forcible one; but high style and vivid conception might overcome this unfitness, in place of which our graceful tenor only brings to bear increased animation, identical in quality with that of his Nemorino, Pollione and Gennaro.'

Grisi, on the other hand, received unstinted praise, as being 'in her best voice, best looks, and best humour.' Chorley was particularly impressed by her execution of Desdemona's aria in the second act. 'This is, perhaps, the grandest song for stage display in the entire range of Italian Opera, and we doubt if it was ever sung with greater force and brilliancy; the divisions on the words "io moriro" were worth many a lesson in solfeggi to all who wish for an example of force combined with volubility.'

The *Times* critic was rather more appreciative of Mario's efforts as Otello. He 'put forth all his energy, as if he were thoroughly aware of the responsibility of the situation. The huskiness of the voice seems gone, never to return and while it is capable of uttering its gentlest tones, its sweetest falsetto, he can force it into an organ of passion and vehemence to a degree which with him is unusual.'

Mario's magnificent costumes—in those days the responsibility of the singer—also received complimentary mention in *The Times*: 'Of course Mario dresses Otello such as no one has ever dressed him before, for he does this with every character he assumes . . . When Otello appears in the first act, Mario sinks the Turkish altogether and wears a complete suit of gilt armour, with a helmet, a blue tunic embroidered and a white flowing bernouse.'

Mario took endless trouble over his costumes. An accomplished artist, he usually designed them himself, obviously with more respect for historical accuracy and period detail than the majority of his colleagues was able to show.

Several times during the latter part of the season, Grisi wrote to Lumley invoking clause seven of her contract—the clause that obliged her to sing not more than twice a week at Her Majesty's. She pleaded fatigue, claiming that if she sang on Tuesday and Thursday she needed rest on Saturday. Lumley accused the singers of tiring themselves at private concerts, at the expense of his theatre, and he certainly had some justification for such a charge; on the other hand, he was always trying to force extra performances from them, whatever the terms of their engagements. As late as 7 August, less than a fortnight before the end of the season, Grisi was still having to remind the manager that 'as much in order to establish my present and future rights as to spare my health, for what remains of the season I will not sing more than twice a week.'

After the usual tour of the English provinces, the Italian singers returned to Paris, where the Théâtre-Italien reopened on 1 October

1844 with Persiani and Mario in *Linda di Chamounix*. Grisi appeared in *Norma* five days later, but neither she nor Mario sang any roles new to them until 5 December, when they both took part in a revival of Bellini's *Il pirata*, the first for several years.

Gualtiero, the eponymous pirate-hero of Bellini's opera, was another of the roles especially written for Rubini. It was, moreover, a part of which the older tenor had been very fond; but Mario, too, found it congenial from the start. 'He was encored, recalled, applauded most enthusiastically and rightly so,' wrote Gautier. 'It would be difficult to find a voice that is fresher, purer and more moving than that of the young tenor; and he is beginning to add to these lucky gifts the illumination of experience and the arts of a consummate singer.'

It was Gautier's opinion that Mario had made enormous progress in the management of his voice. 'At certain moments he used to suffer from a disagreeable huskiness, which is now quite cured; his voice is much more supple and has greatly increased in agility. His acting, awkward to begin with, has become sufficiently dramatic, because expression, for a singer, must be in the voice and not in the movements of his arms and legs. But then we never doubted the promise of Mario,' claimed Gautier, with justifiable self-satisfaction, 'and after his first appearance at the Académie Royale, we drew a horoscope for him that has come true in every detail.'

Grisi also obtained a triumph in *Il pirata*, inspiring Gautier to one of his finest evocations of her stage personality. 'Giulia Grisi sang Imogene for the first time . . . although no woman and no singer has ever been more sure of her beauty and of her voice; or that the public would always receive her with cries of joyous enthusiasm, la Grisi, each time she essays a new part, cannot help being as disturbed, worried, nervous as a pupil at the Conservatoire on her début. It takes a great deal of courage to face that barrier of lights which both dazzle and fascinate. To this emotion, always renewed, the greatest artists owe their finest successes; every night they gamble their reputations on the throw of the dice. The valiant Grisi herself, who with one look can force a whole tribe of Assyrians, a whole school of Druids to their knees, trembles with fear when she has to appear before you and me, before that formidable collection of inoffensive individuals called the public.'

No one else but Gautier has remarked that Grisi—at least at this point in her career—suffered from stage fright. On the contrary, a part of her attraction appears to have lain in her great and obvious enjoyment of singing on stage. Yet when Gautier maintained that 'she was frightened then, that noble and beautiful creature; her Greek brow frowned, her nostrils quivered, her breast heaved', he must be credited with unusual perspicacity. His artist's eye and poet's sensibility gave him an insight denied to most other critics.

When Mario and Grisi appeared in *Lucrezia Borgia*, during January 1845, Donizetti's opera was performed under the title of *La rinegata*. Victor Hugo, from whose play Romani had taken his libretto, objected, not to the libretto itself, but to the French translation which accompanied it at the Théâtre-Italien. Hugo sued the translator, Etienne Monnier and the publisher, Bernard Latte for plagiarism. He won his case, so it became necessary to alter the title and characters of the opera when it was performed in France.

Mario chose *Otello* for his benefit in February, while for hers Grisi offered *Norma* followed by the first act of *Semiramide*. 'Grisi and Norma have become one,' wrote Gautier in another panegyric, 'it is the ideal realized . . . Where did she get that head sculpted by Phidias that she carries so proudly and so nobly on shoulders of polished marble?' he enquired. 'What secret excavation near the Parthenon produced that mask so pure, so classic and so vivacious, that the most violent emotion cannot distort and which remains beautiful during the most dramatic death scene?'

Gautier admitted that there were sopranos who could achieve more difficult technical feats than Grisi ever attempted. 'But if you love real Italian singing,' he continued, 'singing that is generous and expressive, always in tune, the song of a human throat and not the warbling of a flute; if you want to know how love, anger, indignation and pain can sound in the music of the great masters, and how an opera can suddenly become a tragedy or a poem, you must go to the Théâtre-Italien on a night when they are giving *Semiramide* or *Norma*.'

The 'lovely druidess' was in particularly fine voice that night. She sang "Casta diva" with a serene melancholy that made the Théâtre-Italien audience shout with pleasure. In the trio that ends the first act, it was impossible for any Norma to 'display greater energy or a more magnificent violence. The duet and finale of the second act also gave this wonderful singer many occasions for applause. When the black veil was finally lowered over her noble head, the floral bombardment began.'

Intoxicated by the remembered excitement of the scene, Gautier allowed an understandable exaggeration to enter his description: 'An English lady in one of the stage boxes threw a bunch of Parma violets of quite terrifying dimensions; this monstrous bouquet was at least as big as a table seating six people; for a second one feared for the life of the beneficiary; but the perfumed avalanche died politely at her feet.'

DURING APRIL 1845, the Paris newspapers were full of rumours that Mario had been gravely wounded, or even killed, in a duel reported to have taken place in London. Michele Accursi, who acted as Donizetti's agent in Paris, mentioned this duel in a letter to the composer, who was in Vienna, advising him to look for another tenor for the opera that Donizetti was supposed to be writing for the Théâtre-Italien (this opera, alas, never materialized).

The duel was asserted to be the consequence of a quarrel between Giulia Grisi and Jeanne Castellan, the French soprano who took Persiani's place at Her Majesty's that season, over a performance of *Lucia di Lammermoor*. A detailed examination of the performances at Her Majesty's during April quickly proves that no duel involving Mario can possibly have taken place.

Castellan made her first appearance on 1 April in *Lucia di Lammermoor* with the tenor Napoleone Moriani. Grisi and Mario, who had been singing the previous night in Paris at the Italiens, when one act of *I puritani* and one act of *Il barbiere* were performed to mark the end of the season, could hardly have arrived in London before 2 April at the earliest. *Lucia*, with the same cast as before, was repeated at Her Majesty's on Thursday 3 April. Mario sang for the first time that season on 5 April in *La sonnambula*, with Castellan as Amina.

The Queen visited the theatre that night, and noted in her journal that both singers 'sang *quite* beautifully. Mme. Castellan has the loveliest, purest, freshest voice I think I ever heard, with an immense compass. She is very ladylike in her acting. Mario's voice too was splendid, and if possible, it seems to have improved.'

Neither Amina nor Lucia were roles that Grisi considered particularly her own. She sang them on tour but rarely in London, where for several years they had belonged to Persiani. Grisi made her first appearance of the season on Tuesday 8 April in *Norma*, with Moriani as Pollione. On Thursday, an extra, non-subscription night, *Don Pasquale* was revived, with Grisi, Mario, Fornasari and Lablache; the opera was followed by the final scene from *Lucia* sung by Moriani. *Don Pasquale* was repeated on Saturday.

Ernani, the first Verdi opera to be heard in London, which had been produced at Her Majesty's on 8 March, was given on Tuesday 15 April; neither Castellan, Grisi nor Mario sang in it. On 17 April, another extra night, Grisi, with Brambilla, Fornasari and Lablache, sang in *Semiramide*, which was followed by Moriani in the final scene from *Lucia*. The previous day's papers had announced Act II of *La sonnambula* with Castellan and Mario as the second part of the entertainment; this alteration of programme is the only indication that anything might have happened to Mario; but in fact it was to allow Mario and Grisi to sing at a concert in Montague House later that night, when Mario performed two Schubert songs, accompanied by Costa.

Semiramide was repeated for the subscribers on Saturday; *La sonnambula*, again with Castellan and Mario, was given on 22 April. The following night a 'very pretty and elegant party' was, according to Queen Victoria, held at Clarence House. 'Grisi, Mario (in particular) & Lablache sang beautifully.' This time Mario's contribution included Beethoven's 'Adelaïde' as well as Schubert's 'Ave Maria'.

Il barbiere di Siviglia on Thursday 24 April drew the following comments from the *Morning Post* next day: 'What wonderfully gifted performers enact it at Her Majesty's Theatre. But speaking of these, we must express the delight at beholding Mario enacting once more Almaviva. The French newspapers state that he has been killed in a duel—every circumstance is narrated—even the course which the deadly bullet took is related with as much startling detail and veracity as Sir Benjamin Backbite's and Mrs Candour's account of Sir Peter Teazle's fatal duello.' This reference to Sheridan's play, *The School for Scandal*, places the rumours where they belong, in the realm of fiction.

'If Signor Mario be really dead,' continued the *Morning Post* in jocular mood, 'we are right happy he has been considerate enough to leave his ghost behind—a right hearty ghost who last night looked most carnally—the very incarnation of the Caballero and the Hidalgo of those augustan days when Spain could boast of real cavaliers and nobles in bearing as well as lineage.'

Two nights later, when Queen Victoria attended *Il barbiere*, the tenor was not in such good shape. Lablache (as Bartolo) 'was in his highest form and full of new jokes', according to the Queen, 'Grisi in great beauty and in fine voice, but Mario had completely lost his voice, and when he came on to try and sing, said "è impossibile, non posso", bowed, and went off the stage. Upon this Lablache made such a funny, charming face, that the whole audience laughed.'

There is no doubt that Mario's duel was as apocryphal as Sir Peter's

in *The School for Scandal*. By mid-century, duels were greatly frowned
upon in England and had become rare, hole-in-corner affairs. Seven
years earlier, the duel between Castlereagh and de Melcy had pro-
voked an enormous amount of publicity as well as a great scandal. An
encounter between the protectors of two rival prime donne would
certainly have been of equal interest and merited as wide a coverage in
British newspapers. And surely Benjamin Lumley, who was always
looking for facts to discredit Mario and Grisi, would have been the
first to mention such a duel had it ever taken place.

Mario was not, in any case, the sort of man to settle an argument
with pistols. Despite his legendary proficiency as a swordsman—a
skill that he found very useful in his stage career—there is absolutely
no evidence to show that, once he left the Army, he ever touched a gun
of any sort again. He was too lazy and, in the 1840s, far too busy to
fight duels. Then Grisi had nothing to fear from singers such as
Castellan or Persiani, who may have exceeded her in sheer technical
ability but who, in questions of vocal splendour, dramatic ability and
personal beauty, were patently her inferiors. Grisi was quite intelli-
gent enough to realize this and throughout her long career feared
competition from only four other singers; of these Pasta was retired
and Malibran dead, while the other two, Viardot and Jenny Lind, were
not as yet serious threats to her supremacy.

Meanwhile, the season continued. A concert entirely devoted to
music by Prince Albert was given at Buckingham Palace on 2 May, in
which several of the singers from Her Majesty's participated. Mario
sang a Serenata 'Vieni del cor diletto amor', which won the Queen's
approval, as did a duet, 'Siamo nati per amarci', sung by Grisi and
Staudigl. But 'the pearl to my mind was the anthem "Out of the
Deep", which Castellan sang most exquisitely and touchingly, with
her beautiful voice, and she pronounced the English so well.'

Three nights later the Queen gave another concert at Buckingham
Palace; the programme this time consisted of the usual mixture of
songs, operatic arias and ensembles. A duet from *Les Huguenots* sung
by Grisi and Mario was particularly admired by the Queen and her
guests.

Don Giovanni was revived at Her Majesty's, in the presence of the
Queen and Prince Albert, on 8 May. The fine cast included Fornasari
(whom the Queen did not like) in the title role, Grisi as Donna Anna,
Castellan as Zerlina, Lablache as a 'charming and wonderful looking'
Leporello, and Mario as Don Ottavio. 'Il mio tesoro' was, as usual,
encored.

When Bellini's *Il pirata* was performed on Tuesday 13 May, the

London critics followed the example of their Paris colleagues in showering praise on the singers. For once even Chorley had nothing but compliments for Mario: 'we have never heard the tenor to such advantage,' he wrote, 'too frequently his singing has been marked by that gentlemanly indifference which reminds us of first rate amateur performance—promising to sing well rather than achieving it. On Tuesday evening however we had the art he has so frequently approached—so seldom reached.'

Chorley commended the energy with which Mario attacked the part of Gualtiero and the consummate mastery displayed in much of his singing. Even the inevitable comparison with Rubini was not entirely to the disadvantage of the younger tenor: 'In the celebrated and over-rated "Tu vedrai" he did not put forth the intense and tremulous pathos of Rubini, nor has he yet the vocal finish of the Bergamesque tenor, but in the earlier portions of the opera he displayed a force and a fineness (without startling contrast), an animation and a depth of feeling which carried the audience along with him.'

Chorley also noted that Mario had been engaged successfully 'in the task of smoothing and strengthening and sweetening his falsetto, and by his gradual ascent to a high treble note made the stalls scream with delight, just as they were used to scream for Rubini.' Chorley reiterated his dislike of the use of the falsetto, but had to admit that some such artifice was necessary for the singer to make his way through 'the extravagant modern music.' He complimented Mario on his 'improved command over this popular resource, hoping he will use it but sparingly.'

Grisi's Imogene also received unmixed praise from Chorley: 'Mme. Grisi was superb, looking magnificently, acting a most anti-pathetic part with feeling and propriety, and singing with all her old lustre of voice and more than her old volubility of execution.'

During June Grisi incurred Lumley's wrath by refusing to sing in *Roberto Devereux*, but she did consent to appear in Mercadante's *Il giuramento*, which was given on 1 July, with Brambilla, Moriani and Fornasari also in the cast. Two nights later Mario took his benefit in *I puritani*; he also sang Ferrando for the first time when Mozart's *Così fan tutte* was given two performances in the second half of July. The Queen, who attended the first of these, took the audience to task for receiving the opera with such coldness, but herself thought it too long and found 'the story rather uninteresting and absurd.' For once, she enjoyed the ballet more than the opera, as it was the famous *Pas de Quatre*, danced by Taglioni, Cerito, Carlotta Grisi and Grahn.

There was no new Donizetti opera for the Théâtre-Italien to produce during the autumn of 1845, as the composer was already suffering from the illness that eventually caused his madness and death. Instead, Vatel, the manager, fell back on an eleven-year-old work, _Gemma di Vergy_, which failed to please the audience when performed on 16 December, despite the presence of Grisi and Ronconi in the cast.

Vastly more popular was the revival of _Don Pasquale_ in November, with the original singers apart from Ronconi in Tamburini's role of Doctor Malatesta. 'Neither the black spleen of the London fogs, nor the ennui and disillusion of Paris' could resist Lablache in the title role. Gautier goes on to make a very important dramatic point. 'This Titanic prophet of woe, this gigantic jester with the brow of Jupiter, is always immensely effective. In the theatre, actors who play ridiculous parts are usually pathetic . . . Lablache, on the other hand, has only to remove his grotesque make-up and burnt-cork wrinkles, to thunder forth the sublime curse of Brabantio [_Otello_], or the crushing imprecation of Oroveso [_Norma_]; tomorrow Don Pasquale will fulminate in the duet "Suoni la tromba" [_I puritani_] and certainly no more terrible and majestic figure can be imagined. One can therefore surrender entirely to the hilarity he provokes; there is nothing degrading about it, one is not laughing at an infirmity or a misfortune.'

After noting that Grisi was in good voice and looks, Gautier reinforces his previous argument by applying it also to the soprano. 'Norina has never clothed her childish obstinacy, her pretended anger, in such pure and velvet tone. The wild lover of Pollione playing the lively ingénue, is not that an interesting spectacle? Nothing is more pleasing than the charm of strength, the elegance of power. You must see how the lioness coaxes, the statue wheedles, the empress cajoles in her efforts to tease the huge old man.'

Ernesto's Serenade was, as usual, wildly applauded. 'This delicious melody is sung by Mario with a nocturnal limpidity that causes dreams of the moon bathing in the dew, dropping its pearls on the clematis and honeysuckle, or other springlike and poetic fancies.'

Mario was in particularly fine voice that autumn. During performances of _Il barbiere_ and _Il pirata_, 'he enraptured the audience', as Délécluze wrote in the _Journal des Débats_. 'His voice, so fresh and pure, becomes more agile every day, and he is now a remarkable singer.'

But in retrospect much the most important events of that winter were the productions of two Verdi operas, the first to be heard at the Théâtre-Italien; _Nabucco_ was performed in October and _Ernani_ (under the title of _Il proscritto_) in January 1846. Neither work was much to the taste of the regulars in the audience, nor to the Paris critics, but it was nevertheless clear that a new and substantial talent had arrived from Italy. Verdi's early operas sounded crude to Parisian ears, but no one could deny that his music pulsed with irresistible life.

Across the Channel, meanwhile, Lumley was already running into trouble. *Nabucco* was given its first London performance at Her Majesty's on 3 March 1846. Because of the ban forbidding Biblical subjects on stage in England, Verdi's opera was disguised as *Nino*. It was not well received by the public and the critics hated it.

The *vieille garde*, who could not leave Paris until after the closure of the Théâtre-Italien on 31 March, did not appear until Tuesday 14 April, when *I puritani* was performed. Two nights later, *Don Giovanni*, 'which opera, not being popular with the subscribers, is generally reserved for the Thursday public,' as Chorley somewhat acidly commented, rejoined the repertory, with Grisi, Mario, Fornasari and Lablache in the cast.

'The lady looks well,' continued Chorley. 'Time deals gently with her voice; yet there is no denying that its tone has become slightly more metallic than formerly. Signor Mario, to judge by the improvement audible, has not yet reached his meridian as a singer. Signor Lablache is in his highest spirits, having lost not an iota of his consummate power as an artist. These three can sing, as the manner in which their powers tell in Mozart's opera testifies.'

Again and again that summer Chorley complained that not enough first-class singers had been engaged at Her Majesty's, though the season had been shortened and the prices raised. The Italian Opera had one new feature, however, 'its army of trumpeters in the Press who play in any key the manager pleases, himself in person directing the brazen band.' Chorley quotes one of these circulars, written on paper stamped with 'Her Majesty's Theatre' and signed by a secretary, with Mr Lumley's compliments added:

'First comes *Don Pasquale*, so amusing in its libretto and so delightful in its music, especially when rendered by such singers as the splendid Grisi, the exquisite tenor Mario, the handsome and highly gifted basso, Fornasari, and the Don himself, dear old Lablache, who has returned to us as full of drollery as ever. Then after a variety of dances will follow in solemn contrast, the last act of the finest of operas *Nino* . . . A favourite ballet, including nymph Lucille Grahn, the fairy-like Taglioni, Petit Stephan and Perrot, will conclude this irresistibly attractive series of entertainments.'

For his part, Lumley complained when his prima donna and primo tenore refused to sing three times a week, or did not like the parts he proposed to them. He also accused Grisi of demanding the box put at her disposal as a favour on ordinary subscription nights (Tuesdays and Saturdays) for the extra performances on Thursdays as well.

Grisi and Mario made their first appearance in a Verdi opera on 12 May, when *I Lombardi alla prima crociata* was produced at Her Majesty's. Chorley liked the opera even less than *Ernani* or *Nabucco*. He drew up a long list of works on similar subjects—the Crusades— that he much preferred. The list included Benedict's *The Crusaders*, Costa's *Malek Adhel*, Meyerbeer's *Il crociato in Egitto* and Rossini's *Pietro l'eremita*—this last opera, being *Mosé* under another name, for the same reason as *Nabucco* became *Nino*, can hardly be said to count.

However, Chorley continued: 'It is pleasant to close our remarks by commending the scenic magnificence with which the work is presented. As regards its execution, the honours are due to Signor Mario. He is now, we imagine, absolute king of Italian tenors, and seems to show improvement in every new part he studies. Nothing could be more picturesque than Madame Grisi's appearance in her Middle Ages costume, but the part [of Giselda] does not suit her.'

Orontes's cavatina in the second act, 'La mia letizia infondere', was always encored when Mario sang it, and became one of his favourite concert pieces. It was also popular for barrel-organs, 'ere "Il balen" was thought of,' as Chorley afterwards wrote, when the baritone aria from *Il trovatore* had reached the zenith of its popularity.

Lumley's advance publicity for *Il matrimonio segreto*, revived at the end of May, brought down once more the wrath of Chorley on the unfortunate theatre-manager's head: 'When we find it recorded that never before was Cimarosa's opera so admirably cast', fumed the enraged critic, 'how can we avoid recalling a former season in which Persiani, to whose voice the music is better fitted, took the part of Carolina [now sung by Grisi]; Grisi, to whom the shrewish comes more naturally than the sentimental, that of Elisetta; Viardot, who is a contralto and a consummate singer, the part [Fidalma] now perforce handed over to a mezzo-soprano. Then Signor Mario, though improving rapidly, is not yet equal to Rubini; still less so is Signor F. Lablache to Tamburini; whilst *the* Lablache is not charmed against the effects of Time, though wearing its honours as well as they were ever worn by mortal.'

Chorley allowed that Mario sang Paolino's aria 'Pria che spunti' very well, but could not resist a sting in the tail of his notice. 'It is observable how even in music like Cimarosa's, to which a shake is indispensable, he contrives to avoid that grace.'

Grisi wrote to Lumley later in the month to say that she could not sing Lucrezia Borgia the following Tuesday, as she was required to sing Carolina in *Il matrimonio segreto* on the Thursday two days later, 'which is in a completely different style. If you could delay *Lucrezia Borgia* I should be very grateful, as that opera is very tiring and I want to be in good form on Thursday for *Il matrimonio*, in which the voice must be light and youthful-sounding.'

A curious rumour circulated in the London newspapers that summer, to the effect that Mario intended to marry a titled lady and retire from the stage. This rumour was promptly contradicted in another journal: 'Amidst the thousand and one morceaux of mendacity far more fabulous than the thousand and one nights, but without a shadow of their redeeming interest, we may mention the last but three of the inventions all of which may be traced to the same source. Those who in their malice doomed Castellan to death have reported that the greatest tenor of the day was about to marry a noble lady. The tenor, being a nobleman of high lineage . . . might be happy, but not proud except in courtesy of such an union. But there is no truth whatever in the report . . .'

At Her Majesty's, perfomances of *Lucrezia Borgia* and *Semiramide* provided more ammunition for the *Athenaeum*'s crusade against the management of Lumley. The revival of the former opera illustrated how low the theatre's resources had sunk, 'since four or five nameless gentlemen and one chorus-singer had to be thrust into that group in the Prologue which, not seven years ago, was led by Lablache; and the *new* Mdlle. Brambilla (Giuseppina) was allowed to get through the part of Orsini, which the *old* Mdlle. Brambilla (Marietta) sustained so admirably.'

The duets between Grisi and Mario, and the trio in which they were joined by Lablache were, according to the outraged Chorley, 'the only endurable parts of the opera. *Semiramide* suffered yet more cruelly than *Lucrezia*. Mme. Grisi was compelled alone to drag up the opera.'

Anna Bolena, on 9 July, fared rather better. Grisi was in superb voice as Anna, while Lablache, superlatively cast in the role of Henry VIII, was as good as if not better than ever. Mario as Percy was much applauded, particularly after 'Vivi tu'. But his growing proficiency in the use of the falsetto, which so delighted his audiences, displeased the severe and disapproving Chorley, who accused Mario of trying to surpass Rubini in 'the very peculiarities to which Rubini was driven by Time the wronger,' and of revelling in the use of an extensive falsetto when he had chest-notes 'sufficient to serve any tenor's turn.'

Mario was also taken to task for the 'amount of the embroideries laid upon the largo to "Vivi tu". But the difference between artists of the past and of the present schools is curiously illustrated in that one famous song. With limited natural powers, and those impaired, Rubini grew more and more forcible as the air went on, not merely because inspired by his own splendid singing, but in the consciousness of strength enough and to spare. With a voice in its prime, and anything rather than naturally feeble, Signor Mario becomes so obviously fatigued that the last bars of the cabaletta are hurried over with frivolous flourishes to conceal the weariness of the singer.'

As the final 'new' production of an unsatisfactory season, Donizetti's 22-year-old comic opera, *L'ajo nell'imbarazzo, o Don Gregorio*, was given its first London performance under the latter title. The work was under-rehearsed, as the cast had to sing two or three times a week during the period of preparation. 'Signor Mario's improvised recitative,' commented Chorley tartly, 'was not so good as Donizetti's. Mme. Castellan was so much fatigued, as to sing throughout the evening with a distressing uncertainty of intonation.'

The performance, even by the standards of the day, was more of a pastiche than a presentation of Donizetti's *Don Gregorio*: the overture was taken from the same composer's *Fausta*; on her entry Castellan sang 'a grand aria by a M. Maretzek', while her finale was Benedict's brilliant 'Prendi'. Then Mario 'must need interpolate a very unlovely Canzone Toscana by Signor Alary—a national air we presume—tortured out of melody.' Only Lablache, as the embarrassed tutor, Don Gregorio, saved the evening from disaster.

Relations between Lumley and his singers grew more and more strained. Grisi more than once wrote to the manager politely refusing his invitations to Sunday dinner or weekday luncheon, giving a variety of excuses. On Friday 24 July, for instance, she wrote: 'I am not very well and am obliged to stay at home all day, and have even cancelled my concert for this evening. Pity me for thus being deprived of the pleasure of your company, and the opportunity of seeing your lovely garden, but I hope to benefit from them another time.'

The sentiments of Grisi's letter may have been false, but her excuse, on that occasion at least, was perfectly true. She did not sing that evening at Lady Cecilia Des Vaux's concert at 7 Belgrave Square, though Mario did. His contribution to the programme included 'La mia letizia' from *I lombardi* and he also took part in the final trio from *Ernani*. It is interesting to note to what extent the music of Verdi had invaded the drawing rooms of Belgravia; the concert began with the chorus 'Va pensiero' from *Nabucco* and ended with the pilgrim's chorus from *I lombardi*. At an earlier concert that summer, given by Sir William Abdy, Grisi, Mario and Lablache had sung the third-act trio from *I lombardi*; on that occasion Mario had also performed the Canzone Toscana so despised by Chorley.

Just after the season ended, Chorley fired a final broadside against Lumley and his management of Her Majesty's, accusing him again of raising the price of the subscriptions although the company had been much weaker than usual, with only three first-class singers, Grisi, Mario and Lablache. Castellan and Fornasari, the critic considered, 'can count only but as second-rate.' Consequently the only operas which had been in the least satisfactory were those in which the three members of the *vieille garde* took part. Verdi's *Nino*, pushed on whenever the primo tenore was tired, had failed to please, partly because of the weakness of the cast. *I lombardi*, in Chorley's view an inferior work, had been better received because of the excellence of its performance. Several operas, including *Norma, Semiramide, Il matrimonio segreto* and *Don Giovanni*, had suffered from the absence of an efficient contralto or seconda donna.

The subscribers, in Chorley's opinion, had a right to expect an artist of reputation, such as Persiani, to divide first duties with Grisi, while a tenor of the standing of Moriani or Guasco should have been engaged to second Mario, as in previous seasons.

Chorley was not the only person dissatisfied with Lumley's management of Her Majesty's. Michael Costa, the conductor of the Italian Opera and a musician both admired by the critics and popular with the audience, had resigned the year before. When Lumley approached Grisi about the renewal of her contract, which ran out at the end of the 1846 season, she replied, in a letter dated 19 August: 'I can only repeat what I had the honour of saying to you in person. My position precludes me from entering into any engagement for the future and consequently you are free to make what arrangements you think best for your theatre.'

Lumley wrote back on 22 August, urging his reluctant prima donna to sign her usual agreement with him. Grisi replied from Birmingham on the evening of 25 August, to say that Lumley had misunderstood her previous letter and her spoken answer to his offer of re-engagement. 'I said then that your offer came too late, and that if you did not receive a letter from me by the 25th of this month, it would be impossible for me to enter into any arrangement with you. If I had not received your letter today, I would not have written, as I am now engaged with another company.'

This other company was the brain-child of Giuseppe Persiani, whose wife had not been engaged by Lumley at Her Majesty's for the last two seasons. Together with another Italian, Galletti, he had bought the lease of Covent Garden Theatre with the intention of turning it into a second Italian Opera House. Needing further finance, the partners had enlisted the aid of Cramer, Beale and Co., the music publishers. Frederick Beale was appointed manager of the new enterprise, while Costa was to be conductor and musical director.

So much was common gossip by the late summer of 1846. It was further rumoured that the company would include, as well as Persiani, Grisi and Mario, Tamburini, not heard in opera in London since 1841, and Ronconi, who had sung at Her Majesty's during the season of 1842. Thus, of the *vieille garde*, only Lablache remained faithful to Lumley and Her Majesty's. The alterations to Covent Garden were to begin in December.

Mario and Grisi were back in Paris by mid-September and the Théâtre-Italien re-opened on 6 October with *Semiramide*. The first new production of the season, Pacini's *La fidanzata corsa*, was produced on 17 November, with Persiani, Mario and the baritone Filippo Coletti in the chief roles. The opera suffered from an extremely melodramatic plot, but the performance was held to be excellent.

A month later, another Verdi opera, *I due Foscari*, received its first Paris performance, with Grisi, Mario and Coletti. Again the singers, if not the opera itself, were highly praised. The cavatina sung by Mario in the first act, the duet for tenor and soprano, a trio in the second act and the final aria for Coletti were, according to Délécluze in the *Journal des Débats*, 'performed with a rare perfection, so that the most exacting member of the audience was fully satisfied.

'Mme. Grisi sang her part with energy, struggling successfully against the situation of the character of Lucrezia, which is always one of extreme desperation. As for Mario,' continued Délécluze, 'his voice seems daily to become more powerful and more beautiful; though he now controls it quite remarkably, I cannot approve of the spectacular cadenza with which he ornaments his first cavatina, and I warn the singer to beware of the growing power of his voice in the heavy parts of the new dramatic school of music.'

Although *I due Foscari* had originally been produced in Rome just over two years previously, the audience at the Théâtre-Italien on 17 December 1846 was hearing the world première of at least one Verdi number, the cabaletta to the tenor's first-act cavatina mentioned by Délécluze. Mario, who had a much higher voice than Giacomo Roppa, the original singer of the role of Jacopo Foscari, found much of the part uncomfortably low. Accordingly, on 20 September he wrote personally to Verdi, sending the letter via a mutual friend, the composer Prince Josef Poniatowski. Verdi, who was in Milan, did not receive the tenor's letter until 17 October, but replied immediately: 'I understand that the tessitura of the *Foscari* lies uncomfortably for you in many places. The duet can be altered in the manner indicated and, if it is not too high for you, will not lose its effect . . . If this does not suit you, I see no other solution than to transpose it up a semitone for both soprano and tenor.

'With regard to a new cabaletta for the cavatina,' continued Verdi, 'I understand that you would like one that is gentler and more melodious; but let me point out that Jacopo at that moment cannot express tenderness without betraying the dramatic sense. There is also the shortness of time and the work I have on hand to consider; all the same, if I find a theme that can be made suitable, I will send it to you.'

In a postscript to his letter, Verdi added: 'If the cabaletta to the cavatina in *I Lombardi* suits you, why not use it in the *Foscari*? In that way your purpose is achieved and I am spared the reproach of inserting a new piece in an old opera. I do not believe that *I Lombardi* has been given in Paris yet.'

Verdi must have found a suitable theme almost immediately, for only six days later, on 23 October, he wrote again to Mario: 'I am sending you the cabaletta for the cavatina in the *Foscari*. I have had to write it blind because, although I have heard a great deal about you, I should still like to have heard you at least once to hit on the right style and tessitura. But at worst it proves my desire to please you.'

Verdi copied out the verses for the new cabaletta, 'Sì, lo sento, Iddio mi chiama' ('Yes, I feel that God is calling me'), and also a few bars that were 'a bit muddled with the words' in the accompanying manuscript. 'It is unnecessary,' he continued, 'to tell you that the cabaletta should be given with delicacy and passion and that the closing of the periods should be given *smorzando* (fading away), as after the A . . . which is loud, it suddenly becomes *pp*. The same at all points where this phrase occurs. Poniatowski tells me that you employ the falsetto with great effect, and I have not used it, but as this passage seems to me rather awkward, here is a variation of the two bars you will find marked on the manuscript as Nos 1 and 2.'

The two bars mentioned are a setting of the last line of the cabaletta, 'Piu che in terra, in ciel potrò', with the cadenza on the word 'ciel' rising to the high G flat.

'As for the duet,' continued Verdi, 'for which you should already have received my alterations five or six days ago, it seems to me that much the best course is to transpose the whole thing up a semitone and leave it at that. However, do what you find most convenient.'

Mario, as has already been related, scored a triumph with the new cabaletta. Towards the end of December he wrote to Verdi again to suggest some other alterations to the score of *I due Foscari*, and also to propose that Verdi should write an opera for the Théâtre-Italien. In a letter dated 1 January 1847, Verdi politely but firmly turned down both these suggestions, giving as reasons the various obligations he had to his publishers, which must be fulfilled before accepting any new engagements.

'Meanwhile,' wrote Verdi, 'would you very kindly return to me the original of the new cabaletta that I sent you, so that I can dispose of the rights. I rely on your discretion not to keep any copy, as I must guarantee the possessor absolute ownership.'

Mario, renowned for his dilatoriness in putting pen to paper, did not answer Verdi's letter, nor did he return the cabaletta manuscript. There were two more performances of *I due Foscari* at the Italiens during January.

A special performance of *L'elisir d'amore*, given in the Tuileries on 5 February, was attended by Victor Hugo, who described the event in his Journal: 'It was performed by the Italian singers, Persiani, Mario and Tagliafico. Ronconi acted—acted is the word, as he acts very well—the part of Dulcamara, usually played by Lablache. As regards size, though not talent, it was a dwarf replacing a giant.'

In 1847, the theatre in the Tuileries still had its Empire decoration, with lyres, griffins, swans, palm leaves and fretwork of gold on a grey background, which Hugo found very cold and pale. He also complained of the few pretty women present at the performance. 'Mme. Cuvillier-Fleury was the prettiest, Mme. Victor Hugo the most beautiful.' The men were in uniform or dress clothes, though M. Thiers, the statesman, 'who the day before had made a mediocre speech, carried opposition to the point of wearing a black tie.'

Three of the four royal princes were present, wearing lieutenant-general's uniform. There was no applause, which froze both singers and audience. Five minutes before the end of the opera King Louis-Philippe began tidying up. 'He folded his satin programme and put it in his pocket, then he wiped the lenses of his opera glasses, shut them with care, searched for the case in his chair, and put the glasses in the case, fastening the clasp meticulously.'

Three weeks later, one of the Royal princes, the Duc de Nemours, gave a concert in his own apartments in the Tuileries. The occasion was considerably less formal, though King Leopold of the Belgians and his wife—a daughter of Louis-Philippe and sister to Nemours—were present, as well as the Royal Dukes of Aumale and Montpensier. The four royal ladies sat in the front row of armchairs, with King

Leopold; the other ladies were seated behind them while the men stood round the sides of the room and overflowed into the ante-chamber. The singers—Grisi, Persiani, Mario, Ronconi and Lablache—were grouped round the piano. They were accompanied by Auber, and Victor Hugo, who was again in the audience, thought it a pity that none of Auber's own music was included. The programme, however, consisted of music by Mozart, Rossini and Donizetti. Théophile Gautier, who was among the guests, gossiped with Hugo in the interval.

The Italiens closed, as usual, at the end of March; a week later the Royal Italian Opera, Covent Garden, opened its doors.

Chapter 7

In 1834, the year that Giulia Grisi made her London début, the repertory during the Italian season at the King's Theatre had consisted of six operas by Rossini and one each by Bellini, Donizetti and Mozart. Those same four composers were all represented thirteen years later in the opening season of the Royal Italian Opera at Covent Garden, when Rossini and Donizetti clocked up five works each, Bellini scored three and Mozart two. The only newcomer—and a highly significant one—was Verdi, allotted two performances each of two operas.

For many years the three senior Italian composers had resisted all assaults on their virtual monopoly, enjoying enormous popular success and, in the case of Rossini, great critical acclaim as well. But by 1847 Rossini had written no new opera for nearly two decades; Bellini had been dead for more than ten years; and Donizetti was only a few months away from his death. Although their works continued to be performed (and are still performed today) in London's opera houses, it was time for a new star to appear on the horizon.

That star, as in retrospect is perfectly obvious, was Giuseppe Verdi. But in the late 1840s Verdi, though already the composer of ten operas and hugely popular in Italy, was still looked upon with great suspicion by the musical establishments of Paris and London. As so often before, Henry Chorley summed up the official attitude by describing Verdi's operas as 'a mixture of grandeur . . . alternated with puerilities.' The composer was taken to task for choosing ferocious and gloomy stories and for being the most *un*tender of Italians (Chorley did not, unfortunately, live to hear Verdi's *Otello*, with its exquisitely tender love music).

Other accusations made against Verdi included the noisiness of his orchestration—a charge that had frequently been laid against Donizetti in the past—and the banality of both his rhythms and harmonies. It was not until the middle of the following decade, after the productions of *Rigoletto*, *Il trovatore* and *La traviata*, that Verdi was acknowledged as the true successor to the crown of Italian opera, while the official verdict on his style as 'spasmodic, tawdry, untruthful' remained unchanged for many years more.

So, leaving Verdi aside for the moment, the position in 1847 appeared little different from that of the previous dozen years, with the same triumvirate of Italian composers firmly in the ascendancy while honour, usually in the form of *Don Giovanni*, continued to be paid to Mozart. Because of the splendid opportunities offered by the title role to baritones—and to tenors, too, as will become apparent in a later chapter—*Don Giovanni* was easily the favourite among Mozart's Italian operas, with *Le nozze di Figaro* a good second. When, a few years previously, *Così fan tutte* had been given at Her Majesty's Theatre, the performance was a travesty, with Fiordiligi deprived of both her arias—presumably the huge leaps in the vocal line were considered unstylish or unsingable or both—but allotted one of Dorabella's instead, a solecism that today would be found unpardonable.

When *Die Zauberflöte* entered the repertory of the Royal Italian Opera in 1851, it was sung in Italian as *Il flauto magico*. A mere change of language could not, though, transform Mozart's unique mixture of sublime music, pantomime and freemasonry into any familiar category of Italian opera, serious or comic. The audience liked some of the music, laughed at Papageno's clowning and found the plot incomprehensible. While *Don Giovanni* could quite easily be categorized as a romantic opera with comic interludes, *The Magic Flute*, in whatever language, resisted all such attempts at pigeon-holing; consequently the work was dismissed as being beneath serious consideration by the patrons of the Royal Italian Opera.

Public taste, however, despite its seeming continuity, was on the point of a radical change in direction. The opening season at the Royal Italian Opera was the only one ever to justify completely the epithet of Italian. In the following year Rossini, Bellini, Donizetti and Mozart were still represented. Verdi was absent, his place usurped by Meyerbeer, whose enormously popular French grand opera *Les Huguenots*, Italianized into *Gli ugonotti*, was given ten performances, its nearest rival, Rossini's *La donna del lago*, receiving only seven.

From then onwards, the proportion of French to Italian operas in the repertory rose annually, while the number of performances of the French works rose at an even steeper rate. Meyerbeer was not unknown in London, while *Les Huguenots* had previously been heard at Covent Garden in 1842, performed by a visiting company and sung in German. But the immense vogue for his works stemmed from the

date of their appropriation by the Royal Italian Opera and by the
company remaining at Her Majesty's Theatre.

It was not only the grand, spectacular Meyerbeerian type of opera
that crossed the channel from France, either. Works of a more lyrical
nature by Auber and, a little later, Gounod, proved almost equally
popular, with their spoken dialogue transformed into Italian recitative, a fate also suffered by the German operas such as Beethoven's
Fidelio and Weber's *Der Freischütz* that subsequently entered the
repertory of the Royal Italian Opera. This custom prevailed until the
end of the century, when the modern idea that opera should be
performed either in the original language or in the vernacular began to
gain general acceptance.

The changing style of opera brought a new type of singer in its
wake. While the critics deplored the fall in vocal standards from the
high level of the previous generation, as critics have done since the
very beginning of opera, the public welcomed the larger, more
powerful voices needed to cope with the heavier orchestration of the
French school exemplified by Meyerbeer, or the new Italian contingent spearheaded by Verdi. Both schools aimed specifically for
dramatic effect in their stage works and though the older operatic
composers, from Mozart and Rossini to Donizetti and Bellini, had
never lost sight of the fact that they were writing for the theatre, not
the concert hall, some of their interpreters undoubtedly had done so.

Verdi's dramatic genius has never been denied, even by his fiercest
detractors; it was and is an irresistible force easily able to transcend
the changing taste and opinions of succeeding generations. But
Meyerbeer's sense of theatre, wildly acclaimed in his lifetime and for
some 30 years after his death, now appears stilted and lifeless, quite
devoid of that vital dramatic spark still so strongly to be perceived in
all Verdi's operas, even the crudest of his earlier works. The cumber-
some plots devised by Scribe and his collaborators for Meyerbeer and
other French grand-opera composers, which at the time were praised
for their historical accuracy, have retained only the surface realism of a
poor photograph, while Verdi's lurid dramas, often subjected to
ridicule, nevertheless survive because of the marvellous truth and
energy of his characterization.

For the moment, however, Meyerbeer reigned without rival and
both of the London opera-houses were dominated by this German-
born composer of works in the grand French style. In 1847 Her
Majesty's Theatre did perform no fewer than five Verdi operas, including *I masnadieri*, especially written for Jenny Lind. But Lind scored her
most overwhelming successes—in London, at least—in *Robert le diable*

(Meyerbeer) and *La Fille du régiment* (Donizetti), both works originally composed to French texts. Through her total immersion in the
words and music of an opera, Lind was dramatically effective in those
roles, such as Alice in *Robert* or Amina in *La sonnambula*, which lay
within the scope of her own personality. Despite the security of her
technique, she made little impression in parts that required conscious
dramatic insight. Her Norma, for instance, was described as 'maiden-
ly', hardly an appropriate epithet for the priestess bent on liberating
her country from foreign domination who has borne two children to
the commander of the occupying power.

Lind retired from the stage before Verdi's operas gained universal
popularity, but many of his hot-blooded heroines would not have
been to her liking. One of the strengths common to Mario and Grisi,
both of whose careers lasted well over 30 years, was their ability to
adapt, in their private as well as their professional lives, to changing
conditions and tastes. Just as the tumultuous scandals of Grisi's youth,
her disastrous marriage and her highly-publicized affair with
Castlereagh merged into the pattern of complete respectability of
her life with Mario and their children, so her early repertory of Rossini,
Bellini and Donizetti operas was augmented by roles such as Valentine
in *Les Huguenots* and Leonora in *Il trovatore*, two of the greatest
successes of her later career.

Mario's adaptability was even more remarkable. First he was forced
to exchange the comfortable existence of a member of the nobility and
the security of a promising military career for the precarious position
of a penniless political refugee and the hazardous future of a singer.
Then, having discovered his true vocation at the Opéra-Italien as an
exponent of lyric roles, he graduated successfully to the *bel canto*
repertory relinquished by Rubini. Finally, at an age when most singers
are content to trot out their half-dozen warhorses in rotation, he not
only returned to Meyerbeer and discovered several other French
composers, but found in the heroes of middle-period Verdi a reward-
ing new series of congenial characterizations.

Neither Mario nor Grisi was in the very slightest what may be
termed an intellectual singer. Consequently they were despised by
artists such as Pauline Viardot whose attainments were of a more
consciously thoughtful cast and variety. But their instinctive gifts,
both musical and dramatic, were quite sufficient to carry them
through a period of change and transition with surprisingly few
disasters, or even mistakes, en route. Grisi's assumption of the part of
Fidès in Meyerbeer's *Le Prophète* was one such error, prompted no
doubt by the soprano's understandable but unnecessary jealousy of

Viardot. Mario's requisition of the title-role of *Don Giovanni* was another, which failed not because of the violence done to Mozart by transpositions and alterations to the vocal line—such violations were common and accepted at the time, when Viardot herself transposed the role of Lady Macbeth down a whole third—but because the tenor's personality lacked even the slightest touch of the cruelty inherent in Don Giovanni's nature.

But much of this still lay in the future when the Royal Italian Opera opened on 6 April 1847 with a performance of *Semiramide*. Rossini's opera was chosen, according to Chorley, because it contained one of Grisi's best roles; because there was also an excellent part for the new contralto, Marietta Alboni, as well as opportunity for Tamburini to display his now unrivalled ability in florid bass music; and because the overture and grand finales gave the new orchestra and chorus plenty of chances to demonstrate their worth.

'The performance justified the choice,' asserted the *Athenaeum* critic. 'That Mme. Grisi was in her best looks, best voice and best humour, was evident from the first moment of her appearing on the stage. Whether from the excitement of the occasion, or that "coming Linds cast their shadows before", it is certain that she has not sung in London with such force, freshness or brilliancy since the good days of the Haymarket Opera, and that she never sang the part better.'

The mention of 'coming Linds' referred to the engagement by Lumley, as chief attraction of his rival company at Her Majesty's Theatre, of the Swedish soprano Jenny Lind. Grisi, always stimulated by competition to give of her very best, was reacting not only to the imminent début of the Swedish Nightingale at the theatre where she herself had scored so many triumphs during a dozen seasons, but also to the huge success of the young singer making her first London appearance that night in the role of Arsace—Marietta Alboni.

After praising her voice for its extensive range, mellow tone-quality and flexibility, Chorley continued: 'The countenance of Mdlle. Alboni is pleasing. She is very "fat", however, as well as very "fair", happily for operas to come, *not* very forty.'

Tamburini was also given a great welcome back after his long absence from London; the chorus and orchestra, the musical direction of Costa and the general ensemble all earned high praise, and the new venture was judged to have got off to a magnificent start.

The Queen made her first visit to the Royal Italian Opera at Covent Garden on 17 April. 'The House, beautifully fitted up, looks like a foreign theatre, such as La Scala, Albert says,' wrote the Queen in her Journal. 'The orchestra conducted by Costa was admirable, *Semi-*

ramide was beautifully got up, very fine scenery, decoration, dresses, etc. Grisi sang beautifully but is grown very large. Mdlle. Alboni, who appeared as Arsace, has a fine contralto voice and sings very well. Tamburini also sang very well. The performance was immensely long . . .'

Mario made his first appearance in the new house on Tuesday 20 April, when 'one of the most perfect representations of *La sonnambula* ever given in England took place. Barring an occasional sharpness in Mme. Persiani's voice, it is difficult to conceive singing more perfect than hers in Amina.'

Jenny Lind, herself a much admired Amina, was in the audience and, in the words of Chorley, 'sat watching the stage with eager interest . . . Signor Mario re-appeared as Elvino. At first he seemed slightly indisposed, or slightly shaken by the cordiality of his reception. In the [first-act] finale, however, and in the second act, he had wakened thoroughly or recovered himself, and his performance of the aria satisfied us that he is some steps nearer to Rubini than he was last year.'

Jenny Lind made her London début at Her Majesty's on 4 May as Alice in *Robert le diable* (translated, of course, into Italian). Queen Victoria and Prince Albert were present and shared in the general enthusiasm. 'The choruses were bad and the orchestra very often went wrong,' wrote the Queen, 'but Jenny Lind was absolute perfection . . . She has a most exquisite, powerful, & really quite peculiar voice, so round, soft & flexible & her acting is charming & touching & very natural. Her appearance was very ladylike & sweet & though she is not beautiful, she has a fine tall figure, is very graceful, has fine blue eyes & fine fair hair.'

The Lind fever, which raged so violently in London, had begun; it was to last for exactly two years, ending on 10 May 1849, again with a performance of *Robert le diable*, the Swedish Nightingale's last appearance on any stage.

Meanwhile at Covent Garden the new company continued to give performances of a general standard never before achieved in London. The production of *Lucrezia Borgia*, with Grisi, Alboni, Mario and Tamburini, on Saturday 15 May, was a good example. 'Let whosoever will have this or the other favourite singer,' wrote Chorley, 'Covent Garden keeps its promise and has the *Opera*. The distinction was clear as the difference is wide; we desire after some weeks' experience to record our judgement; and our pleasure in perceiving that a high style of performance is so warmly relished by the audience.'

The singers, too, benefited greatly, in Chorley's opinion, from the overall excellence of their surroundings and were spurred on by the rivalry with the other company. 'Mme. Grisi, with whom this part [Lucrezia] has always been her best, is now at her best in the part. She seems to have studied it anew. Her by-play has a sinister and voluptuous delicacy, and her grand scenes have a force, without her olden violence, which make it surpass any of her former efforts; and her voice was poured forth with such fulness and brilliancy as if she wished the Amina at that moment on her former throne to hear the challenge.'

The remainder of the cast also received praise from Chorley, though his compliment to Mario, who 'has not yet reached his maturity, though already incontestably the best tenor in Europe,' was typically two-edged. Alboni, who sang the travesty role of Maffio Orsini, had to repeat the Brindisi three or four times. 'Great is the virtue of opposition.'

Twelve days later, while the first London performance of Donizetti's *La Fille du régiment* was being given at Her Majesty's, in the presence of the Queen, with Lind, the tenor Italo Gardoni and Lablache in the cast, the Royal Italian Opera offered a *Don Giovanni* at Covent Garden, with Grisi, Persiani, Mario and Tamburini. 'The present cast is, perhaps, unprecedented in its ensemble,' wrote the critic of *The Illustrated London News*. 'In addition to the powerful phalanx of leading singers, Costa has taken especial pains with the score; restoring the triple orchestra in the finale of the first act and the military band in the last scene.' (A reference to the on-stage musicians in the Supper scene—the final sextet was always omitted at this period, the opera ending with the descent of Don Giovanni to hell.)

Almost every number had to be repeated: Persiani (Zerlina) and Tamburini (Don Giovanni) were encored in 'Là ci darem'; Taburini had to repeat 'Finch 'han dal vino' twice; Zerlina's 'Batti, batti' and the Trio of masks, sung by Mario, Grisi and Corbari (Donna Elvira) also had to be repeated twice; Mario was encored in 'Il mio tesoro'—'the finest specimen of tenor singing we have ever heard'—and several other encores were demanded but not given.

'To add to the effect of this glorious ensemble,' continued *The Illustrated London News* critic, 'Fanny Elssler and Dumilâtre danced in the Minuet in the Ball scene, and were encored . . . The cast and mise en scène of *Don Giovanni*, with its triple orchestra and double chorus, must be reckoned, like the *Lucrezia Borgia*, an epoch in the annals of lyrical art. Never did the matchless orchestra achieve greater triumphs, for every player's heart was in the cause. It would be vain to point out each successive beauty, developed in the interpretation of the score by the genius of Costa.'

Both Donna Anna's 'Non mi dir' and Donna Elvira's 'Mi tradi', frequently omitted, were restored, though Mario, to the critic's disappointment, did not sing 'Dalla sua pace,' which he could 'render as divinely as he does "Il mio tesoro". On the whole this has been the most perfect adherence to the original text ever heard in this country.' This notice makes one wonder what performances of *Don Giovanni* in London can have been like before 1847.

The following night the singers from both companies, including Grisi and Lind, took part in a concert at Buckingham Palace. This was the first time that the rival prime donne had appeared together—at a previous royal concert on 3 May, Lind did not sing, presumably because it was the evening before her début at Her Majesty's—and Grisi must have displayed her resentment and jealousy of the younger singer. A fortnight later, on 12 June, Queen Victoria wrote to her Uncle Leopold, King of the Belgians: 'Tonight we are going to the Opera in State, and will hear and see Jenny Lind (who is perfection) in *Norma*, which is considered one of her best parts. Poor Grisi is quite going off, and after the pure angelic voice and extremely quiet, perfect acting of J. Lind, she seems quite passée. Poor thing! she is *quite* furious about it and was excessively impertinent to J. Lind.'

Furious and impertinent Grisi may well have been, but passée she was not. As every review testified, she was in particularly fine voice that summer. Jenny Lind's Norma, popular in Sweden and Germany, was a comparative failure in London, where audiences continued to prefer the more forceful, imperious characterization of Grisi. They were not accustomed to a ladylike *Norma*. But the Queen never really forgave Grisi for her behaviour towards her rival. References to Grisi in the Journal ceased almost entirely, though Mario remained as much a favourite as ever. Needless to say, Grisi and Lind were not invited to sing together again at Buckingham Palace.

Verdi's *I due Foscari*, which had already been given at Her Majesty's earlier in the season, entered the repertory of the Royal Italian Opera on Saturday 19 June; the composer, in London for the forthcoming production of *I masnadieri*, the opera he had written specially for Lind, was present at Covent Garden that night and, 'it is more than probable,' as Chorley put it, 'had never before the opportunity of hearing one of his works given with so signal a perfection.'

Chorley disliked *I due Foscari* even more than the three other operas by Verdi already heard in London. The excellence of the performance, in his opinion, 'but strengthens our judgement of the utter worthlessness of the music. Greater trash as a whole has been rarely gone through by such an orchestra, chorus and trio of dramatic singers . . . The puerility of Signor Verdi's instrumentalisation—the platitude of his melodies—the almost ungrammatical crudity of his modulations, and the total disregard of tone in colouring are too poorly compensated for by the accomplishment of certain effects to permit us to unsay one word of our former strictures.'

Chorley awarded the dramatic honours of the performance to Ronconi, who took the part of Francisco Foscari, the Doge: 'his singing was instinct with musical feeling and fine apprehension; but his acting was sublime.' Grisi as Lucrezia also received praise, 'doing her utmost with a most ungracious and monotonous part of sorrow without relief—looking like some grand Venetian portrait by Giorgione.'

Mario, as Jacopo, the Doge's son, 'won an encore for his cavatina; his cadence, however, in spite of the immense compass of the falsetto it disclosed—to G flat above the line of the treble stave—was strange and startling rather than in harmony with the deep and sad expression of the andante it ended.'

The *Times* critic thought Mario's Jacopo a graceful and finished piece of acting, while 'his singing was so natural and elegant as to elevate much that was commonplace in the music into sentiment and even passion. An air which Verdi wrote expressly for him, "Si, lo sento", in the first act (one of the happiest and least affected *morceaux* in the opera), gave the accomplished artist an opportunity of exhibiting the beauty and extensive register of his voice and his mastery over the *portamento* and passages demanding flexibility of utterance to extraordinary advantage.'

Gaetano Fraschini, the tenor who had sung the role of Jacopo at Her Majesty's earlier in the season, had sung the original cabaletta, 'Odio solo, ed odio atroce,' so Mario's performance of 'Si, lo sento' was the first to be heard in London.

There was apparently some gossip in the newspapers about Verdi's failure to get in touch with or congratulate Mario after his great success as Jacopo, and the tenor wrote to the composer to complain about some criticism that Verdi was reported to have made about his, Mario's, behaviour. Verdi replied on 24 July, two days after the première of *I masnadieri* at Her Majesty's, in a dignified letter that says the final words on the subject of the cabaletta: 'It greatly surprises and displeases me to learn from your letter that you suspect me of criticizing your behaviour towards me from a motive of self-interest, when if you knew me better you would have the opportunity to discover that my way of thinking is quite different.

'In my own defence I should like to relate the circumstances which have probably given rise to the gossip about which you complain in your letter. Having been reproached by certain persons for failing to get in touch with you, someone who occupies so distinguished a position in the artistic world, in order to avoid their insistence and not to be accused of arrogance, I was obliged against my will to explain what has passed between us.'

Verdi gives a résumé of the correspondence between himself and Mario the previous autumn, as a result of which he wrote the cabaletta for Mario to perform in the Paris production of *I due Foscari*, 'and for which I did not dream of asking any recompense whatsoever. I was very willing,' continued Verdi, 'to attribute to forgetfulness the fact that I did not receive any acknowledgement from you until about two months later, in a letter in which you also asked me what you should do with the cabaletta. It upset me, therefore, to learn that, after I had consequently told you that I wanted to dispose of the rights, you continued to use the cabaletta, as you have done here in London.'

Stressing the frankness of his character, which did not allow him to conceal the truth of what had happened in any way, Verdi cites his preoccupation (with *I masnadieri*) at the time when the rumours occurred: 'It did not seem worth the trouble to raise the matter between us again, and I hope that you, as well as I, will never refer to it any more.'

Anna Bolena was presented at Covent Garden on 10 July for Grisi's benefit, with Alboni as the page Smeaton, Mario as Percy and Tamburini in Lablache's usual role of Enrico. At the end of the month, *La gazza ladra* was revived, with Grisi 'as ever brilliant and pathetic— wondrously little changed indeed, since she bounded on the stage to sing "Di piacer" in the year 1834, on her first appearance; Signor Tamburini [is] still incomparable as the Deserter-father.' Mario sang Gianetto, while Alboni, doomed to travesty roles, which she hated, was a splendid if overgrown Pippo.

The last production of the season, during August, was Rossini's *La donna del lago*. Grisi, singing the role of Elena, 'spurred to the utmost by the popularity of the contralto in her own company and of the soprano at the house over the way, seemed resolved to surpass herself in care, taste and brilliance.' Grisi's duet with Alboni—once more a reluctant young man as Malcolm—was the finest heard in London 'since Sontag and Malibran took the town by storm.'

Mario, who had hitherto sung the part of Rodrigo in *La donna del*

Iago, this time impersonated the King, in which role 'he has not much to do of the kind he loves best; but he has improved greatly in accent and flexibility—and the beauty of his voice in the romance "Aurora" suited well the beauty of the music.'

Despite the undoubted artistic success of this first season given by the Royal Italian Opera, the costs, both of the rebuilding of the theatre and of the running expenses incurred during the season itself, were so great that an enormous deficit had accumulated. Giuseppe Persiani and Galletti retired diplomatically to Paris, and Frederick Beale had to send his son Willert, then barely out of his teens, to persuade Persiani to return. Eventually sufficient money was raised to cover the deficit and Persiani sold the lease of the theatre to Beale, who in his turn sold it to Edward Delafield. Delafield, a rich brewer, engaged Frederick Gye to help him run the theatre. After two seasons, Delafield had lost so much money that he went bankrupt; in 1850 Gye found himself sole manager of the Royal Italian Opera, Covent Garden, a position he was to keep for more than twenty years.

Chapter 8

IN RETROSPECT, THE dominant event in Paris during the winter of 1847–48 was of course the revolution which broke out on 21 February 1848, and resulted in the abdication of Louis-Philippe and the proclamation of a French Republic. Mario and Gaetano Grisi, Giulia's father, watched as the Citizen King and his wife, Marie-Amélie, drove away from the Tuileries on their journey to exile. Gaetano, who had lived through two previous revolutions in Paris, one far bloodier than the '48 disturbance, must have felt that history was repeating itself with somewhat monotonous regularity, especially when another Bonaparte, Louis Napoléon, was elected President of the Republic in December.

The season at the Théâtre-Italien had opened as usual at the beginning of October 1847, with a performance of *Don Giovanni* in which Grisi, Persiani, Mario, Coletti and Lablache took their accustomed parts. There were no new productions and the Italiens audiences, even more conservative in taste than their London counterparts, appeared content to exist on a diet of Rossini, Bellini and Donizetti, varied occasionally by the one Mozart opera—*Don Giovanni*—that could be termed popular. But change, even in this stronghold of tradition, was on the way.

At the end of November Mario became ill and did not sing for a month. The theatre put on *Semiramide*, which did not require the presence of the first tenor. Mario was well enough to sing in *Lucia* on 28 December, and in *Il barbiere* on 1 January 1848, when his Almaviva was a well received. Ten days later, a major revival of *La donna del lago*, with Grisi, Alboni, Mario, Gardoni and Coletti, evoked eulogies from Délécluze in the *Journal des Débats*: 'Mme. Grisi, as in *Semiramide*, demonstrated as the Lady of the Lake that she is a fine actress and delightful singer. Rossini's lovely music, whose naturally expressive melody does not need to be pushed to the extremes of piano and forte, shows Mme. Grisi's beautiful voice and her pure and delicate singing to their best advantage, to the delight of those who really love music, and hate mere noise.'

After remarking on the 'charming verve and grace' with which

Mario had been singing since his recovery from serious indisposition, Délécluze noted once more that 'Rossini's music, just now much in favour again with the public and singers alike, seems to have influenced the manner in which Mario has been singing. His admirers, who become uneasy at the slightest alteration in his voice, do not like to hear him sing music that makes him use his vocal resources to their limits. They fear that such occasional forcing of his voice may become a habit, and that the smooth timbre, which gave such great charm to his singing during the early years of his career, will lose its sweetness and purity.'

But Mario, in the opinion of Délécluze, realized the advantage in discreet shading of his music over the achievement of vulgar dramatic effects, and never let his singing degenerate into mere shouting. 'There is nothing therefore but praise to offer him for the way he sang his role in *La donna del lago*. The big duet with Mme. Grisi in the first act was done brilliantly and it is unnecessary to say how perfectly he managed all the music he had to sing in the ensembles.'

Mario's greatest triumph in Rossini's opera was, however, obtained from 'a pretty cavatina composed by Tadolini, the conductor, on a theme of Pacini. This stylish and elegant piece brought out perfectly all the skill with which our tenor uses his voice, and Mario gained a great and deserved success.' Giovanni Tadolini was also the composer of an aria, 'Arder piu sempre', that Grisi sang in concerts at this period.

Performances of *Il pirata* and *La gazza ladra* followed, then at the end of February the revolution forced all the Paris theatres to close. The violence did not continue for long and on 1 March a special performance of *I puritani* was put on at the Théâtre-Italien in aid of the wounded. Two days later Frédéric Chopin, in a letter to Solange Clesinger, the daughter of George Sand, commented that 'Paris is quiet, with the quiet of fear. Everyone has rallied to the cause of order. Everyone has joined the National Guard. The shops are open—no customers. Foreigners, passport in hand, wait for the damage to the railways to be repaired.'

The Italiens gave spasmodic performances until the end of the month, closing on 31 March after a performance of *Otello* which proved to be the last appearance of Mario and Grisi in Paris for five years.

The second season of the Royal Italian Opera, now under the management of Delafield, had opened on 9 March with Alboni in Rossini's *Tancredi*. The main batch of singers arrived from Paris at the beginning of April and *Don Giovanni*, with Grisi, Persiani, Mario and Tamburini, was announced for Thursday 11 April.

On the morning of that day, however, Grisi sent a note to Costa: 'I am in despair at having to tell you that I have a sore throat, so bad that I fear it will be impossible for me to sing this evening. Please let Mr Delafield know at once so that he can send me a doctor immediately to give me a proper certificate, and then get in touch with Castellan. She has already sung the part of Donna Anna and might be very pleased to help out this evening if she can. I had hoped that perhaps later I might be a little better, but now I fear I can hardly swallow and also have a fever.'

Grisi was not able to sing that night and was, as she suggested, replaced by Castellan. Mario, making his first appearance of the season as Don Ottavio, was in very good voice. At the beginning of May he sang Don Ramiro in *La Cenerentola*, with Alboni in the title role, but then himself became the next casualty.

Pauline Viardot, engaged by Delafield for the Royal Italian Opera, had not been able to leave Paris, where she was singing at the Opéra, until the beginning of May. She and Mario were billed to appear in *La sonnambula* at Covent Garden on Tuesday 9 May, but at the last minute Mario was taken ill and replaced by Signor Flavio. The usual rumours, that Mario's indisposition was caused by Grisi's jealousy of Viardot, at once began to circulate. There is little reason, however, to find anything sinister in this particular cancellation of Mario's. He suffered from indisposition, whether real or imaginary, no more and no less than any other star tenor whose reputation rests on the condition of his voice.

By Friday 12 May Mario was well enough to sing in the *Stabat Mater* at a concert, then the following evening he and Viardot appeared together in *La sonnambula*; both singers were much applauded.

All indispositions were forgiven or forgotten on 23 May, when Donizetti's *La favorita*, with Grisi in the title role of Leonora and Mario as Fernando, was presented by the Royal Italian Opera. 'A painful story, set to generally uninteresting music,' was Chorley's opinion of the work. But he continued: 'All that could be done for *La favorita* by mise en scène, orchestra, chorus and two principal artists has been done at Covent Garden. There has been nothing to approach Signor Mario's singing of the part of Fernando since Rubini left the stage. His Romance in the fourth act was encored with that sort of applause which must be "corn, wine and oil" to an artist hungering for triumph . . . The subsequent duet, too, was something like the *ne plus ultra* of dramatic singing.'

Chorley also praised Mario for his acting, though in the third act he found him less impassioned than Duprez, who had created the part of Fernand in the original French version of Donizetti's opera in Paris. The critic of the *Athenaeum* had similar commendation to bestow on Grisi's Leonora: 'That rivalry and comparison have helped, not harmed, Mme. Grisi is susceptible of mathematical proof. The long array of notable dramatic vocalists who have been heard since 1834, when she first appeared in London, have not among them robbed her of a single great part; Norma, Anna Bolena, Semiramide, Lucrezia [Borgia], Donna Anna, Susanna, and the like . . . assigning to her a place peculiar and not be disputed among the six rival songstresses at present here.'

The six rival songstresses were Persiani, Alboni and Viardot at Covent Garden, Lind, Cruvelli and Eugenia Tadolini at Her Majesty's. Chorley ended his eulogy to Grisi by stating that 'the alternate delicacy and lustre of her voice, the finish and power of her singing in the duet [with Mario] which closes a long and trying opera, will henceforth be among our remembered marvels.'

When Queen Victoria attended a performance of *La favorita* on 4 July, she admired the decorations and choruses, but thought 'the only one who really sang well was Mario.'

Fernando became a favourite part with Mario, while 'Spirto gentil', the Romance from the fourth act of *La favorita*, rivalled the Serenade from *Don Pasquale* as his most popular concert piece. He sang it on the afternoon of 23 June at 99 Eaton Place, the home of Mrs Sartoris who, as Adelaide Kemble, had had a successful career as a singer, until her retirement in 1843.

This occasion was notable as the first public concert given in London by Chopin, who had already played at several private parties since his arrival in England early in April; at one of these functions, the christening on 15 May of the Duchess of Sutherland's baby, to which the Queen stood godmother, at Stafford House, Mario, together with Tamburini and Lablache, had also participated.

In a letter to a friend in Paris, Chopin wrote: 'I gave a matinée here (very elegant). Mrs Sartoris (Miss Kemble) lent me her house; Mario sang three groups while I played four—that was all. They found this arrangement both novel and charming. I had a select audience of 150 at one guinea each, as I did not want to crowd the rooms. All the tickets were sold the day before.'

Wilhelm Kuhe, who was present at the concert, noted that Mario sang, as well as 'Spirto gentil', Beethoven's 'La Pénitence' ('Busslied'). 'He looked extremely handsome in his velvet coat,' continued Kuhe, 'presenting a strong contrast to the death-like appearance of the great pianist, and singing as he alone could sing.'

The climax of the London season of 1848 was undoubtedly the Royal Command performance on 20 July of Meyerbeer's *Les Huguenots*, or *Gli ugonotti* as it became at the Royal Italian Opera. It was Queen Victoria's first state visit to Covent Garden since the establishment of the new company and if 'the magnificent decorations of the theatre for the reception of Her Majesty in state and the presence of the Court for a while distracted the attention of the audience,' the house soon settled down to 'such a performance that has never before been seen or heard in England.'

The Queen herself was delighted: 'The decorations, dresses, mise en scène, pageantry and choruses could not have been better.'

Chorley, too, emphasized that 'too much credit cannot be awarded Signor Costa and the forces under his disposal; too many acknowledgements cannot be made to the management for a liberality which becomes Oriental when we recollect that no Government purse is at its back to pay for supernumerary embellishments.'

The seven principal characters of *Les Huguenots* were sung by Viardot, Castellan, Alboni, Mario, Tamburini, Joseph Tagliafico and Ignazio Marini. 'Collectively [they] defy rivalry; while what is of even more consequence, Covent Garden possesses an orchestra and chorus distancing those of any foreign theatre of our acquaintance—save the Académie as it was in 1836'—the year of *Les Huguenots'* first performance at the Paris Opéra.

The Valentine of Viardot was highly praised. The Queen thought she 'acted and sang well though one longed for Lind.' Chorley was more enthusiastic: 'she was in excellent voice, making the utmost of the difficult music; while her acting in the Conspiracy scene and in the following duet and terzet was of the loftiest tragic excellence, fearfully, but always poetically, natural.

'Signor Mario's Raoul,' continued Chorley, 'was as a musical whole the most satisfactory one which has been seen since the original Raoul of Nourrit, the part having been always difficult for Duprez . . . Signor Mario's acting in the grand duet [with Viardot] was admirable.'

In the Queen's opinion, 'Raoul, personified by Mario [was] quite perfection as to singing & acting.' She also liked the Urbain of Alboni, for whom Meyerbeer had written a special aria, which was encored.

Les Huguenots was a tremendous popular as well as critical success. The opera was given ten times during the remaining four weeks of the season and was chosen for Viardot's benefit on Thursday 3 August.

On the morning of that day, according to the Reverend T. Cox, 'Madame Viardot was waited upon by a gentleman of great influence in the theatre, who had to convey to her the intelligence that Mario was too ill to sing at night, but that under such untoward circumstances Mme. Grisi would sing the *Norma* for her, if that opera were substituted.' After conveying her thanks to Grisi, Viardot asked: 'Do you not know that Roger is still in town? I will ask him to play Raoul; but if he cannot do so, let *Norma* be given; only I shall play Norma.'

Gustave Roger, the French tenor who was to create the title role of Meyerbeer's opera *Le Prophète* the following spring, agreed to sing Raoul, a part he had performed in France, that evening. Meanwhile at two o'clock in the afternoon, Mario sent a letter to Covent Garden, addressed either to Delafield or, more probably, to Frederick Gye:

'I can imagine the embarrassment and annoyance that my position is causing you, but it is impossible for me to risk singing in my present state. Make what arrangements you can, as you cannot count on me for tonight. I am all the more upset because evil tongues will not fail to ascribe the cause to Mme. Viardot's benefit. If you want to do me a service, please contradict them.'

The performance of *Les Huguenots* that night was a great success. Roger, who did not know the Italian translation, sang in French, and by the time of the duet in the fourth act, Viardot had learnt her part in it in French too. This, to quote Cox once more, 'so excited Roger that he threw his whole soul into the scene, which was then sung and played as it had not previously been witnessed, creating an immense furore, and a double call, both for the Valentine and for the Raoul. It is needless to say that Roger was never again permitted to appear as Raoul, neither did it happen that Mario was ever afterwards indisposed when *Les Huguenots* had to be repeated.'

The facts may be as Cox stated them, but his interpretation is not correct. The following day, 4 August, Mario wrote another letter to Gye: 'I take advantage of the messenger you sent to Mme. Grisi, to give you my news. My chill is a little better, thanks to the pills of Dr Billing, but I don't know what my voice will be like by tomorrow, Saturday. As Roger helped you yesterday by replacing me, I think it would only be justice to let him sing the role for the subscribers, which would be quite alright as far as I'm concerned. In that case you should remove my name from the poster for tomorrow.'

In fact Mario was well enough to sing on the Saturday, but his letter to Gye surely exonerates him from the malicious behaviour implied by Cox.

Performances of *Les Huguenots* continued through August; for

Mario's benefit on the 17th, *I puritani*, with Grisi, Tamburini and Marini was given, followed by the rondo finale from *La Cenerentola* sung—and encored—by Alboni, and the third act of *Les Huguenots*, with Viardot and Mario 'creating extraordinary enthusiasm.' The season ended with Grisi and Mario in *Lucrezia Borgia* on Thursday 24 August.

Mario and Grisi, with a party consisting of Mdlle. Vera, Tagliafico and others, conducted by Julius Benedict, left London immediately for Dublin. They opened at the Theatre Royal on Tuesday 29 August with *Norma*. During the twelve-day season there were two perform-ances each of *Norma*, *I puritani* and *La sonnambula*; one each of *La gazza ladra* and *Don Pasquale*; and a grand matinée concert. Grisi and Mario sang at all performances.

The Italian singers then went on an extended tour of the British Isles. They were in Edinburgh on 10 September, when Henry Greville attended their concert. Afterwards he wrote: 'If one may judge by the enthusiasm they excited, the Scotch [sic] must be very fond of music. There were 2,000 people present, and I never saw so many hideous women congregated before.'

Jenny Lind, Chopin and many other musicians also visited Edin-burgh that autumn. The general state of unrest in Europe during 1848 had resulted in an unusually large number of visiting artists in Britain, and it was not only London and Edinburgh, but many smaller provincial cities that also benefited.

The revolt in Piedmont proved as abortive as those in Sicily, Venice, Parma and Milan, but during the short-lived truce with the Austrians an amnesty of political offenders against the Sardinian government had been declared, and Mario was able to return to Italy after thirteen years of exile. His father had died, apparently without learning that the son he had treated so harshly had become the most popular tenor in Paris and London. Mario paid a brief visit to Cagliari to see his mother. While in Sardinia he was deluged with requests to sing, but refused, mindful of his vow never to sing in public in Italy.

Another political exile, Marco Aurelio Marliani, had returned to Italy the year before. When the various states rose against the Austrians, he had joined the Republican army as a Captain and for his bravery was promoted Major. When the Austrian army stormed Bologna in May 1849, Marliani was killed.

Grisi was pregnant again that winter and Rita, the second of her daughters by Mario, was born on 11 March 1849 at Ashburnham House, Chelsea. The birth of the child was registered on 28 March, the father's name being given as John Mario de Candia, Gentleman, and

that of the other as 'Joséphine de Candia, formerly Colonna.' Poor
Grisi was unable to put her own name on the birth certificates of her
children. Had she done so they—and their potential earning power—
would automatically have become the property of her husband, de
Melcy.

The birth of Rita delayed the opening of the 1849 season of the
Royal Italian Opera from 10 March to 15 March. The opera was
Auber's *La Muette de Portici*, or *Masaniello*, as the Italian version was
usually entitled. Masaniello was Mario's fortieth role since his début
just over ten years before. Although it was a part that, for various
reasons, he came to dislike, there is no doubt that on this occasion he
won great popular and critical success as the Neapolitan fisherman
who leads a revolt against the Spanish occupying forces.

'Signor Mario is assuredly the best Masaniello since Nourrit,'
asserted Chorley, 'and his mellifluous voice, clear of the brilliant
Frenchman's nasality, enables him to throw into certain portions of
the opera a charm which we have never enjoyed in them before.
Though he was tired by rehearsal, and possibly by his amazing
brilliancy in the duet of the second act, his romance [sung] by Fenella
sleeping was deliciously said.'

Fenella, Masaniello's sister and the 'dumb girl' of the original title,
was played by the dancer Pauline Leroux, 'who in pantomime remains
unsurpassed on the stage—save by Mdlle. Fanny Elssler. The dresses
are gorgeous,' continued Chorley. 'The scenery is in the best manner—and there is an eruption of Vesuvius which in times past would
have been placarded all over London in letters half as high and quite as
red as the Burning Mountain.'

Queen Victoria, who attended a performance of *Masaniello* on 24
March, also admired both Mario's picturesque appearance as the
Neapolitan fisherman and the production: 'The decorations, dresses
and mise en scène were magnificent & on a grand scale, hardly
equalled yet in England. At the end when the eruption of Mount
Vesuvious [sic] takes place there must have been 200 people on the
stage.'

Two nights later, when Mario sang at a Philharmonic concert, the
Queen was again present. The programme included Beethoven's
Fourth symphony, the overture to Weber's *Der Freischütz* and
Mendelssohn's incidental music to *Athalie*.

Mario wrote to Delafield on Thursday 12 April to say that he had a
bad cold which would prevent him from singing in *Masaniello* that
evening. The tenor Lorenzo Salvi took over the title role for that
performance. The following Tuesday 17 April, Grisi made her first

appearance since the birth of Rita, in *Semiramide*. The next day Mario wrote to Gye: 'I have just informed Mr Delafield that I am still unable to appear at the theatre, as my recovery is not yet complete—and to warn him to change the announcement for tomorrow. I have also written to him about a certain letter which should guarantee my salary for the whole season, and which from day to day is delayed, for one reason or another. Nor have I received the payment due on 19 April. Would you kindly remind him that if by my contract I am obliged to forfeit £100 if I break my engagement, the same contract binds him too, and for a similar obligation to pay.'

Delafield was already in the financial difficulties which led to his bankruptcy and was finding it more and more of an impossibility to obtain sufficient money to pay his singers. Later in the week, on Saturday 21 April, it was Grisi's turn to complain: in a letter to Gye she wrote: 'I am very vexed to have to inform you that I cannot sing tonight, as I am not well enough; besides, I do not care to sing for directors who do not hold to their engagement with me; I was promised that I should be paid yesterday, Friday, the remaining money, but I have seen no one; therefore do not count on me for this evening, and please relay this to Mr Delafield.'

Grisi and Mario, both recovered and in the best of health, sang in *Lucrezia Borgia* on 1 May and both of them also appeared in *Don Giovanni* on 17 May. A week later, *Les Huguenots* was revived, with a largely new cast from that of the previous year. Only Mario as Raoul and Marini as Marcel remained the same. Marguerite de Valois was now sung by the Belgian soprano Julie Dorus-Gras, who had created the role; the page Urbain was sung by Mlle. Angri, in place of Alboni, who had gone over to the rival establishment at Her Majesty's that season; and, owing to Pauline Viardot's engagement at the Paris Opéra, where she was appearing in Meyerbeer's new opera, *Le Prophète*, the part of Valentine was sung by Grisi.

In Chorley's opinion, 'Mme. Grisi's singing and acting are nothing short of wonderful. To carry away her public as she did on Thursday, in a style of opera new to her, at the present stage of her career and immediately succeeding in the part to one of the subtlest and most impassioned tragic actresses [i.e. Viardot] whom the world has ever seen, argues a power for which even we were unprepared, highly as we have always rated her.'

Grisi's determination to beat, as it were, her rival at her own game, and the satisfaction she obtained from her success, can readily be imagined. Not every critic admired Grisi's Valentine so whole-heartedly as Chorley, but 'the duration of [her] gifts, the versatility of her talent, her beauty of voice and person, and her impulsive dramatic energy' could not be denied.

During one week in mid-June, both opera houses gave performances of *Il matrimonio segreto*, providing an occasion for direct comparison between the two companies. Despite the matchless Don Geronimo of Lablache at Her Majesty's, Chorley awarded the palm without question to Covent Garden: 'the exquisite singing and sparkling shrewish comedy of Mme. Persiani and Mme. Grisi as the sisters', Tamburini's Don Geronimo, 'older, feebler, more stupid than Lablache's angry old gentleman . . . but not less true and individual . . . the capital and coxcombical Count' of Tagliafico and the Paolo of Mario, whose '"Pria che spunti" is next in beauty and grace to Rubini's', all combined to make up an irresistible performance.

During that summer, as Austria regained control over the provinces of Northern Italy one by one; as Garibaldi entered Rome and then, after a seven-week siege, had to abandon the city to the French, the hopes of the Italian exiles and the supporters of a united Italy, raised so high by the early successes of their armies, fell to a new low level. In a letter from London to an Italian friend in Paris, Mario expressed some of this profound distress:

My dear Luigi, you will understand all the sorrow I feel for our country and families, our forebears must be laughing, or perhaps crying! In my case, the trouble and disgrace of poor Serafino [his younger brother] is an additional burden, and for the honour of my name I am obliged to pay at once the sum of 760 francs to M. Vincent, bookseller and Commissaire in the rue St André-des-Arts, Paris. For this I am enclosing half a bank draft for £40—the other half I have sent to Cabecchia, in my name, to be forwarded to Pagello in Turin as soon as he receives the letter. Ask Commissaire Vincent to write at once to Pagello in Turin that he has the same amount. Also please ask if he has received a draft from Turin for 500 lire, sent and signed by Serafino de Candia. If so, he can return it to you, if not, just get a receipt for the money.

It is strange that Serafino, the only de Candia of that name, has not received one of my letters in which I told him to present himself to Count Galli, my friend in the Ministry of War, in order to regularize his affairs, both of money and of conduct. It was sent last March 29 to the Grand Hotel Trombetta, the best in Turin, and would have assured me, if not of his financial stability, at least of his security this year from Austrian bullets. [There is a pun here in the Italian, on *palle*—bullets—and *palto*—overcoat or hide.]

Dear Luigi, I am really unhappy and only my little girl consoles me; everything else adds to my sorrow, disgrace piled on disgrace. So as not to risk the mail I will draw a draft payable at sight for £140 sterling, which can be cashed at any bank for Lire just like English currency. Tell me when, so I can leave the money in Piccadilly and thus pay my debts. Goodbye dear Luigi, I haven't the heart to write more. Giulia is well and sends her love, also little Rita, whom God turn into a virtuosa, though not of singing. Mario.

Please send the two ghastly portraits of my parents which are in the bedroom. Love, JM. xx—the mark of Giulia.

Meanwhile Viardot had arrived in London, fresh from her triumph as Fidès in Meyerbeer's *Le Prophète*, which had received its first performance at the Paris Opéra on 16 April. She was to take the same part in the Royal Italian Opera production of the work at Covent Garden, where *Il profeta* was already in rehearsal. Despite the financial crisis which resulted in Delafield's bankruptcy on 14 July, the singers and musicians were persuaded to carry on and Meyerbeer's opera was produced on Tuesday 24 July, to even greater critical acclaim than *Les Huguenots* the previous year.

Chorley, who had been to the Paris première in April, reiterated his 'formerly expressed judgement of the Fidès of Mme. Viardot as an incomparable piece of art and nature.' In the title role, Jean of Leyden, Mario shared with Roger, the Paris Prophet, the disadvantage of having to sing a part intended for Duprez, 'whose weight of voice and breadth of style were obviously from first to last present with M. Meyerbeer while he was writing.'

Moreover, like the other members of the London cast new to their roles, Mario had had comparatively little time to prepare a role that even to 'a Duprez would have been no piece of mere Italian song singing or child's play.' Even so, Chorley preferred Mario's Prophet to Roger's in many respects: 'His pastorale in the first act is deliciously sung. The largo before the final hymn of the second act too, is finely given and the lyric itself with great animation . . . Signor Mario is more noble and less mannered than M. Roger in the Baccanale which closes the opera. In the Cathedral scene his presence is splendid—nothing less than a figure which has walked out from the frame of a Van Eyck or Memlinck picture.'

In the great scene where the Prophet's imposture is detected, Mario's acting was as yet less subtle than Roger's; but Mario 'habitually improves in a new part nightly; and already his is a most picturesque and satisfactory representation of the hero, as his success must have assured him.'

Le Prophète was given ten times in the month that remained of the season. Even Cox, by no means one of the tenor's greatest or most uncritical supporters, considered Mario's John of Leyden a remarkable characterization: 'The make-up of his face was realistically, painfully beautiful,' wrote Cox, 'and his demeanour was so graceful and noble, energetic and subdued, that he seemed to be the very man he represented, and not an actor merely playing a part.'

At the beginning of August Chorley wrote another piece about the new opera: 'Since our last notice, the English performance of *Le Prophète* has gained much in ripeness, ease and accuracy. Signor Mario now surpasses M. Roger as Jean of Leyden.'

It would be difficult, if not impossible, in Chorley's view, for any one tenor to encompass the threefold aspect of son, lover and 'Enthusiast . . . In Signor Mario we must not look for the enthusiastic fanaticism or the mysterious reverie of the Prophet, but he gives us the tenderness of the lover and the repentance of the son. Unequal to the brilliancy demanded by the martial scene in the second act, he still delivers the final chaunt (which is much shortened) with rare beauty of voice. Then, though uninspired in the earlier part of the cathedral scene . . . he throws great agony and remorse into the by-play betwixt himself and Fidès, which is a finer piece of acting than any that we have hitherto seen from him.'

In the Baccanale of the final banqueting scene, when Jean, but not the other guests, knows that the powder-magazine below is about to explode, Mario sang 'with a voluptuous abandon which is irresistible.'

After the Royal Italian Opera season had closed with a performance of *Don Giovanni*, Mario and Grisi, together with most of the singers from both opera houses, as well as many other artists, took part on August 27 in the opening of the new Liverpool Philharmonic Hall.

From Liverpool the singers went to Manchester, where Mrs Charles Hallé was pressed into service to look after the six-month-old Rita while her parents were busy. On the morning of Saturday 1 September Grisi wrote to the conductor's wife: 'Very dear and beautiful Lady, you have been so good and kind in giving hospitality to my little baby, that I can only offer you my warmest thanks and take the liberty of asking you again today, as I am obliged to go out without taking her with me, for fear of tiring her too much.

'Would you very kindly keep her for a couple of hours so she can breathe the fresh air, and send her back to me at the Hotel about five-thirty, when I shall return after a long and tiring day. Please present my compliments to your good kind sisters, as well as to M. Hallé, and believe me always your affectionate Giulia Grisi.'

On the back of the letter Mario added: 'I regret infinitely, Madame, that I am unable to call on you today, and thank you for your kind reception. My compliments and friendship to M. Hallé. J. Mario.'

The next day the singers travelled to Birmingham, where Mendelssohn's *Elijah*, which had received its first performance at the Festival of 1846, was to be given on 4 September. Henry Greville, who had also been in Manchester, and Adelaide Sartoris and her husband were among the visitors to Birmingham that autumn.

The customary tour of the British provinces was curtailed in 1849, as Mario and Grisi were off to conquer another foreign capital; they had been engaged to sing in St Petersburg.

Chapter 9

ST PETERSBURG WAS a city where it was possible for singers to earn huge sums of money, where favourite artists were received with costly gifts as well as overwhelming applause. Their engagement at the Théâtre-Italien every winter had prevented Mario and Grisi from going to Russia before. There had been rumours in the London newspapers the previous year that they had been invited to St Petersburg for the 1848-49 season, but Grisi's pregnancy and the birth of Rita precluded a visit then.

The Italian Opera in St Petersburg was under the patronage of the Tsar, Nicholas I, and owing to the death of his brother, the Grand Duke Michael, in September, it was feared that the season might have to be postponed. Public mourning, however, was for only three weeks and on 13 October the Italian Opera was able to open with a performance of *Semiramide*.

Grisi's first appearance was greeted by a storm of applause. Further bursts of acclamation punctuated the entire performance and at the end of the opera Grisi was called before the curtain twelve or thirteen times. Mario made his first appearance in *I puritani* and 'it is needless to state how he was received, how he sang, and how he was applauded,' wrote a correspondent in *The Illustrated London News*. 'The ladies threw their bouquets at him—a custom which would not be much approved of in London or elsewhere.' Elvira was sung not by Grisi but by the Italian soprano Erminia Frezzolini.

Excitement was intense before Grisi's first Norma in St Petersburg. The theatre was crammed full and 'the effect she produced in every part of the opera cannot be described. After the trio the public rose as one with a deafening shout, which lasted some minutes. In the last scene, the ladies wept aloud; certainly La Diva was never heard to such perfection before; her voice was in the finest condition, and her spirit and energy untiring.'

After four performances of *Norma*, *Lucia di Lammermoor* was presented with Mdlle. Corbari and Mario. 'Despite Rubini's great triumph in St Petersburg as Edgardo, Mario's success was enormous.' By now it was mid-November, but the weather was still as mild as in

London. The Tsar and his family had not yet returned to the capital and the real season, with its endless round of parties and concerts, had hardly begun. A performance of *Linda di Chamounix* raised little enthusiasm, perhaps because neither Grisi nor Mario sang in it.

Lucrezia Borgia, in which they both appeared, was a great deal more popular. Every place was taken days in advance and a packed house wildly applauded the two singers. The part of Maffio Orsini at that performance was sung by Mdlle. de Meric, daughter of the soprano Henriette Meric-Lalande, who had created the title role of Lucrezia Borgia at Milan in 1833.

In St Petersburg, as in Paris and London, Mario had to combat memories of Rubini, great idol of the Russian public, in many of his Italian roles. Which perhaps explains why for his benefit at the end of January 1850, Mario chose *Les Huguenots*. As the religious disputes between Catholics and Protestants, culminating in the massacre of St Bartholomew's Eve, that formed the basis of Scribe's original libretto were unacceptable to the Russian censor, Meyerbeer's opera had to be given as *Les Guelfes et les Gibelins*.

Mario had met Tsar Nicholas when the Russian Emperor was on a visit to London in 1845. Among various stories told about the tenor's first engagement in St Petersburg, one rings particularly true. Whatever the weather, Mario liked to wander round the streets of any city in which he happened to be singing. He also liked, above all, to smoke and, except when actually on stage, was always to be seen with a cigar in his mouth. Walking one day in St Petersburg, where smoking in the streets was forbidden, as many of the houses were still built of wood, the tenor saw the Tsar's sleigh approaching and hastily hid his cigar in the wide sleeve of his overcoat.

Nicholas, well aware of the concealed—and forbidden—cigar, kept Mario talking for several minutes; then, relenting, he gave the tenor a special dispensation, allowing him to smoke in the street.

By the beginning of April, Mario and Grisi were back in London. They made their first appearance of the 1850 season at Covent Garden on Tuesday 9 April in *Lucrezia Borgia*. 'The climate of the Czar's country,' commented Chorley, 'which has rained crowns and diamonds on the lady (or Gossip Rumour lieth) has agreed with Lucrezia's voice; since Mme. Grisi used her topmost notes on Tuesday with the vigour and fearlessness of former years, and sang and acted throughout the evening with all her passion and all her brilliancy.'

Grisi was received with great appreciation by the audience. So, too, was Mario, 'for whom an apology was made on the score of a cold, evidently a transient indisposition, since he too gave tokens of his best power and passion.'

Two days later Mario, apparently still not recovered from his cold, wrote to Gye, now sole manager of the Royal Italian Opera: 'I think it would be a thousand times better to give *Norma* tonight—it would spoil *Lucrezia Borgia* forever, and wrong the theatre, to give another performance like Tuesday's. As Mlle. [de] Meric has not yet arrived we are more or less obliged to give *Norma*—I know the subscribers will be pleased, it will give me a rest and we can put on *I puritani* next Tuesday.'

Mlle. d'Okolski, deputizing for de Meric as Orsini, had not, apparently, pleased the audience the previous Tuesday.

Norma was duly presented on 11 April with Grisi and, as Pollione, the Roman-born tenor Enrico Tamberlik, who was singing that season for the first time in London. Evidently Mario continued indisposed, as there were no performances of *I puritani* that year.

A revival of *La donna del lago* on 25 April brought the two tenors together on the same stage for the first time, when Mario sang the King and Tamberlik took the part of Roderick. It was some years since Mario had had to compete with a flesh and blood rival—though memories of Rubini grew more, not less potent with the passing of time—and the advent of Tamberlik, ten years younger than himself, had a wholly beneficial effect on Mario.

Mario 'is this year singing like one determined to keep his throne let tenors be ever so many and Tamberliks ever so brilliant and passionate,' wrote Chorley. 'In an interpolated scene from Pacini's *Amazila* he works all manner of falsetto wonders: which amazing feats we never admired in Rubini, and have not yet learned to relish. But beautifully and gracefully impassioned was the cantabile which opened the aria, given with such a union of charm and fervour as marked the beau ideal of tenor singing in sentimental music.' Grisi sang Elena as usual while de Meric, now arrived in London, took the part of Malcolm.

A month later the two tenors sang together again, when *Robert le diable* was produced for the first time by the Royal Italian Opera, on Thursday 23 May. Mario, having already ceded the title role of *Masaniello* to Tamberlik without regret, now allowed him to take over Robert, a part which Mario himself had not sung since leaving the Paris Opéra, with equal lack of sorrow. Instead, he sang the less important role of the minstrel, Raimbaut or, in Italian, Rambaldo. Alice, the part associated in London with Jenny Lind—whose operatic career had ended a year previously—was sung by Grisi who, somewhat surprisingly, won great success in a character very different from the imperious, temperamental heroines she was used to portraying.

'Mme. Grisi's Alice deserves the first mention as admirable,' wrote Chorley, 'whether in its vocal force and finish or in its simple and spirited acting. There are few facts in the annals of music comparable to this lady's entering upon grand French opera after so many years of practice in the dramatically slighter Italian school and in such new and difficult occupation distancing every competitor—one alone excepted . . .' That one alone was, of course, Pauline Viardot, who in Berlin had once sung both Alice and Isabella in the same performance, when the singer of the latter role was taken ill.

Tamberlik was judged a splendid Robert and Castellan a more than competent Isabella, but 'the gem of the opera' in the opinion of Cox, 'was Mario's Rambaldo, the music of which part can never be sung better by any one else, and never had been before, nor has been since, equalled. To have heard the descriptive song of Roberto in the first act, and the duet with Bertram in the second, was little else than priceless.'

As Mario only sang Raimbaud at the six performances of *Robert* given that season and then never again, 'the beauty it added to the general effect of the opera was so transient that it can be remembered but by very few. By those few, however, it must always be referred to with unmeasured pleasure and pain, pleasure at its having been witnessed—pain on account of the utter impossibility of its repetition.'

Meyerbeer was certainly in the ascendancy that season, as apart from the six performances of *Robert le diable*, there were also twelve of *Les Huguenots* and ten of *Le Prophète*. The Queen and Prince Albert attended a performance of *Le Prophète* on 25 June. Victoria found the story of interest and the music beautiful, while 'the acting of Mario & Viardot & the singing of the former most exquisite. His appearance, very striking & handsome . . . The most beautiful scenes, & the most striking music, are in the Finale to the 2nd act, where Jean sings the Hymne Triomphale, which is quite thrilling & the whole of the Coronation scene in the Cathedral, beginning with the March & Procession & ending with the scene between the Prophète & his mother—one of the most touching ever imaginable.'

The Queen made some sketches of Mario as John of Leyden (see illustrations following page 44) which give a very good idea of Mario's appearance in *Le Prophète*. She also returned to the subject of Meyerbeer's opera in a letter to her Uncle Leopold written on 2 July. After mentioning a concert at Buckingham Palace the previous night—at which Grisi, Viardot, Mario and other singers from both opera houses took part—she continued: 'The *Prophète* is quite beautiful and I am quite sure would delight you. The music in the *Scène du Couronnement* is, I think, finer than anything in either *Robert* or the *Huguenots*; it is highly dramatic, and really very touching. Mario sings and acts in it quite in perfection. His Raoul in the *Huguenots* is also most beautiful. He improves every year, and I really think his voice is the finest tenor I ever heard, and he sings and acts with such *intense* feeling.'

Mario's next new role, Eléazar in *La Juive*, became the subject of more controversy and gossip. Halévy's opera, with Viardot as Rachel, the Jewess of the title, and Mario as her father, the goldsmith Eléazar, was announced for production at Covent Garden on Thursday 25 July. On the morning of that day, Mario wrote to Gye: 'I am in despair, but it is impossible for me to sing this evening—I waited in case, but no use, *La Juive* will have to be postponed till Saturday, for this evening don't think of it, it's quite impossible for me to sing, it is the evil eye!'

Mario did not sing that evening, but the performance of *La Juive* was not postponed. As in the case of Roger in *Les Huguenots*, a tenor was found who knew the role of Eléazar: Enrico Maralti, who had sung the part in Brussels, stepped in at the last moment, singing in French and without rehearsal.

Rumours immediately began to circulate implying that Mario's indisposition was caused by Grisi's jealousy of Viardot, but in fact there is plenty of evidence that the tenor was genuinely ill. He sang in the second performance of *La Juive* on Saturday 27 July when, according to the critic of *The Illustrated London News*, 'he still laboured under such severe indisposition that he merely walked through the part [of Eléazar] and sang with evident languor.'

Mario was not the only member of the cast of *La Juive* to fall sick. Karl Formes, the German bass 'who had left his bed to play at the opening performance, was replaced on Saturday by Zelger, who has frequently enacted the Cardinal in Belgium.' By the following Tuesday 30 July, both Mario and Formes were recovered and *La Juive* was performed as announced, without untoward incident.

But though Mario was evidently back in his finest vocal form, he was criticized for his dramatic characterization of 'Lazzaro' by *The Illustrated London News*. 'The first great mistake is in the making-up of the head. The face is not furrowed as it should be by the wrinkles of age and cunning, and he looks more like the brother of Rachel than her father. The form of Signor Mario is too erect and his gait is too steady for the restless, suspicious Shylock of Constance. That the popular tenor will improve in the part there can be no doubt; everybody recollects how he played Raoul and the Prophète the first times, and how he acts these characters now . . . Mario, if he have the will, has unquestionably the intellect and power to render Lazzaro one of his finest creations.'

Mario, however, did not have the will; he disliked the role of Eléazar and, after two more performances that season, never sang it again. Perhaps the great stage lover was unwilling to disguise his still youthful good looks and upright carriage; more importantly Mario, as Chorley had pointed out in his notice of *Le Prophète*, could not portray fanaticism, so the hatred and desire for revenge motivating Eléazar were outside his range.

The 1850 season ended on a brighter note with a revival of *L'elisir d'amore* in which Viardot sang Adina, Mario was the incomparable Nemorino, Ronconi acted superbly as Dr Dulcamara and Tamburini, 'the Belcore of Belcores', completed a perfect cast.

The Queen, the Prince and their children had already moved to Osborne House, their private summer retreat on the Isle of Wight. An informal concert was to be held there on the evening of 5 August, and during the afternoon the Queen went to hear the rehearsal: 'Mario, Lablache & Castellan, with Costa at the piano, which was a real treat,' she wrote in her Journal.

'I had never heard Mario sing so "con amore", so quietly & was able to most thoroughly enjoy his heavenly voice.' The singers only rehearsed part of the concert, but 'Mario was kind enough to sing twice over that glorious Hymne Triomphale [from *Le Prophète*] which Mario said was a sort of Gregorian Chant, which Meyerbeer had heard in a Convent in Genoa.'

The Queen and the Prince talked with the artists, finding Mario 'very pleasing and gentlemanlike.' The concert took place after dinner, and was by common consent considered a great treat by Victoria and her household.

'We were all in ecstasies with the power, volume & rich quality of Mario's voice, & the feeling, fire & facility of his singing. It is quite beautiful & really touches one to hear. The duet from the *Huguenots* was beautifully given. Altogether the Concert was a great success.'

Grisi did not sing at that concert, nor indeed at any subsequent entertainment at Osborne in which Mario took part. Evidently the Queen had not forgiven her impertinence to Jenny Lind; and no doubt the unconcealed nature of the Mario-Grisi ménage was also a contributing factor. Grisi could be invited to appear at official or semi-official functions at Buckingham Palace, but not to take part in private affairs at Osborne.

At the end of August, Mario arranged a special concert for Mazzini, in aid of the Italian refugees in London, now more numerous than ever since the fall of the short-lived Roman Republic the year before and the collapse of resistance against the Austrians in the north of Italy. Most of the singers who had not yet left London took part and the following day Mazzini wrote to his English friend, Mrs Matilda Biggs: 'Two words about the concert. It was successful. I do not know now the profits; but all calculations tend to make me believe that we shall have, the expenses, some forty pounds, deducted, about 150 pounds left.

'The artists were brilliant, Mario, Mad. Grisi, Ronconi and Baucarde especially. It lasted from eight o'clock till half-past twelve. The audience very enthusiastic. The gas went off and the room was in sudden complete darkness for five minutes at least but nobody was alarmed, two or three old ladies excepted. About the practical result I will tell you more in a few days.'

Grisi was once again pregnant and her third daughter, Maria Angelina, was born in Paris during December. Life in the French capital had long ago returned to normal after the revolution, but there was no question of either Mario or Grisi singing there for the moment, as their old adversary Benjamin Lumley was now manager of the Théâtre-Italien. A rumour that Mario was to sing at the Italiens that season was immediately contradicted in a letter to the newspapers. At the end of the year Mario went alone to St Petersburg.

While in Russia that winter, Mario made friends with a young nobleman, whose aspirations to become a composer he encouraged in a letter dated 19 March 1851:

Dear Friend, I do not want to leave Petersburg without saying goodbye to you. Frezzolini goes to Moscow, having arranged matters with the Theatre Direction of St Petersburg. The portrait of me that you own is very bad—I will send or bring you one from London that is better, so that the beauty of the drawing makes me *piu simpatico* in your memory.

Mario's amused acceptance of his own good looks, the very opposite of personal vanity, was one of his most endearing traits. His letter continued:

Work, my dear Count, and study, that is the only true happiness on earth. God has given you so much talent it would be a crime not to use it . . . Send me your compositions when you write anything. I will write to you from London, and will send you any news I think

Mario, Grisi, Tamburini and Lablache in *Don Pasquale*

THE MARIO VALSE.
BY
F. G. TINNEY.
LONDON T BOOSEY & SONS 28 HOLLES STREET OXFORD STREET.

Mario as the Duke in *Rigoletto*

Left: Grisi—marble bust by C. F. Fuller, 1858
Right: Mario—marble bust by C. F. Fuller, 1857

Mario as Jean de Leyden in *Le Prophète*—drawing by
Queen Victoria

Grisi and Mario in *Les Huguenots*

might interest you. Goodbye, I must catch the train at seven o'clock which is why I write so briefly and so badly, but I love you well. J. Mario.

1851 was the year of the Great Exhibition, which opened in London on 1 May. Visitors flocked to the capital from all over the British Isles and also from abroad. The Royal Italian Opera season, which had begun on 3 April, continued until the end of August. As in the preceding two years, the operas of Meyerbeer dominated the repertory; there were performances of *Les Huguenots* with Grisi and Mario, *Le Prophète* with Viardot and Mario, and *Robert le diable* with Grisi and Tamberlik.

During May, both Grisi and Mario caught influenza and went to Brighton for a few days to recuperate. Gye had evidently sent Grisi the score of Auber's opera *L'Enfant prodigue* and on 28 May she returned it to him with a letter in which she refused the role he had proposed: 'You know it is not a part for me, and that I don't want to do it, as I have already told you; I am astonished that you have sent it to me.'

Gye's next suggestion was a revival of *La favorita* and Grisi replied:

Costa tells me that you want to give *La favorita* next Thursday—I must warn you that it is impossible for me to do it, first because I have been ill with a bad cold and I don't think I shall be able to sing at all until next Tuesday; and secondly because *La favorita* is practically a new role for me, and I need to study it and rehearse it well, neither of which I can do while I am so ill . . . The week after next I think I could be ready.

La favorita was eventually produced on 12 June. The opera was a great success with the public and Mario and Grisi, now back in their best voice, were both much applauded.

Neither singer appeared in any opera new to them until 10 July, when *Die Zauberflöte*, or more precisely *Il flauto magico* was chosen by the Queen for her state visit to Covent Garden. Despite a cast that included Mario as Tamino, Grisi as Pamina, Ronconi as Papageno and Viardot in the unlikely role, for a noted tragic actress, of Papagena, Mozart's opera was coldly received.

Before the Queen left London for Osborne, she went again to *Le Prophète,* staying for the last act, which she had seen only once before. 'We admired the music & the whole, more than ever,' she wrote. 'Mario, though still obliged to save his voice, sang beautifully, & in the last act, with all his accustomed force & vigour.' Some ten days

later, describing a concert at Osborne in which Castellan, Mario and
Formes sang, she observed: 'Mario's head is quite "une tête de Christ"
& he wears a beard & his hair parted down the middle as in the
Prophète . . .'

In the autumn, after the closure of the Royal Italian Opera season,
Mario and Grisi returned to St Petersburg. The tenor made his first
appearance in *I puritani* and B. Damcke, writing in the French-
language *Journal de St Petersbourg*, found it very natural 'that the rentrée
of Mario, a singer with such an admirable range, has caused a sensation
and aroused enormous interest. Is it necessary to describe Mario's
talent, his thrilling chest notes, his falsetto, so pure and clear it
resembles the voice of a woman, and his expressive and noble diction?'
asked Damcke, answering his own question with an emphatic
negative.

'To say Mario,' he continued, 'is to evoke tenderness, poetic
sentiment; to raise his great qualities to the highest level of artistic
perfection. In the role of Arturo, more perhaps than in any other part
in the Italian repertory, all Mario's most individual and most precious
gifts are shown to their greatest advantage.

'The fine cavatina of the last act, especially, gains a magic and an
inexplicable charm from Mario's voice and diction, which reaches its
peak in the last chromatic phrase. When these marvellously expressive
notes leave the lips of the singer like sighs of love, all breathing
stopped, all hearts ceased beating. The existence of the whole audience
was concentrated in the vibrations of that unique voice, which has no
equal in the memories and souvenirs of a lifetime.'

The enthusiasm with which the St Petersburg public greeted the
return of its favourite tenor 'made one think of the ancient Greeks
awarding the crown to the winner of the Olympic Games.'

This notice, which does not even mention the name of Rubini, must
have given Mario as much pleasure as the warmth of feeling demonstrated by the audience. But both critic and public could prove fickle.
On 8 November Mario appeared in *Lucia di Lammermoor*. The tenor,
who was obviously not well, sang the first two acts as best he could; an
announcement was then made saying that he could not appear in the
third. Damcke commented tartly that 'Mario's indisposition spoiled
this fine opera. The crowds were disappointed. Let us hope that he will
soon make it up to them.'

Mario replied to this criticism in a letter dated 23 November, which
was published in the *Journal de St Petersbourg* on 5 December: 'It seems
to me that many people, after reading the *Journal* for 17 November,
might think that I had failed in my duty to the Italian Opera . . . For

the sake of my reputation, which I hold dear, I must deny this accusation. The *Lucia* in which I did not sing the last act was my third consecutive performance, and considering the very bad weather, it was hardly surprising that I became indisposed. If there was a fault on my part, it lay in my consenting to sing at all that night.

'I am very anxious that the St Petersburg public should know that I am more concerned with my reputation as an honest man than with the vain glory of an artist, and you will oblige me by publishing this letter.'

Any temporary coldness in the relationship between Mario and the St Petersburg audiences was soon forgotten. In January 1852 there were further performances of *I puritani* and a revival of *Il barbiere di Siviglia*, in which opera, according to Damcke, Mario was charming. 'He sang with particularly good humour and spirits. He was, moreover, in admirable voice, which made his Almaviva a worthy pendant to his Arturo . . . In short, we must again recognize that when he wishes, Mario is undisputed king of all the tenors alive, and that his throne is solidly and magnificently established.'

When *Les Huguenots*, still under the guise of *Les Guelfes et les Gibelins* was given during February with Mario and Grisi as, respectively, Raoul and Valentine, their duet roused the audience to a frenzy, expressed by endless applause and innumerable calls before the curtain. The final opera to be presented, before Lent brought the season to an end, was *Sardanapale* by Giulio Alary, which was receiving its first performance, with Grisi, Mario and Ronconi in the principal roles.

Sardanapale was Mario's 45th role in just over thirteen years. He sang no new part during the 1852 season at Covent Garden, when Meyerbeer was again the most favoured composer: there were eleven performances of *Les Huguenots*, of which two were attended by the Queen; on 1 May Mario, having started the evening in good voice, broke down in the second act, while Formes 'seemed a little husky too.' A week later, when the Queen made her second visit to *Les Huguenots*, 'Mario was in his old beautiful voice again, singing quite exquisitely & Formes in splendid voice. Grisi, as well, sang & acted extremely well & the whole was perfection, we stayed to the end.'

The Queen gave a concert at Buckingham Palace on 10 May, the last occasion, almost certainly, that Grisi sang there. Mario, who contributed a touching account of 'Du pauvre, seul ami fidèle' from *Masaniello* to the concert on 10 May, sang at Buckingham Palace again on 4 June, when he included two Schubert songs, the Serenade and 'La douce peine' ('Lob der Thränen'), to the programme. Then his name, too, disappears from the lists of performers at Queen Victoria's concerts.

A performance of *The Magic Flute* at Covent Garden on 11 May earned the Queen's displeasure: 'the opera itself was performed in a slovenly manner. The 3 black ladies [sic] sang very badly, the scenery, etc., very inferior & Mario really only walked through his part.' Though Tamino was certainly not one of Mario's favourite roles, he could have no excuse for walking through it. The performance of Mozart's opera was saved by 'the inimitable drollery of Ronconi [as Papageno] who kept one in constant fits of laughter with his tricks.'

In addition to *Les Huguenots*, nine performances of *Le Prophète* were also given that season. As Pauline Viardot was not engaged at the Royal Italian Opera in 1852—she had a baby at the end of May—the role of Fidès was taken over by Grisi, who would have been better advised not risk direct comparison with her rival in one of the latter's finest characterizations.

'Mme. Grisi has made so few mistakes during her long and brilliant career,' wrote Chorley in the *Athenaeum*, 'that the very great one she has at last made by attempting the part of Fidès in *Le Prophète* shall not be further descanted on here.' Other critics were not so forbearing, but the popularity of the opera itself, and the enthusiasm aroused by Mario's performance in the title role, ensured that *Le Prophète* was as successful with the public as ever.

Grisi never sang the part of Fidès again. When *Le Prophète*, under the title of *Le Siège de Gand*, was given for the first time at St Petersburg during February 1853, it was Viardot who took her accustomed place in Meyerbeer's opera opposite the Jean of Leyden of Mario. 'As soon as the public heard the voice of Mario, as soon as it saw the grace, the acting and the simple manner of the great tragedian Viardot,' wrote Damcke in the *Journal de St Petersbourg*, 'that public found its old emotions and applause, cheers and encores were heard with all the old enthusiasm. Meyerbeer should be more than ever grateful to these same artists who have come to introduce his masterpiece to the music lovers of the 60th degree of latitude, as they have already done in London and Paris.' Mario had not, of course, sung in *Le Prophète* in Paris.

Earlier performances at the Italian Opera in St Petersburg had not been received with quite such enthusiasm as usual. Viardot, returning to Russia after several years absence, and Mario were, however, heartily welcomed in *Il barbiere di Siviglia* on 15 January. Then Mario succumbed to indisposition just before another performance of Rossini's opera was due to take place, giving rise to the usual rumours of jealousy, although in Grisi's absence Mario surely had no reason for jealousy. Viardot sang in *La Cenerentola* instead.

It was, as on previous occasions, Grisi's pregnancy that had stopped her from going to Russia with Mario that winter. Their daughter Cecilia was born in London at the beginning of March. Mario left St Petersburg at the end of the month and did not return there for more than fifteen years.

In June, Grisi replied to a Court official who had written offering her and Mario engagements for the following winter season in St Petersburg:

Excellency, I dare not express what pleasure your kind letter has given me. No one could reply adequately to such a letter, and this proves the truth of something I have read, that sometimes silence is more eloquent than words. In this silence please read all my gratitude.

Nevertheless, M. le Comte, I am very unhappy to state that I cannot accept an engagement for next winter in St Petersburg, as a long-standing promise to go to America forbids it. The Imperial family have been so kind and the public have been so indulgent to me that I should have to push vanity to great heights to believe myself worthy of all the flattering souvenirs that St Petersburg has left me.

My duty to my family has prevented me from turning down the engagement in America, and that is the sole reason for the ingratitude which I feel in refusing your offer; my heart is bitter at the idea of going to America instead of St Petersburg, but what can one do? In this world one must make sacrifices for those one loves.

As will be seen, Grisi and Mario went neither to America nor to Russia the following winter. Grisi never visited St Petersburg again, while the next time that Mario sang there, Nicholas I was dead and Alexander II reigned as Tsar.

Chapter 10

THE PROFESSIONAL RELATIONSHIP between the two singers had naturally developed and altered considerably since their first appearance
together fourteen years previously in *Lucrezia Borgia*. Then, it had
been Grisi who, already at the zenith of her own career, had dominated
the partnership, taking the inexperienced young tenor under her
wing, helping him with encouragement and advice. Mario, profiting
both from Grisi's patronage and her example, learnt his trade rapidly;
from the mid 1840s, after the retirement of Rubini, he enjoyed equal
status with the prima donna and for nearly a decade the couple ruled
with joint and undisputed sovereignty.

Now that Grisi's voice was beginning to show the wear and tear of a
quarter of a century before the public, Mario inherited the dominant
role. Unlike Grisi, whose tendency to stoutness was aggravated by
four pregnancies in five years, the tenor had kept his youthful figure.
On stage he could still—and would be able to for many years
yet—play the ardent lover with complete conviction, while his voice,
retaining the sweetness and agility necessary for lyrical Italian music,
had acquired new power and expressiveness, enabling him to add the
heavier and more dramatic French operas to his repertory.

The 1853 season at the Royal Italian Opera was a particularly
successful one from Mario's point of view. Once escaped from the
rigours of the Russian winter, he was in exceptionally good voice,
while the stimulus needed to combat his inborn laziness was about to
be provided by a new and most congenial part—the Duke in *Rigoletto*.

Mario arrived in London from St Petersburg at the beginning of
April and made his first appearance of the season at Covent Garden on
Tuesday 26 April in *I puritani*. The theatre was full to overflowing and
The Times next morning carried an enthusiastic notice: 'How great has
been Mario's progress of late years need not be told. As an actor he has
attained an eminence to which few tenors on the Italian stage have ever
aspired, while, though he cannot challenge comparison with Rubini
as a bravura singer, or as a master of ornament and fioriture, he
has acquired a perfection in the art of phrasing, a command of
vocal declamation and what may be justly called a manliness of

style, to which with all his accomplishments, Rubini could hardly lay claim.'

These qualities, continued the *Times* critic, 'united to a voice which has rarely been approached in richness of tone, and a person singularly well adapted to the purpose of scenic illusion, have helped Mario to the position he now maintains as one of the most admirable dramatic singers of whom the history of the art makes mention.'

Turning to the actual performance of *I puritani*, the anonymous writer—in all probability J. W. Davison, music critic of *The Times* for over 30 years—was no less complimentary: 'The manner in which the first stanza of the renowned quartet "A te o cara" was delivered by the great tenor proved to the satisfaction of the audience that the keen winds of Russia had not frozen up the springs whence the melody is drawn that imparts such power and beauty to his voice. It was sung by Mario in Mario's best style.' The quartet was encored and the second stanza had to be repeated.

Grisi meanwhile, having recovered as rapidly as usual from the birth of her daughter, had already made her début for the season on 21 April, in *Norma*. Both she and Mario, together with Ronconi, appeared in *Lucrezia Borgia* on Thursday 5 May when, according to *The Times*, the house was crammed to suffocation while soprano and tenor had never sung better.

Rigoletto was produced, for the first time in London, on Saturday 14 May, with Ronconi in the title role, the Italian soprano Angiolina Bosio as Gilda and Mario as the Duke of Mantua. Heartily disliked by most of the critics, Verdi's opera immediately became a huge popular success. The singers, all superbly cast, were grudgingly praised by Chorley, who allowed 'that the performance throughout had been perfectly prepared and was highly finished.' But, he added, 'how long [the opera] will endure time must show.' Time has indeed shown the exceptional endurance of *Rigoletto*.

The Duke quickly became one of Mario's favourite roles and he sang it more often than any other, with the exception of Raoul, Almaviva and Gennaro, in his repertory. 'La donna è mobile' was invariably encored, as well as the quartet.

Mario's health, so excellent at the beginning of the season, now began to deteriorate under the strain of singing four and sometimes five nights a week. He was in a very fine voice on 30 May, when Lady Howard gave a so-called town breakfast at Craven Cottage, Fulham. 'Mario sang to perfection,' noted one of the guests, 'everything was charmingly done and the entertainment lasted till after seven o'clock.' The tenor was still in good form on 2 June when, according to the same young lady, who found both Mario and Grisi superb in *Les Huguenots* that evening. But on 13 June Mario cancelled his appearance at Lady Antrobus's concert—'thanks to the influenza'—while a week later he refused to sing at a concert at Buckingham Palace, where 'the Cologne singers performed some very fine choruses.'

This refusal perhaps explains the disappearance of the tenor, while still indubitably at the top of his profession and the height of his powers, from subsequent court concerts. The fact that he had to sing the Duke in *Rigoletto* the following night, 21 June, and Gennaro in *Lucrezia Borgia* on 23 June, was not, presumably, accepted as sufficient excuse for disobeying a royal command.

The diarist whose social life took her frequently to the opera and to private as well as court musical parties, was Princess Mary Adelaide, daughter of Adolphus, Duke of Cambridge (who had died three years previously), and first cousin to Queen Victoria. The Cambridge ladies—the Duchess and her two daughters, Augusta, Grand Duchess of Mecklenburg-Strelitz, and Mary Adelaide, who later became Duchess of Teck—were passionately fond of music, in particular of Italian Opera.

Princess Mary Adelaide recorded her first impressions of Mario and Grisi in her Journal at the age of thirteen and a half, when she was taken to hear them in *I due Foscari* at Covent Garden and thought the performance quite magnificent. She was now nineteen years old. She dined with the Duke and Duchess of Hamilton on 9 July; afterwards 'there was an evening party and a splendid concert—Mario, Grisi and Ronconi did their best to please.' Lady Howard gave another town breakfast at Craven Cottage on 15 July. It poured with rain and 'as Mario *se fit attendre*, we had a *déjeuner dinatoire* first, and then a charming concert, in which Mario was sole performer.'

The following day, Saturday 16 July, *La favorita* was revived at Covent Garden, with Mario and Grisi both, apparently, in good voice. 'Spirto gentil' was, as usual, encored; it was, in the opinion of Davison, 'without exception the most perfect specimen of im-passioned vocalization that has ever emanated from his [Mario's] matchless voice.'

A second performance of *La favorita* was announced for Tuesday 19 July, but Grisi had such a bad cold that the opera had to be changed at the last minute to *Le Prophète*, to the acute disappointment of Princess Mary Adelaide. *La Favorita* was again announced for Saturday 23rd, but this time it was Mario who fell ill, and *Otello*, with Tamberlik and Grisi was given instead.

Mario went to Brighton for a couple of days to recuperate, returning on Tuesday 26 July when he wrote to Gye: 'I shall be able to sing tonight, but I think you should ask the audience for their indulgence, as my chill has not yet gone, being as tenacious as the bad weather!' Despite his chill, the tenor apparently got through the performance of *La favorita* that night without disaster.

By 5 August Mario was in good voice again; with Grisi and Bosio he sang at a concert given by Henry Greville for the Duchess of Cambridge. Greville gave at least one musical party each season and the Duchess and her daughters were frequently the guests of honour. Princess Mary Adelaide found the singers 'all in high force, and the music well chosen.'

Mario and Grisi made their last appearance for the season on Monday 15 August in *Lucrezia Borgia*. Gye had tried to postpone the performance until the following day, but Mario wanted to make a short visit to Florence, where he had acquired a property, before the autumn tour of the British provinces. He wrote to Gye saying that he needed time to put his affairs in London in order, it being impossible to do anything on the day of a performance. Gye acceded to the request.

It was announced in the papers that the two singers were going to America that winter and that on their return they would retire from the operatic stage, to live on Mario's Italian estate. In the *Athenaeum* Chorley commented on this news: 'It is said, on good authority, that Mme. Grisi's approaching departure for America is equivalent to her retirement from our Opera stage; 20 years of supremacy in the same capital for a dramatic soprano singer constitute a phenomenon of rare occurrence.'

Not merely, continued Chorley, 'was Mme. Grisi one of the most sumptuously handsome women that ever trod the stage, not merely did she possess a strong, sonorous, sweet extensive voice, a legitimate dramatic soprano, ready at its owner's call, seldom disabled and capable of conveying almost every emotion that its owner pleased to imagine, but her performance displayed an essential fitness for the theatre, and a power of fairly carrying through every part which she undertook, in conjunction (when the character suited her) with those bursts of spontaneous emotion and energy which are more popular than the sublimer and finer qualities of a Pasta.'

Chorley complimented Grisi on the respect that she had always shown her public, by never presenting herself unprepared in her music. He also remarked that 'the number of apologies, postponements, etc, etc, to which she has given occasion, is small without precedent in the history of the Italian prima donna.'

Turning to Mario, Chorley considered his retirement a heavier loss, 'since so far as regards the state of his voice, it is a totally unnecessary measure. With a little more care, and with a little more respect for his obligation as a public servant (distinct from his obligingness as a private favourite) we might have looked to him as to the Almaviva, the Don Ottavio, the Nemorino, the Elvino, the Arturo and even the Raoul in *Les Huguenots* for the next 10 years.'

But while 'in the annals of Mayfair and Belgravia Signor Mario will live as the most fascinating singer of romances that ever trod velvet pile, and as a courteous and courtly recipient of homages such as have been hardly paid to any singer . . . in the chronicles of Opera, he can be recorded only as possessing a charming voice, and being (of late) a passionate actor, but not as a complete vocalist, and not as even a respectable musician.'

In the event Mario and Grisi did not go to New York that winter—the impresario had been unable to find sufficient money to guarantee the season—and nor did either of them retire, though Grisi did not sing for several months. At the end of September the three-year-old Maria Angelina died in Paris, and was buried in Père Lachaise cemetery beside her sister. Meanwhile Grisi was already pregnant again.

Mario, after his return from Florence, made a short provincial tour under the management of Willert Beale, who had taken over that aspect of his father's business. Then the tenor appeared at the Théâtre-Italien in Paris for the first time since 1848. The Italiens opened for the season on 15 November with Alboni in *La Cenerentola*. A week later *Lucrezia Borgia* was given, with Mario in his usual role of Gennaro, to be followed on 1 December by *I puritani*, with Mario and the soprano Erminia Frezzolini.

'The Théâtre-Italien seems to be in fashion again,' wrote Délécluze in the *Journal des Débats*. 'The reappearance of the tenor Mario and the debut of Mlle. Frezzolini in our city have drawn a great many people to the theatre and stimulated unusual curiosity . . . But an end to generalities and let us come to Mario. It has been rumoured that the voice of this charming tenor has altered. Thank goodness this is not so, and the five years that have passed since we last heard him in Paris have hardly affected his beautiful voice.'

In the opinion of Délécluze, 'his range has extended at the top, while the middle and lower notes have gained a mordancy and strength, with the result that in the role of Arturo, where tender passages are as frequent as those demanding a great deal of force, Mario now unites all the qualities necessary to make the best of this character.'

Mario, who had been greatly applauded as Gennaro in *Lucrezia*

Borgia, scored a veritable triumph as Arturo in *I puritani*. He was made to repeat the third-act cavatina, and a shower of bouquets rained on his head at the end of the opera.

Early in January 1854 the Théâtre-Italien presented *Il barbiere di Siviglia* with Alboni, Mario and the veteran Tamburini, still marvellously youthful as Figaro. Mario also sang in *La sonnambula*, *Don Giovanni, La donna del lago, Otello* and, in April after the opera season was over, in Rossini's *Stabat Mater*, which was given three performances.

'Mario was much admired at the first performance,' wrote Délécluze, 'particularly in the duet sung by him and [the baritone Francesco] Graziani. But the third performance totally bewitched those young listeners on whom Mario's voice and art were leaving a first sweet and indelible impression.'

At the end of March or the beginning of April, Clelia, Grisi's and Mario's fifth daughter, and the third to survive infancy, was born.

Mario was still in Paris on Wednesday 26 April, as on that day he received a letter from Gye, which he answered immediately:

I only received your letter of the 24th today, and do not understand the delay—it was the same with a letter to Mme. Grisi. I cannot promise, or even consider singing in London on Tuesday [2 May]; the best I could manage would be to sing in *Il barbiere* on Thursday, as I could not be ready for *Rigoletto* until Saturday, needing to restudy my role in the latter work and also requiring some rest beforehand.

I do not understand your lack of repertory, as you have two newly arrived celebrities in Mlle. Cruvelli and Lablache; and forgive me if I am a little angry with you—you are too much the *gentleman* to forget Mme. Grisi's present position. This is not the moment to discuss business matters with her, still less is it the time to ask her to give up a role, something an artist always does unwillingly.

That is my complaint, now it is your turn, because I must warn you that I shall need money on my arrival in London, and though I am sure you have not forgotten our contract, nevertheless I feel I should give you notice in advance.

Life in Paris was undoubtedly expensive for Mario and his growing family. At that period he lived in a second-floor apartment in the rue de Rivoli, where Henry Greville had called on him earlier in April. Mario told Greville that the apartment cost 950 francs per month, and 'everything is dear in proportion.' The move to London, a major undertaking with three children, one a few-weeks-old baby, was accomplished and Mario made his first appearance of the season at Covent Garden on Tuesday 9 May in *Il barbiere di Siviglia*.

This performance was also the occasion of the début of Lablache at the Royal Italian Opera. With the great bass as Bartolo, Bosio as Rosina, Ronconi as Figaro and Mario as Almaviva there was, according to Chorley, 'no incompleteness in the execution, which was worthy of the best days that are gone; as pure and joyous a specimen of Italian mirth in music as could now be presented—worth studying as a lesson, and meriting every handful of the applause showered upon it.' Mario also sang in *I puritani* and *Rigoletto*.

It was again announced that Grisi would definitely retire at the end of the year and that the current season would be her last in London. She appeared for a limited number of performances in *Norma*, *Lucrezia Borgia* and *Les Huguenots*—the only roles 'belonging' to her that Sophie Cruvelli was allowed to take over were Desdemona and Donna Anna—then on 29 June *Don Pasquale* was presented for the first time at the Royal Italian Opera, with the three of the original cast: Grisi, Mario and Lablache. Ronconi sang the Tamburini role of Dr Malatesta. Princess Mary Adelaide and her mother attended the second performance of *Don Pasquale* on 1 July; the Princess thought 'Lablache perfect, Grisi very good, Ronconi and Mario ditto.'

Early in July Gye asked Grisi if he could announce a benefit in her name and also if she would give two extra performances. She replied:

> I have thought over what you said to me this morning about the benefit, and whether I could fit in two extra nights at the beginning of August. Briefly, dear Mr Gye, my answer is that you may announce a benefit in my name for which ever day suits you, and you will pay me four hundred pounds for that evening, and two hundred pounds each for the extra nights. Frankly, I don't particularly want to do either the benefit or the extra nights, especially the benefit, which makes it look as if I was demanding the charity of the public, but if I do, it is only fair that I should make some profit too.

La favorita was revived on Thursday 13 July, with Grisi, Mario and Lablache. 'The principal soprano and tenor,' according to the *Morning Post*, 'were both a little out of voice, and did not sing or act with all their usual energy; still, their performances presented many beauties of the highest order—perfections of conception and style—which no other Italian singers in their respective genres could reach.'

Mario was made to repeat 'Spirto gentil' and a large audience, that included the Queen and Prince Albert, warmly applauded the three principal singers at the end of the opera.

Next day, Friday, there was to be a Grand Morning Concert at Covent Garden, which had been widely advertised for several weeks as not only the last concert of the season, but also the last that Giulia Grisi would ever give in London.

When the audience began to arrive (the doors opened at one o'clock), 'the first thing that disturbed the proverbial equanimity of the British Lion was a horrible placard posted at the doors and putting forth in large and wet, but painfully clear type, that the great star of the morning (Madame Grisi) could not sing, the cause being sudden indisposition.'

There were murmurs of disappointment, but the members of the audience took their seats quietly enough and the concert began. After the Overture to Weber's *Oberon*, conducted by Julius Benedict, and a chorus from Auber's *Masaniello*, there should have followed a complete performance of Rossini's *Stabat Mater*. Owing to the absence of the prima donna, only excerpts could be given. The audience listened attentively to the opening quartet with chorus, *Quis est homo*, and to *Pro peccatis*, sung by Tagliafico, then suddenly awoke to the fact that the performance was proceeding without a tenor and that *Cujus animam* had been missed out. Where was Mario? (His celebrated name was pronounced in no gentle terms by some dozens of voices.)

The storm was temporarily diverted by the authority of Lablache, who sang *Videt suum dulcem natum* in respectful silence, but as soon as he had finished, the tempest burst out with redoubled fury. The quartet *Sancta Mater* was shouted down and Augustus Harris, the stage manager, came forward to say that 'Signor Mario had not yet arrived but that he was momentarily expected and would of course sing the aria set down for him.'

Temporarily pacified, the audience consented to listen to *Sancta Mater* and directly afterwards 'Signor Mario, the hero of the morning, made his appearance and was received with mingled applause and sibilations, the latter predominating. He, however, went through the *Cujus animam* without interruption, but its close was the signal for a renewal of hostilities, and the great Italian tenor retired, perhaps for the first time in his life, amid a shower of hisses.'

Fac ut portem, sung by Viardot, and the final chorus of the *Stabat Mater* were followed by Mendelssohn's pianoforte concerto in G minor and a solo on the French horn. 'Then *should* have been performed the finale from Rossini's *Zora* [*Mosè*], but the storm had already recommenced with increased violence, for Mario *should* have sung again twice before this, and had not appeared at all since his first ill-received effort. Furious cries for Mario once more resounded through the building, and Tamberlik, evidently in a rage, rushed precipitately from the stage, followed leisurely by his scared companions. Mr Harris now stepped forward to assure the audience that the object of their indignation had quitted the theatre suffering from indisposition. This was met by cries of "Humbug!" and "It won't do!" and several indescribable noises, ending in general uproar.'

Finally Harris came forward again and announced that dissatisfied patrons could have their money back if they wished. Part of the audience then left, still complaining bitterly, and the rest, after discovering a new cause for dissatisfaction in the non-arrival of Ronconi, who had also been billed to appear, regained its good humour and settled down to listen to the remaining items of the concert in peace, even granting Bosio an encore for her rendering of Verdi's 'Ernani involiami'.

Under the two-column description of this concert in the *Morning Post*, a short paragraph stated without comment that the same evening Lady Manners gave a reception at her house in Upper Brook Street, at which Mario, Ronconi, Bosio and Viardot, accompanied by Benedict, all sang. The Duchess of Cambridge and Princess Mary Adelaide, together with '300 of the élite of society' attended this reception.

Gye apparently wrote to Mario in order to pacify the tenor, who most certainly was not accustomed to being received with hisses. Mario replied next day, Saturday 15 July: 'I admit your letter did me good, and it was kind of you to write it. I blame my own anger, and am sorry to have left the London public with such a disagreeable memory. Thank you again for your kindness and friendship.'

Mario and Grisi sang in *La favorita* that Saturday night and again in the same opera on Monday 17 July (one of the extra nights promised by Grisi to Gye). On Thursday they sang in *Lucrezia Borgia*, and later the same night took part in Henry Greville's annual concert for the Duchess of Cambridge—according to the host, the selection of music was good and all the singers gave of their best. *Don Pasquale* on Saturday 22 July and *Les Huguenots* the following Monday (another extra night) found both Mario and Grisi still in good voice, despite an incredibly busy ten days, during which they had sung five performances of four different operas and taken part in one concert at least, quite possibly more.

Lucrezia Borgia was announced for Thursday 27 July, Donizetti's opera to be followed by *La prova d'un opera seria*, a one-act piece by Gnecco in which Viardot and Lablache were to appear.

The Prologue and first act of *Lucrezia Borgia*, with Grisi in particularly fine voice, were received with enthusiastic applause. There was then a very long interval and after more than half an hour Harris came before the curtain to announce the 'unwelcome news that Signor Mario having been taken suddenly ill, it would be impossible for him to go through the last act of the opera, and that consequently the audience must be good enough to be satisfied with its omission.'

The audience was manifestly *not* satisfied, and scenes reminiscent of the concert took place, with cries of 'Mario!' 'Tamberlik!' 'Fetch Sims Reeves' and 'Give us our money back' echoing through the theatre. Harris came out again to say that 'Signor Mario was *really* ill,' which occasioned roars of laughter and more hisses. Harris stood his ground and said the opera could not be continued without one of the principal characters, and Tamberlik was not in the house.

'What is the matter with Mario?' enquired an individual from the stalls.

'He is seized with sudden hoarseness, sir, which was perceptible through the first act, sir,' replied the stage manager.

Costa tried to quell the tumult by playing the overture to *Guillaume Tell*, but there was so much noise he had to stop in the middle of it. After another pause the curtain rose on the set for *La prova d'un opera seria*, and the shouting broke out again with redoubled force. Harris came out yet once more to announce that Mme. Grisi had kindly consented to sing an aria as compensation for the missing act of *Lucrezia Borgia* and this statement was received with hearty applause.

Grisi sang 'O mio Fernando' from *La favorita* and was cheered to the echo. Finally *La prova* was allowed to begin, to everybody's satisfaction.

Princess Mary Adelaide attended this performance and her account of it differs slightly from that of the *Morning Post*: 'Poor Mario was taken suddenly hoarse, and quite unable to sing the last act, in consequence of which the audience got up a *row*, and would not suffer the orchestra to play the overture to *Otello*. At last the people were pacified . . . and Grisi sang (to *calm* the public mind) an air out of *Anna Bolena*.'

This time there was no doubt that, in the words of the unfortunate Harris, 'Signor Mario was *really* ill.' The performance of *La favorita* announced for Saturday was cancelled and *L'elisir d'amore* given instead. On Monday Grisi sang in *Norma* with Tamberlik, then on

Tuesday 1 August Mario was recovered sufficiently to appear in *La favorita*.

Grisi's 'farewell' benefit, consisting of the first act of *Norma* and three acts of *Les Huguenots*, took place on Monday 7 August. The theatre was not entirely full, presumably because of the high prices charged, but the blame was laid at Gye's door, not Grisi's. The audience, rather cold at first, soon warmed up and at the end recalled the prima donna three times. 'Mario and Grisi were *beyond*,' commented Princess Mary Adelaide in her Journal, 'and the house rose to give her a last cheer. We threw her our bouquets, and she must have received a hundred. She left the stage much affected—almost in tears.'

There was no time, however, for retrospective emotions. Terms satisfactory to both parties had been agreed with the American impresario and, overcoming her reluctance to leave her children as well as her extreme dislike of the sea, Grisi, together with Mario, took the train to Liverpool on the very day after the Benefit performance. The two singers spent the night at the Adelphi Hotel and on the morning of Wednesday 9 August 1854, accompanied by the impresario, James H. Hackett, they embarked in the United States Mail Steamer *Baltic*. After many postponements and delays, they were on their way to America.

Chapter 11

THE NIGHT BEFORE the *Baltic* sailed, the two singers had scanned the passenger list to make sure that it did not contain a certain name. For over two years, Mario had been subjected to a form of silent persecution that had upset and annoyed Grisi even more than it did the tenor himself. At a reception in St Petersburg given by the composer Michael Balfe, Mario had been formally introduced to an English lady, Miss Giles. They had never met nor spoken to each other again, but ever since, Miss Giles had followed Mario all over Europe and had attended every performance he gave in London and Paris, always sitting either in the front stalls or in a stage box where everyone, the singers included, could see her.

Though Miss Giles was apparently middle-aged and also extremely plain, her admiration for Mario made him nervous and aroused Grisi's latent jealousy. When, therefore, the *Baltic*'s passenger list did not contain the objectionable name, the Diva, according to Willert Beale, gave a sigh of relief, supposing that the pursuit was given up. 'Stormy weather prevailed after the ship had left Queenstown,' continued Beale, 'and all but the most adventurous of the passengers remained below. Mario, ever the first and foremost to enjoy a storm, paced the deck and took delight as usual in braving the elements.'

What follows may not be the strictly literal truth, as Beale often embroidered his stories, but it undoubtedly contains a germ of fact: 'While walking to and fro, [Mario] stumbled over some tarpaulin and, vainly trying to regain his balance, fell heavily upon it. A scream was heard and the tarpaulin being raised, the form of Miss Giles, in a green silk dress, was discovered lying on the deck beneath it.'

The Atlantic continued stormy and Grisi, who suffered badly from seasickness, kept to her cabin for most of the voyage. The *Baltic* docked in New York at four in the afternoon on 19 August and the singers were driven to the St Nicholas Hotel, on Broadway at Spring Street, where they were to stay.

The venue chosen for the first appearance in America of Mario and Grisi was Castle Garden, which later became an immigration station. Hackett had offered the singers $85,000 for 63 performances ($50,000 had already been deposited in a London bank as guarantee) and the price of tickets for the opening performance on Monday 4 September was raised from $1 to $3 and $5. Consequently the house was not quite full, while the opera, *Lucrezia Borgia*, was given only a tepid reception. The following Monday, 11 September, when *Norma* was performed to an audience of more than 4,000 people, a very different atmosphere prevailed in Castle Garden and success was assured. 'The performances of the two distinguished artists were undeniably very fine,' wrote Richard Grant White. 'Grisi, although showing in person and in voice that she was past her prime, was superb and Mario, who was in his prime, both of voice and person, sang exquisitely.'

Grisi's Norma overwhelmed the critics, even the sternest. 'What a perfect embodiment of the varying passions and feelings of the human mind does she present in her rendition of this character,' wrote 'Meerschaum' in the *Spirit of the Times*. 'Joy, fear, hope, love, jealousy, revenge, all these and more are depicted with a vividness and truthfulness to nature that are perfectly startling.'

Richard Grant White, having prefaced his review in the *Courier and Enquirer* of 12 September with the statement that Grisi's interpretation differed little from that of others heard in New York, then proceeded to describe in vivid detail the ways in which her Norma was outstanding, in particular the scene in which she listened to Adalgisa's relation of the birth and growth of her own love: 'Grisi stood with her back to the girl and, as the tale was told and the memory of the dawn of her own passion was awakened by the timid confession of her companion in guilt, the face of the Arch-Druidess beamed with tender joy; she clasped her trembling fingers, timidly; her breathing was as gentle as a child's; her eyes were bright with the light of youthful love; and then for the first time, we saw how lovely Grisi must have been.'

In the following scene, where Norma confronts Pollione with his unfaithfulness, 'her eye flashed his doom upon him; her arms waved the vengeance of heaven down to him; she spurned him with her voice, as a man spurns with his foot the thing that he most loathes; she looked a beautiful Fury. Her vocalisation . . . was incomparably fine—brilliant, powerful, impetuous. Her voice seemed unrestrained by consciousness and abandoned to the sway of her all-controlling rage.'

It was not only her outburst of passion that Richard Grant White admired in Grisi's Norma. In the final scene, the pathos of her acting touched him profoundly. 'As Pollione knelt at her feet repentant and again her lover, but too late, there was a silent moment; one hand fell from her averted face upon his shoulder; she drew it gently but firmly away and, as it passed across his head, it lingered for an instant and its mute fingers told an agony of love and grief beyond the utterance of words.'

Norma was such a success that it had to be repeated six times; meanwhile, the next opera to be given was *I puritani*, on Monday 25 September. Mario was much applauded in 'A te o cara' and in the final scene. The presence of Miss Giles at every performance in which Mario sang had not escaped the notice of the New York Press. Luigi Arditi, the conductor for the season, quoted one newspaper article on the subject in his *Memoirs*: 'Poor thing! Everybody but Grisi must pity her in their hearts. There she sits, solitary and alone, in her spacious box, dressed in the costliest of laces and brocades, perfectly indifferent to everything but Mario.'

Immune to the curious glances of the chorus ladies, the gentlemen of the orchestra and the members of the audience, who stared at her through lorgnettes and opera glasses, Miss Giles 'heeds nobody and when not looking over the fringe of her splendid fan or through the parted petals of the white camellias of her bouquet, at the object of her burning passion, she sits like a sphinx, a tremendous riddle, which nobody has yet been able to solve.'

After the four-week season at Castle Garden was finished, the company moved to the new Academy of Music on Fourteenth Street and Irving Place, which was destined to be the home of opera in New York until the building of the first Metropolitan Opera House nearly 30 years later. The Academy opened on 2 October with Grisi and Mario in *Norma*. Performances of *Lucrezia Borgia* and *I puritani* followed, then on 16 October *La sonnambula* entered the repertory. Mario was indisposed and after a second performance of *La sonnambula* on the Wednesday, he became seriously ill and was unable to sing for nearly a month.

Grisi appeared in *Semiramide*, but it was not until Friday 17 November that Mario was sufficiently recovered to sing once more, in *Il barbiere di Siviglia*. The following week *I puritani*, followed by Mario in the final scene of *Lucia di Lammermoor*, was repeated, to be succeeded by three performances of *La favorita*.

Semiramide was given again for Grisi's benefit on 11 December, when Mario sang the role of Idreno for the first time. Richard Grant White thought that 'Grisi never appeared to such advantage, in New York at least, as in *Semiramide*. Her port and person suited the character of the semi-barbarous Assyrian queen, and the splendid costume with its trailing robes suited her.'

Grisi's mature beauty and queenly bearing as Semiramide was no doubt admired by all the men in the audience, while Mario, appearing unwontedly in the minor tenor part, 'charmed the female half of his audience by the beauty and quaint richness of his costume, one noted item of which was a pale green India shawl, so fine that it could have been drawn through a lady's bracelet, which he wore as a girdle.'

This exotic garment was very probably the Cashmere shawl presented to Grisi by the Tsar and reputedly worth over 4,000 roubles. The *Athenaeum*, reporting Mario's appearance as Idreno, stated that he introduced the last scene of *Lucia* into the final scene of Rossini's *Semiramide*. Needless to say, Mario never sang the role of Idreno again after his return from America.

The season at the Academy of Music ended on 27 December with a performance of *Don Pasquale*, then the company went on a short tour, to Philadelphia, Washington and Boston. In Washington, where *Norma* was performed on Monday 8 January 1855, the weather was so cold that, according to Arditi, Grisi was obliged to wear a huge fur cloak over her traditional white robe. Later in the evening, as the snow on the roof began to melt as a result of the warmth of the gas lighting inside the theatre, Mario appeared holding a large coachman's umbrella, under which he and Grisi sheltered.

A week later, on 15 January, the company opened in Boston with *I puritani* at the new Boston Theatre, where presumably the roof did not leak. During the two-week stay in Boston, the receipts averaged nearly $12,000 a week, an unprecedented amount at that period. Back in New York, they gave six farewell performances at the Metropolitan Theatre. In *Don Giovanni*, 'Mario distinguished himself as Don Ottavio (a part in which great tenors are reluctant to appear, as they are in that of Pollione), and he sang "Il mio tesoro" with a purity and grace which seemed the perfection of vocalisation.'

The American visit ended, as it had begun, with *Lucrezia Borgia*, on 20 February, after which Mario, Grisi and, presumably, Miss Giles returned to Europe. Grisi was never to leave her children for such a length of time again and never to embark on any strip of water wider than the English or Irish Channel. She did not, as had been announced the previous summer, retire from the stage. After 25 years she seems to have found it impossible to abdicate from her position as reigning prima donna, while her voice remained—as the American tour had amply proved—in such relatively good state.

No doubt her jealousy of Mario, who obviously had many years of career still to come, played a part in her decision not to retire; and there was also the question of money. For the last fifteen years both singers must have been earning vast sums—Mario told Willert Beale that he earned more than £10,000 a year, which did not include trips to St Petersburg or New York—but they also spent money with great prodigality. There was the percentage of her earnings to be paid to Grisi's husband, de Melcy; then, with three children and a retinue of nurses, maids and valets to provide for, their living expenses were enormous.

In London they always rented a large, furnished house for the four or five months of the season. For the sake of the children's health, this was situated in Fulham or Clapham or some equally pleasant suburb, which necessitated two carriages and a stable of horses for getting to and from the theatre. During several summers they also took a flat in Brighton, so that the children could benefit from the sea air.

In Paris they had a permanent apartment, until Mario bought a plot of land in the rue des Bassins, off the Champs-Elysées, on which to build their own house. This luxurious establishment was supposed to have been financed by the sale of the jewels that he and Grisi had been given in Russia. Mario never wore jewellery of any kind, while Grisi was notoriously casual about the great amount she owned herself, with the exception of the magnificent rope of black pearls presented to her by the Tsar, which she kept and wore to the end of her life.

But the most expensive of all their residences was undoubtedly the Villa Salviati in Florence. Mario had bought the Villa in the early fifties; he spent thousands of pounds in restoring and refurnishing it, and in filling the innumerable rooms with paintings, statues and other *objets d'art*. At first the two singers had little time available to spend in Florence, apart from brief visits in the spring or autumn between their various engagements. But after their return from America, Grisi sang much less often and Mario, though appearing as frequently as ever, was free from the continual grind of studying up to eight new parts a year, as in the first half of his career.

After the 1855 season at Covent Garden, when neither of them sang anything but familiar roles in familiar operas—including two performances, the last ever given, of *Don Pasquale* with its original cast of Grisi, Mario, Tamburini and Lablache—they were able to spend several weeks in Florence. Grisi was again pregnant and her sixth and last daughter was born in Paris on Christmas Day, and christened Bella Maria.

Mario made his rentrée at the Théâtre-Italien on Friday 18 January, 1856, in *Il barbiere di Siviglia*, with the young mezzo-soprano Adelaide Borghi-Mamo as Rosina. Ten days later, on 28 January, he appeared for the first time as Manrico in Verdi's *Il trovatore*, with Rosa Penco as Leonora (the role she had created three years previously in Rome) and

Borghi-Mamo as Azucena. Manrico quickly became one of Mario's finest roles in the second half of his career.

A new opera, *L'assedio di Firenze*, by the conductor at the Italiens, Giovanni Bottesini, received its first performance on 21 February. Mario sang the role of Lodovico Martelli, champion of the Republic, adversary (and rival in love) of Giovanni Bandini, a supporter of the Medici. Michelangelo also appeared in this opera, as a friend of Martelli's. The work was repeated two or three times and revived a few years later in Florence. Then it disappeared.

Grisi, recovered from the birth of Bella Maria, made her first appearance for eight years at the Théâtre-Italien on 3 March. The opera chosen was *Semiramide*, which had always been more popular with Paris audiences than *Norma*. The only other role that Grisi sang that season was Lucrezia Borgia, at the end of the month, but before that an event occurred which had a direct influence on the careers of Mario, Grisi and many other of the Italian singers.

Very early in the morning of Wednesday 5 March, after a masked ball the previous evening, Covent Garden Theatre burnt down. Gye was in Paris, making arrangements to hire singers for the following season and returned to London immediately. Although he had lost not only his theatre, but all the sets, costumes and scores it contained as well, by the end of March he had planned a season at the Lyceum Theatre and was back in Paris, from where he wrote to Costa on 31 March:

> I have now seen all the artists who are here, all have in the *kindest* and *most willing* manner agreed to my proposals; these include Mario, Grisi, Gardoni, Bosio, Tagliafico, Luchesi, Graziani, etc. I have also had letters from Ney, Marai and Tamberlik—Lablache not yet arrived. I hope to be home on Thursday, but I thought you would like to hear how our affairs progressed. Calzado [manager of the Théâtre-Italien] will lend me scores, orchestra, chorus and voice parts of *Rigoletto*, *Traviata* and several other operas. Lumley is here and they tell me making engagements . . .

The news that Lumley was planning to give a season at Her Majesty's, the first for several years, was enough to make the remaining members of the *vieille garde* such as Mario and Grisi agree to Gye's proposals with alacrity, even if it meant accepting a reduced salary. The Théâtre-Italien closed on 31 March with a performance of *Il trovatore* given for Mario's benefit and followed by Act II, scene 1 of *Il barbiere*, in which Rosina was sung by Alboni.

By the beginning of May, Gye had managed to launch his season at the Lyceum; the size of the theatre, considerably smaller than Covent Garden, prevented him from mounting any of the spectacular Meyerbeer operas, but the return of Ronconi, who had not sung in London the previous summer, allowed the run of *Rigoletto* to be resumed on Thursday 22 May, when 'the opera bid fair to prove one of the court cards of Mr Gye's provisional season,' as Chorley wrote in the *Athenaeum*. 'We have not heard Signor Mario to such advantage for three years,' he continued, 'using his voice without misgiving or management.' Bosio, whom Chorley did not much care for, was conscientiously praised for her Gilda, while Ronconi, 'throughout in his best voice on Thursday, cannot be replaced in characters such as that of the Jester.

'The orchestra and chorus are irreproachable, the opera is put on the stage superbly and with taste, the public, more's the pity, likes the shocking story of the opera, the quartett in the fourth act is Signor Verdi's most attractive inspiration of the kind: for all which reasons we fancy *Rigoletto*, poor though the opera be, may draw as well as ever during the present season.'

Meanwhile Gye had inaugurated a series of operatic concerts in a building that could hold more than twice as many people as Covent Garden—the Crystal Palace, now reconstructed at Sydenham. The first concert was given on Friday 16 May, when nearly 3,000 persons attended. The acoustics were found to be surprisingly good from all parts of the enormous hall and the programme was popular in the extreme. Mario sang the Serenade from *Don Pasquale*, Grisi the *Inflammatus* from Rossini's *Stabat Mater* and the baritone Francesco Graziani obliged with the piece whistled by every errand-boy, played on every barrel-organ and slaughtered by every amateur baritone in Europe—'Il balen' from *Il trovatore*.

At the second concert, the following Friday 23 May, more than 4,000 out of a possible 6,000 places were taken. Mario sang 'Il mio tesoro' from *Don Giovanni*, which was encored, as was the duet from *Don Pasquale* sung by Grisi and Mario. The Crystal Palace concerts continued every Friday throughout the season and soon became a regular feature of London musical life.

Mario sang Manrico for the first time in London (the previous year the part had been taken by Tamberlik) on Thursday 12 June, when *Il trovatore* was produced at the Lyceum. 'Few will deny,' wrote Chorley, 'that the burning out of M. Meyerbeer's operas, for this season, has been attended with one benefit, the refreshed state of Signor Mario's voice . . . [his Manrico] may become as popular as his

Duke in *Rigoletto*. Almost all the music suits him; and the romantic position of the hero (for character there is none) furnishes the actor with just those opportunities of which Nature and picturesque taste enable him to avail himself thoroughly. Few figures have been seen on the English stage more graceful than his in his Condottier armour, cap and floating scarf.'

Queen Victoria visited the Lyceum to hear *Il trovatore* on Saturday 14 June and again the following Saturday, 21 June. She particularly admired Mario's Manrico and thought she had 'never heard him sing more beautifully or with more "verve".'

In August, after the end of Gye's hastily improvised but successful season at the Lyceum, Mario and Grisi, together with Josefa and Édouard Gassier, went on an extended tour of the British Isles under the management of Willert Beale. Instead of the usual miscellaneous concerts that were given in towns too small to possess a proper theatre, Opera Recitals (as Beale called them) were given: complete performances of *Don Giovanni, Lucrezia Borgia, La sonnambula, Norma, Don Pasquale* and *Il barbiere di Siviglia* were sung in concert halls throughout the country. For the last fortnight of the tour, at the beginning of November, Beale leased the Theatre Royal, Drury Lane from E. T. Smith, and staged performances of Italian opera, at ordinary play-house prices, that filled the house every night. A second series was arranged, but Mario had to leave to keep his engagement at the Théâtre-Italien, where he appeared on Saturday 15 November in *Il barbiere*, again with Alboni as Rosina.

Mario also sang in *Il trovatore*, then on Saturday 6 December he sang the role of Alfredo in *La traviata* for the first time. The performance provided the occasion for the Paris début of Marietta Piccolomini, the very attractive and talented 22-year-old soprano who had sung Violetta for Lumley at Her Majesty's in the London première of Verdi's opera that summer. The role of Germont was taken by Graziani, and it was in a performance of *Il trovatore* given for the baritone's benefit on Sunday 11 January, 1857, that Grisi sang the part of Leonora for the first time.

Rigoletto returned to the Théâtre-Italien repertory on 19 January, and by the end of the season on 31 March, there had been thirteen performances of *Rigoletto*, fifteen of *La traviata* and 23 of *Il trovatore*; Mario had sung in all but four or five of these performances.

The same three Verdi operas also provided the mainstay of Gye's second season at the Lyceum and the chief tenor roles in all three were sung by Mario. Mario and Grisi appeared together in *Il trovatore* on Thursday 23 April and, as Chorley wrote two days later in the

Athenaeum, 'the tenor was in his best voice. The character, half condottiere, half lover, fits him exactly, he sang, acted and looked with due romantic fire, unusual force, and delicious vocal pathos.'

Chorley was even more impressed with Grisi's performance as Leonora, a long and arduous role, that makes heavy demands on the voice. 'In what magic cauldron the lady has had a dip, we know not, but on Thursday she was marvellous from first to last; equal to the music, without stint, strain or sacrifice, flinging out those rich high notes which of late she has used so charily, as though she had found some spell which makes Time roll back, and was resolved that this new part should be her most brilliant one—we remember nothing comparable to the renovated force, purity and lustre of her voice. Her appearance was magnificent—her acting, especially in the Miserere scene, impassioned and touching.'

Chorley was rather fond of demanding rhetorically of his readers in what magic cauldron had such and such a singer taken a dip, but his notice is evidence that Grisi as well as Mario had benefited from singing fewer and less heavy roles at the Lyceum.

La traviata was performed for the first time at the Lyceum on Saturday 16 May and again Chorley had nothing but praise for the performance, but grave reservations when it came to the opera: 'The part of Violetta suits Mme. Bosio's voice, as that of Alfredo belongs to Signor Mario . . . but make what the actress will of it, the character of Violetta is a painful one, the position of her lover even more repulsive. Signor Mario sings his music with force, passion, voluptuous tenderness. He looks the part as no tenor we have seen could look it, but his odious position seemed thereby brought into a prominence which it had not held before.'

Mario did not, in fact, much like the role of Alfredo, and sang it far less often than either Manrico or the Duke of Mantua. Nevertheless, the public flocked to the Lyceum nine times that season to hear the 'unpleasant' drama of *La traviata*. Among the audience at one performance was Lady Geraldine Somerset, lady-in-waiting to the Duchess of Cambridge and an even more fervent admirer of Mario than her employer's daughter, Princess Mary Adelaide.

Lady Geraldine was also an industrious diarist. She thought the performance of *La traviata* was 'too too beautiful!!' She also went to *Il trovatore*, afterwards confiding to her journal: 'I cannot attempt to describe how beautiful it was, for if I did but half express a portion of its beauty 'twould sound like raving—words are so inadequate; Mario and Grisi are perfection in it—their acting and singing beyond description and it is such a beautiful opera!'

Henry Greville gave his annual *soirée musicale* for the Duchess of
Cambridge on 22 June, when Mario, Grisi and the English soprano
Louisa Pyne were the main attractions. Greville, Princess Mary
Adelaide and Lady Geraldine all recorded the evening in their re-
spective diaries.

The Friday concerts at the Crystal Palace remained as popular as
during the previous summer. Grisi sang at every one except for that on
24 July. The evening before, she had written to Gye: 'Dear Mr Gye,
someone very dear to me, who is leaving for India next Saturday, is
coming to see me tomorrow for probably the last time, so it is
impossible for me to leave the house tomorrow, and I shall be unable
to go to the Cristal [sic] Palace—as I have never missed once you could
excuse me for tomorrow, couldn't you? A thousand compliments, G.
Grisi.'

The 'someone very dear' to Giulia Grisi was, of course, her
son. Frederick Ormsby, now nearly eighteen, and newly gazetted
Lieutenant in the 2nd (The Queen's) Regiment of Dragoon Guards,
was sailing for India, where the Mutiny had broken out the previous
March. Lieutenant Ormsby saw action at Azzingleur, Jamo, Burwah,
Musseapore and Bungaan. He was awarded a medal and returned to
England with his regiment in 1859.

Meanwhile Willert Beale had engaged Mario, Grisi, Alboni and
other singers for a second tour of the British Isles during the autumn of
1857. One publication, the *Press*, commented that it was curious to
find 'that Alboni, who has pertinaciously refused to appear at Her
Majesty's Theatre in contralto parts, is going to do for Mr Beale what
she certainly in common justice ought to have done for Mr Lumley . . .
We notice also,' continued the *Press*, 'that Mario, who would have
raved at Mr Gye if the director had asked the great tenor to play Pollio
[Pollione] in *Norma*, is about to do so for Mr Beale. We consider that in
the line of conduct on the part of the Italian singers there is much
ingratitude as well as inconsistency.'

Willert Beale emphatically denied that the singers named were ever
ungrateful, inconsistent or capricious to any manager on his account.
'It was not their thirst for gold,' he pointed out, 'that led them to do
that for me which they declined to do for Gye and Lumley. In the
aggregate, they probably received larger sums from me than from any
other director, but not for that reason were my suggestions complied
with when similar requests were refused to others by Mario and his
companions. Their compliance in my favour is attributable to
friendship and good-nature on their part, and to no other motive
whatever.'

Willert Beale, who as a child had played with the infant Fred Ormsby and had learnt his impeccable Italian from the lips of Giulia Grisi herself; who had toured with the singers from the age of eleven or twelve; who had spent many a stormy night-crossing of the Irish Channel walking the deck of the packet-boat with Mario and even more train-journeys the length and breadth of the British Isles playing chess with the tenor, understood the Italian singers and their some-times extraordinary foibles. He laughs at them, pokes gentle fun at them in his accounts of their travels together, but is never malicious or cruel at their expense.

Beale's tour opened in London at the end of August at the Princess's, the theatre managed by Charles Kean, with a repertory of four operas. Kean allowed Beale the use of any sets, properties or costumes in the theatre and himself attended many of the rehearsals. Alboni sang the contralto parts in *Rigoletto* and *Lucrezia Borgia* as promised, but Mario did *not* sing Pollione in *Norma*.

In mid-September the company travelled north to Manchester, where two concerts were to be given in the Free Trade Hall, on 16 and 19 September. On the morning of the first concert, it was announced in the *Manchester Guardian* that Madame Grisi had just received news of the death of her mother—in fact, her step-mother, Gaetano Grisi's second wife—and consequently would not be able to sing on either evening, but that Madame Gassier, Alboni and Mario would all perform extra pieces in compensation. The second concert ended with the Miserere from *Il trovatore* 'by request'.

The following day Beale's party crossed to Dublin, where on Monday 21 September they began a two-week season at the Theatre Royal with *La traviata*, in which Madame Gassier sang Violetta and Mario took the part of Alfredo. The next evening *Il trovatore* was given with Mario and Grisi, followed on Wednesday by *Norma*—in which Mario again did not sing Pollione—and on Thursday by *Lucrezia Borgia*. During the second week *Semiramide, Don Giovanni* and *Les Huguenots* were added to the repertory. Mario did not appear in either of his usual roles in the Mozart or Meyerbeer operas, nor did he sing in the concert given on the morning of 2 October, the penultimate day of the season. His place was taken by the tenor Benedetti.

During the company's stay in Dublin, it was discovered that Miss Giles, who had as usual followed the object of her admiration, but must have been disappointed by his non-appearances, had bribed Mario's valet to tell her the itinerary for the rest of the tour. Presum-ably she followed the singers from Dublin to Liverpool and then on their six-week tour of the provinces.

On the way south, the train in which the company was travelling was involved in an accident just outside Stafford. The night-express ran into a stationary goods train. No one was injured, but the passengers were shaken up; Willert Beale found himself catapulted into Grisi's lap, while Mario's travelling chess-set was scattered all over the compartment. There were no corridors in the trains of the period, and the doors of first-class compartments were usually locked to keep out third-class passengers. Beale gave a graphic—and probably apocryphal—account of Grisi's exit through the window, with the aid of himself and Mario, in order to discover what had happened to the train. Returning with the guard, she was able to re-enter the compartment by the normal method.

January 1858 found Mario back in Paris at the Théâtre-Italien, singing in the three ever-popular Verdi operas, as well as in *Don Pasquale* and *Il barbiere*. Flotow's opera *Martha* provided him with a congenial new part in Lionel, the love-sick hero. After the first Paris performance on Thursday 11 February, Délécluze wrote in the *Journal des Débats* that, in the third act, Lionel 'arrived in the forest, pale and mad with love for Martha, which gave Mario the opportunity to sing an agreeable air so admirably he was made to repeat it.' This was 'Ach so fromm' or, in Italian, 'M'appari', which immediately became one of Mario's most popular encore pieces.

The tenor was also made to repeat 'a charming song which he sang with exquisite taste' in *Don Desiderio*, a comic opera by Prince Josef Poniatowski given for the first time in Paris on Tuesday 16 March. Mario took the part of Federico. Grisi sang in *Il trovatore*, *Norma* and *Otello*. She and Mario also appeared together in *I puritani*, when their thoughts must have turned sadly to the original Giorgio, Luigi Lablache.

The great bass had died on 23 January in Naples, where he had been born and where he had made his operatic début 45 years before. 'Lablache died a short time ago,' wrote Henry Greville in his diary. 'A funeral service was performed by his old comrades Grisi, Mario, Tamburini etc, at the Madeleine Church in the presence of Rossini and an immense concourse of the artistic world of Paris.'

Chapter 12

IN LONDON, MEANWHILE, frantic activity was going on in an effort to finish the building of the new Covent Garden theatre in time for the opening of the 1858 opera season, which Gye had announced for 15 May. When the contingent of Italian singers arrived from Paris at the end of April, the builders were still in possession of the theatre, but somehow everything was made ready in time and punctually on the evening of Saturday 15 May 1858 the third—and present—Covent Garden theatre opened its doors to the patrons of the Royal Italian Opera. Gye himself was not there to welcome them; he was suffering from a nervous breakdown.

The opera chosen was *Les Huguenots* and for the occasion Meyerbeer had made some alterations and additions to the last act (the fourth, in the Royal Italian Opera's version). 'The new theatre is a superb building,' wrote Chorley. 'The effect of the interior, at once stately, simple and gorgeous, is instantaneous.' The *Athenaeum* critic also praised the performance of the opera. 'Not for many years past have we heard Signor Mario give such fullness and freshness of voice throughout an entire opera; he burst forth at the close of the septuor with the force of a trumpet, in perfect tune. Madame Grisi the marvellous, too, was in her best order. Both, it is needless to say, were applauded to the echo, as Signor Costa had been on taking his place.'

Chorley found the costumes superb, the scenery, 'though hardly yet in its place, fine and real. The excusable delays of the evening, however, drove everything so late that, at the end of the third act, it was found best to drop the curtain and sing the National Anthem, leaving the fourth act with its novelties for the next performance.'

Though it was long past midnight when Costa struck up 'God Save the Queen', part of the audience was not best pleased at being sent home before the end of the opera, considering that it had not received its full money's worth.

The Cambridge party attended the performance of *Les Huguenots* the following Saturday 22 May. 'We were lost in admiration of the new house,' wrote Princess Mary Adelaide in her journal. 'It is in perfect taste, the soft red of the curtains relieved by the white and gold decorations.'

Lady Geraldine, who also committed her opinions on the new theatre to paper, was rather less matter of fact: '*Huguenots!* oh joy to be once again going there,' she wrote, 'dear, dear Covent Garden—oh how it revived thoughts of old days to hear and see Mario and Grisi in the *Huguenots* at Covent Garden again!!! Oh the opera was so beautifully given! my dear dear *Huguenots*, the greatest enjoyment of my life is to hear that 3rd act with Mario and Grisi—and I *do* rejoice to have heard it once again.'

The breathlessness of Lady Geraldine's style should not blind one to the basic good sense of many of her observations. 'My perfect enjoyment of it,' she added at the end of her effusion on *Les Huguenots*, 'was disturbed by the talking in the box and remarks about the House and Mario and Grisi etc.' Whenever possible she preferred to sit not in the Cambridge box, but in the Stalls, where there was less conversation during the opera.

Throughout the first half of June, Gye was still too ill to return to the theatre, consequently he wrote almost daily letters to Costa about the repertory and other details of the season. 'I am getting strong fast,' he wrote on Thursday 3 June, 'and hope in a few days to be allowed to go to the theatre. With regard to the new operas, *Martha* is the one I think we ought to do as soon as possible, and Mdlle. Bosio and others ought to have their parts if they have not already got them. I suppose Mario has Alary's alterations in *Don Giovanni*, please ask him about it as Tamberlik will be here the end of the month and it must be done immediately.'

The alterations in *Don Giovanni* mentioned by Gye were the transpositions necessary to enable Mario to sing the title role. Though such a cavalier treatment of Mozart's masterpiece would today be found shocking, it must be remembered that during the first half of the nineteenth century many tenors sang the part of Don Giovanni, among them Manuel Garcia, considered by many the finest Giovanni ever heard or seen, and Nourrit, who also had a great success in the role.

It was undoubtedly the dramatic aspects of the part which gave Gye the idea that Mario would make a good Don Giovanni, and the manager went ahead with his plans, writing to Costa again on 10 June that 'I shall be delighted to see Ronconi in Leporello. I fear there is no dependence to be placed on Formes. I am very glad you will begin the rehearsals of *Martha* on Monday. Do you think it can be done on Saturday 19th?'

Five days later Gye, still convalescent and obliged to stay at home, wrote once more to Costa: 'I arranged with Alary yesterday about *Don Giovanni*, Ronconi's part [Leporello] included. Thus cast the opera ought indeed to be attractive . . . I am getting much stronger and hope to be allowed to go to the theatre on Thursday or Friday. When do you think *Martha* can be played? It is always so much better when a long announcement is made.'

Martha was not in fact given until Thursday 1 July, when the production, 'noticeable for its picturesque richness', and the cast, that included Bosio, Nantier-Didiée and Graziani as well as Mario, ensured the opera's success. Meanwhile Gye was at last back in personal charge of his theatre and, a couple of nights before the first *Martha* performance, just before the curtain rose on *Les Huguenots*, he apparently made a tactless remark to Mario, probably a suggestion that the tenor should give up one or other of his roles. Mario replied the next day in a letter dated—in English—'the 29 of June 1858.'

I am annoyed that you chose a bad time last night to talk to me of business—the moment before an artist sings he is always too nervous and preoccupied to think of anything other than the theatre . . . Naturally you must arrange your affairs as you think fit, but I cannot stand aside to such an extent as to allow myself to become an old hanger-on of the theatre. I have never pushed myself forward, so if others are now of more use to you than I, it is right you should take advantage of it, but in that case you must allow me to withdraw.

Mario offered to resign the role of Almaviva in *Il barbiere*, 'for which I am getting too old, and I told you in Paris to make other arrangements for *Rigoletto*, and even *Ugonotti*, but chiefly I think it is useless for me to undertake or study the role of Don Giovanni, as I could never consent to replace my good friend Tamburini, while to come to London just to trot out *Don Giovanni* and *Il barbiere* on extra nights—either I am still capable of something better, or I would prefer to do nothing at all.'

Mario asked Gye if the manager wished to use his right to continue the season to the end of August, as 'I have been asked to sing at the Birmingham festival and must answer them immediately. I beg you therefore to give Alary's alterations to another tenor and dispose of my other roles as you think fit.'

In his answer Gye must have reassured the offended tenor and managed to smooth his ruffled plumage, for the following evening,

Wednesday 30 June, Mario sang at a private concert at Bridgewater House, in radiant voice and his habitual lazy good humour. A young English baritone, Charles Santley, also took part in this concert. He had made his stage début in Italy only the year before, and was now experiencing his first London season.

Henry Greville gave his annual musical party on 9 July; Mario sang 'Goodbye Sweetheart', a song by John Hatton, at that time Charles Kean's director of music at the Princess's Theatre and composer of many popular songs and ballads. According to Lady Geraldine, Mario 'pronounced English quite *perfectly*, only he makes it fifty times a prettier language than anybody else ever did.'

Mario, despite his outburst to Gye, continued to work with Alary on the role of Don Giovanni, and Mozart's opera was given on Thursday 29 July. Chorley described Mario's libertine as 'a first class drawing in water colours. His presence is excellent,' continued the critic, 'a Velasquez portrait of a hidalgo in a black dress, which walked out of its frame. His demeanour is gracious and graceful—but there was not sufficient triumph, nor defiance, nor artfulness, not enough, in short, of the devil . . .

'This was curiously felt in the scene "La ci darem" where Signor Mario's chivalresque wooing—a tone too refined—made it hard for peasant Zerlina (Bosio) to yield, without her showing a tone too much of willingness.' In the first-act finale, Chorley found Mario 'not so much spiritless as polite, astonished and acquiescent.' With Donna Elvira he was over genteel. In the Supper Scene he was more self-assertive. 'Probably he may, according to his usage, strengthen and enrich his conception and performance as he repeats the character'; but Chorley was inclined to think that Don Giovanni, like Otello and Eléazar in *La Juive*, was one of the characters that lay outside Mario's dramatic range, though 'he sang throughout with great firmness and finish.'

With Grisi in very fine vocal and dramatic form as Donna Anna, Tamberlik as Don Ottavio and Ronconi (whose music had also had to be transposed and rearranged by Alary) as Leporello, the performance was greatly enjoyed by the audience, if not the critics. The season ended on 14 August with *Martha*; Mario did not, as he had intimated in his letter to Gye that he might, sing at the Birmingham Festival.

Instead, that autumn Mario, Grisi and their four daughters (Rita was now nine years old, Cecilia five, Clelia four and the baby, Bella Maria, nearly three) spent some months at the Villa Salviati in Florence. An English friend, John Woodford, accompanied them, and was suspected by the police of being the 'arch-conspirator' Mazzini

Mario and Viardot in *Le Prophète*

Mario as Lionel in *Martha*

Faure, Patti and Mario in *Faust*

Mario as Raoul in *Les Huguenots*

Mario after his retirement

Grisi and Mario from a photograph by Caldesi

himself, come secretly to Florence and sheltered in the house of a known sympathizer of the United Italy movement. Though the regime in Tuscany was less oppressive than in some other Italian states, life there was full of petty restrictions and annoyances, while Mario's Italian friends were liable to arrest and banishment without reason or trial.

After Christmas, Mario returned to Paris and during January 1859 appeared at the Théâtre-Italien in *Rigoletto*, *Martha* and *Il trovatore*. In February there were performances of *Il barbiere* and Poniatowsky's *Don Desiderio*, while in March Mario repeated his performance of the title role of *Don Giovanni* for the Paris public.

Grisi did not sing at all in Paris that spring, but in the last week in March she accompanied Mario and a company of singers, including Viardot and Graziani, with Luigi Arditi as conductor and managed by Willert Beale, to Dublin, where they were to give a three-week season.

The season opened on Monday 28 March with *Il trovatore*. A review the following day in the first number of the *Irish Times*, commented that 'the renowned Prima donna of now more than a quarter of a century, exceeded her ancient fame in her brilliant sustainment of the difficult part of Leonora. It was vain to seek for any indication of decay in her splendid vocal powers. The rich and thrilling tones of her glorious soprano voice were heard with delight and admiration in almost every one of the songs and duettos which she sang.' Mario, according to the *Irish Times*, 'frequently afforded extreme pleasure by the peculiar sweetness of his notes.'

In fact Mario was suffering from slight hoarseness, which was even more pronounced the following night, when he redeemed his promise to Beale and appeared as Pollione in *Norma*. Both Mario and Grisi had a night off on Wednesday 30 March, when Dublin was treated to the first performance in what was then the British Isles of Verdi's *Macbeth*. Viardot sang Lady Macbeth and Graziani took the title role. According to Arditi, who conducted the performance, Viardot's music was transposed down a third; it was not only Mario who sang parts composed for a different type of voice.

The audience, with the exception of the gallery, received *Macbeth* with respect rather than enthusiasm. The Dublin Theatre Royal gallery, always vociferous in its opinions and quick to show pleasure—or the reverse—was in particularly noisy mood during this season and several times had to be called to order by the manager. During intervals, not content with the official programme, the gallery was in the habit of providing its own entertainment by singing popular songs and choruses and even solos, though intrepid tenors were usually shouted down with cries of 'Mario's listening!'

On 1 April, the day after *Lucrezia Borgia*, there was a concert at the Ancient Concert Rooms in Great Brunswick Street; Grisi sang 'Qui la voce,' the Mad Scene from *I puritani*, while Mario obliged with 'Le Chemin du Paradis', a song by Jacques Blumenthal, which was encored. The second week at the Theatre Royal opened with *Don Giovanni*, in which Graziani sang the title role and Mario reverted to Don Ottavio; he was rewarded with rapturous applause for 'Il mio tesoro,' which he had as usual to repeat.

Martha was given its first Dublin performance on Saturday 9 April and proved rather more to the audience's taste than *Macbeth*. Flotow's opera benefited from one of the finest casts it can ever have enjoyed, with Grisi in the the title role, Viardot as Nancy, Mario as Lionel and Graziani as Plunket. The *Irish Times* critic wrote that 'The Last Rose of Summer', under its Italian disguise of 'Qui sola vergin rosa', was 'sung with much sweetness and feeling by Madame Grisi.' At a concert the following Friday, Grisi sang the piece in English and 'The Last Rose of Summer' thereafter joined 'The Minstrel Boy' as one of the most popular ballads in her repertory. The season, which ended on Saturday 16 April with the fourth performance of *Martha*, was considered to have been one of the most successful, both financially and artistically, ever given in Dublin.

By the time that the touring party returned to London, the Royal Italian Opera's second season in the rebuilt Covent Garden theatre had already begun. Mario made his first appearance early in May as the Duke in *Rigoletto*, with, as Chorley rather tartly remarked, 'some of his voice and all of his grace. Signor Ronconi,' he continued, 'having next to no voice left, does marvels.'

There were seven more performances of *Don Giovanni* with Mario in the title role and otherwise the same cast as the previous year, with the exception of Zerlina, now sung by Penco. Bosio, aged only twenty-nine, had died in Russia early in April.

'As usual Signor Mario,' wrote Chorley, 'has with practice improved in his acting of the part, particularly in the last scene of the opera. Nothing more picturesque than his appearance ever was seen on the stage; but our feeling as regards his assumption of the character, with the musical transpositions involved, is what it was—that the effect does not justify the temerity.'

Mercadante's *Il giuramento*, a 22-year-old adaptation of Victor Hugo's play, *Angelo, tyran de Padoue*, was performed on Saturday 9 July, but despite the presence of Grisi, Mario and Graziani in the cast, the opera did not please and was not repeated. Otherwise Mario and Grisi both sang in *Les Huguenots* and *Lucrezia Borgia*; Mario appeared in *Martha*, Grisi in *Norma* and one performance of *Otello*.

Although Luigi Arditi was conductor at Her Majesty's, rival establishment to the Royal Italian Opera at Covent Garden, he remained a close friend of Mario and Grisi after their shared experiences in America and in Dublin. Arditi's first child, a daughter, was born on 13 July 1859 and Mario and Grisi were to stand sponsors at the christening a few days later, when the baby was named Giulietta. 'As Mario had never, within the memory of man, been known to arrive in good time at any function whatsoever,' wrote Arditi, 'we anticipated his advent with anxiety not unmixed with apprehension.' But for once Mario was not late. Together with Grisi he arrived at the Arditi's tiny apartment a full quarter of an hour before time, 'laden with flowers for my wife and several beautiful silver presents of unusual splendour for my firstborn.' Grisi sailed into the room and gave Arditi and his wife each a hearty kiss.

'There,' she said triumphantly, pointing to Mario who stood in the doorway beaming with self-satisfaction. 'This is the first time Mario has ever been known to be punctual; I hope you appreciate such an unheard-of event, for I feel sure it will never happen again.'

Towards the end of September, Mario and Grisi went to Madrid. They were to sing at the Teatro Oriente and already before they had even arrived in the Spanish capital, there were ominous paragraphs in the newspapers, which expressed the hope that the two singers would live up to their reputations, which had preceded them by so many years.

The season opened with *Norma* on Thursday 6 October and Grisi, who had been in excellent voice both in Dublin and in London earlier that year, was unfortunately not in her best form. To quote the *Museo Universal*, 'the public heard la Grisi and then la Grisi heard from the public something that cannot have pleased her.' Not only the soprano, but the rest of the company, the orchestra and even the chorus, earned the audience's displeasure. Grisi rescinded her contract and for a while it looked as if she would not sing again in Madrid. Other operas—*La traviata*, *Ernani*, *Il trovatore*—were given. Then in November it was announced that 'the Teatro Oriente has sold all tickets for the first performance of *Les Huguenots*, in which Grisi is to reappear. Therefore those who have not already got places need not bother to apply. It is said that great improvements have been made in the company—let us hope that is ture.'

The performance of *Les Huguenots* was a triumphant vindication for

Grisi, who was loudly applauded; her great duet with Mario made its usual tremendous effect. Mario felt very much at home in Madrid, where the disregard of time was carried to even greater lengths than in his native Sardinia and where a constant supply of his favourite Havana cigars was provided by his admirers. He was even reputed to have been allowed to smoke on stage by the indulgent Madrid audience, instead of having the cigar snatched out of his mouth by a stage-hand as he made his entrance, as happened in other theatres.

Gye, meanwhile, had been having some difficulty in engaging his artists for the 1860 season. He wrote to Costa from Paris on 21 March to say that he was getting on pretty well with his arrangements, though Calzado, the manager of the Théâtre-Italien, would not let Graziani go to London before May. However, in his place, Gye had engaged Jean-Baptiste Faure, a baritone from the Opéra-Comique, who had created the role of Hoël in Meyerbeer's *Dinorah, ou le Pardon de Ploërmel.* 'He has a fine voice, is an excellent actor, young and handsome, a good musician, a professor at the Conservatoire indeed, and has great flexibility of voice, sings Assur [in *Semiramide*] well, he has determined to leave the French stage and go on the Italian—with us he will sing Hoël, Alfonso in *La favorita*, Fernando in *La gazza ladra* etc.'

Gye was having even more trouble with his contralto singers than with his baritones. 'I fear Didiée will not be able to come until the end of May,' he informed Costa, 'as she is *not yet* accouchée. De Meric has only last week unburdened herself of her load, so *she* can't come to begin the season—how prolific must be the air (or something else) of St Petersburg!!!'

Despite Gye's difficulties, the Royal Italian Opera re-opened punctually on 10 April and a fortnight later Grisi and Mario made their first appearance of the season in *La favorita* which, according to Chorley, 'was produced on Tuesday [24 April] with consummate care and splendour. The last scene may be cited as one of the most picturesque and pompous stage-pictures ever displayed in any country. The artists were received with enthusiasm by a crowded house.' Faure, as predicted in Gye's letter, sang Alfonso.

During May, Mario sang in *Il barbiere*. The performance on Tuesday 8 May was particularly brilliant. 'For seasons past we have not heard Signor Mario in such complete possession of vocal power,' asserted Chorley. A fortnight later he declared that the performance of *Il barbiere* on 19 May 'if possible, outdid its predecessor. Signor Mario must either have signed the black parchment, or else taken a dip in Medea's cauldron.'

During June, Mario and Grisi, both in excellent voice, sang in *Les Huguenots*. Mario also sang four more performances of the title role of *Don Giovanni*, his last in London; the following year it was Faure who took on the part.

That summer of 1860 the Italian exiles in London, as elsewhere, followed with hope and excitement the news of Garibaldi's landing in Sicily, the lightning campaign by which he captured Palermo and then the rest of the island. In August, Garibaldi landed on the Italian mainland and on 7 September, ahead of his army, he entered Naples, to be welcomed with wild enthusiasm. Two weeks later, Garibaldi linked up with the Royal army of King Victor Emmanuel of Piedmont outside Naples. United Italy, from being just the dream of a few thousand patriots, had become a reality, with only the Papal States still holding out in the centre of the peninsula and Venice still occupied by the Austrians in the north.

Grisi and Mario, however, were immersed in a private tragedy of their own. Bella Maria, the youngest of their four daughters, died at the end of October in Brighton, where Grisi had taken the child in a last attempt to save her life. Mario was already in Paris, as he wrote to Grisi from there on 25 October, addressing his letter to the Lord Warden Hotel in Dover. Bella Maria was buried in Père Lachaise Cemetery in Paris with her two baby sisters on 1 November, and three days later Mario had to sing at the Théâtre-Italien.

The opera that Sunday, 1 November was *Il barbiere di Siviglia* and during the autumn Mario also appeared in *Rigoletto*, *Il trovatore* and *Martha*. In January 1861 *Un ballo in maschera*, Verdi's most recent opera, was given its first performance in Paris, providing Mario with a new and congenial role. Censorship trouble in Rome before the première two years previously had already forced Verdi to change the setting of the opera from eighteenth-century Sweden to seventeenth-century Boston, while King Gustavus III became Riccardo, Count of Warwick. Mario flatly refused to appear as the Governor of Boston, so the setting was changed once more and at the Italiens Riccardo was transformed into the Duke of Naples, a Grandee of Spain.

Mario was now fifty, but he still retained his youthful figure and, on stage at least, his exceptional good looks. The part of Riccardo suited him to perfection and with Penco, Alboni and Graziani also in the cast, Verdi's opera became very popular in Paris and was repeated a dozen times before the Théâtre-Italien closed at the end of March.

That winter the long persecution of Mario by Miss Giles came to a tragic end. While dressing to go to the first performance of *Un ballo in maschera* at the Italiens, the unfortunate woman overturned a lamp.

She was badly burnt and died a few days later. The role of a Don Juan did not suit Mario, either on or off stage and after four more performances of Don Giovanni in Paris, he abandoned the part for ever, returning to the more suitable role of Ottavio.

Mario's contract with Gye came up for rewewal in 1861 and all through April and part of May, copies of the agreement were sent from London to Paris, annotated by the tenor and returned to Gye, who found the alterations unacceptable and sent the contract back to Mario again. At last a three-year engagement was agreed upon by both parties. Mario would sing for two months in 1861 for a round sum of £1,400; and for three months in 1862 and 1863, for £2,500 each season.

By the middle of May, Mario, Grisi and the three little girls were installed at Mulgrave House, Fulham, where they had lived during the past two summer seasons. Surrounded by a large garden that led down to the river Thames, Mulgrave House allowed the singers to have the relaxed, informal family life they preferred, and which they were so seldom able to enjoy. Mario could sketch, paint and model in clay to his heart's content, and also indulge in his new passion for photography. If he never rose before noon, he rarely went to bed before three o'clock in the morning. Letter writing, unless absolutely necessary, was left to Grisi, who was by temperament as energetic as Mario was lazy.

Both dispensed hospitality as prodigally as they spent money; not one of the scores of uninvited guests who arrived at Mulgrave House was turned away without being offered a meal, a handful of sovereigns or at the very least one of Mario's expensive Havana cigars. The children, though treated as little princesses and waited on by a retinue of nursemaids and governesses, were not spoilt by their parents. Discipline was firm, if not exactly strict, and the girls were brought up to be trilingual in English, French and Italian. A little later they acquired a German governess and added German to their accomplishments.

Not surprisingly, the girls sang almost as soon as they could speak. They also loved to dance, with Grisi providing the music at the piano and Mario taking turns as partner to the three children, in a polka or a waltz. On other evenings it was the children—better pianists than their mother—who played the latest Johann Strauss pieces, while Grisi knitted and Mario played patience. Mario also read widely, his favourite subject being history, of which he had an extensive library.

Grisi's decision to retire from the stage in 1861—a firm decision this time—was almost certainly taken as a result of the death of Bella

Maria. After that loss, which appeared to affect her even more deeply than the deaths of her other two daughters, she seemed to resent being parted from the remaining three girls, Rita, Cecilia and Clelia, for even the shortest period of time. A performance in the theatre represented several precious hours that could have been spent in their company. Her career had lasted 33 years, during which she had never quite learnt to control the impulsiveness that was an essential facet of her character and which expressed itself mainly in the generosity with which she lavished her talents on stage as well as her love and affection in private life.

Now the time was approaching when, needing to husband those talents and resources, she preferred to direct them all on her family.

Chapter 13

THE 1861 SEASON of the Royal Italian Opera at Covent Garden was marked by two events of particular interest. On Tuesday 14 May an unknown soprano of eighteen, Adelina Patti, made her London debut in *La sonnambula*; on Wednesday 24 July, the fifty-year-old Giulia Grisi took her farewell of the stage. Between them, the careers of these two prime donne spanned nearly 70 years, from 1828, when Grisi made her début, to 1895, when Patti made her last appearance at Covent Garden.

Grisi made the first of her farewell appearances on 18 May in *Norma*, followed ten days later by *Lucrezia Borgia*. Mario made his first appearance of the season on Monday 3 June in *Il barbiere*. According to Davison in *The Times*, 'so brilliant a Count Almaviva as his has not been witnessed by the present generation of opera-goers. Incomparable as an exhibition of vocal skill, it is also a pattern of high-class comedy—natural and refined in equal measure, easy, elegant, and in every sense attractive.'

After deploring the fact that no other contemporary tenor, Italian or non-Italian, could execute the music of Rossini's hero with the required grace and fluency, Davison continued: 'to these qualities, rare as they are just now, Signor Mario joins unflagging spirits and a kind of gentlemanly humour as agreeable as it is peculiarly his own. Last night he fairly eclipsed his previous achievements.'

The next opera in which Mario appeared was *Les Huguenots*, on 11 June, the third in the series of farewell performances given by Grisi. Chorley considered that Mario's Raoul was 'the best presentation of the character offered by him for some seven years past. He seemed to court, not evade, those great if extravagant effects in the part which were not planned for any voice like his.'

Davison, though he admitted that many of Grisi's admirers might have liked to hear again 'the Anna Bolena and the Semiramide that long ago consoled them for the loss of Pasta', thought that 'few will be disposed to quarrel with two representations of the *Huguenots*, in which Mario's Raoul figures side by side with Grisi's Valentine. How much Mme. Grisi has owed to Signor Mario need not here be discussed, but probably as much, of late years, as Signor Mario owed to Mme. Grisi when their names were first publicly associated.'

If *Lucrezia Borgia* a couple of weeks previously had aroused less enthusiasm than usual from the public, it was not because Tamberlik made a bad Gennaro, but because, in Davison's opinion, 'Mario was not present to augment the interest and share the honours of the evening. Last night,' he continued, 'no such drawback intervened. There was the Raoul de Nangis to whom the patrons of the Royal Italian Opera have been accustomed since 1848 . . . the greatest Raoul, probably, ever witnessed. Thus supported, Mme. Grisi surpassed herself. . . Signor Mario exerted himself with uncommon ardor, and the magnificent duet that follows the benediction of the swords, magnificently given from end to end, brought the curtain down amid a storm of applause.'

Another member of the audience that night was Lady Geraldine Somerset. 'To Covent Garden to hear Mario and Grisi in the *Huguenots*,' she wrote in her diary. 'Once again to have the *ineffable* delight—oh, it was too beautiful that 3rd act—what in all the length and breadth of all the earth is like it?'

The following evening, Wednesday 12 June, Henry Greville gave his annual concert for the Duchess of Cambridge. 'Mario and Grisi sang admirably,' he wrote, 'there have been more perfect *artists* than Mario, but no one ever gave me the same pleasure in a room. Grisi's voice was wonderfully fresh and limpid, and I have never had a concert which went off so well.'

After a lengthy period of rehearsal and several delays and postponements, *Un ballo in maschera* was produced at Covent Garden on Thursday 27 June. Meanwhile, twelve days earlier, J. H. Mapleson's company at the Lyceum Theatre had stolen a march on the Royal Italian Opera and had presented the first London performance of Verdi's opera. At the second performance at the Lyceum, on 18 June, Mario and Grisi were in the audience.

Despite the relative smallness of the theatre and the very short time spent in preparing the new work, the performance was a great success, mainly owing to the superb Amelia of the German soprano Therese Tietjens. The rest of the cast was good, Arditi conducted and was judged to have done his best with the small orchestral and choral forces at his disposal. But as Davison in *The Times* pointed out, 'that anything like adequate preparation can have been bestowed at the Lyceum Theatre it would be foolish to assert.'

No such excuses were necessary for the Royal Italian Opera's production of *Un ballo in maschera*. 'Seldom is an epithet so well deserved,' declared Chorley, 'the performances at Covent Garden Theatre are for the most part "royal" in their completeness—the union of choral and orchestral force, and care bestowed on the scenic portions of the operas given, distance anything of the kind till now enjoyed in this capital, and to be found in any other metropolis at the time present.'

After praising the Amelia of Penco, whom he preferred to Tietjens, Chorley continued: 'Signor Mario is, this season, bewildering (no other word will do) as compared with what he has been of late years. He would appear to have no more need to manage his voice—no more fear of its betraying him—no more misgiving—no more stint—but to fling himself into the action and singing of every part, with as much enterprise as if "the world was all before him where to choose".'

That Riccardo was a role very much to Mario's liking, the tenor had already discovered in Paris. Covent Garden abided by the Neapolitan setting as presented at the Théâtre-Italien. 'He wears three different costumes,' wrote Davison, 'which all become him well (especially the picturesque one of a Neapolitan sailor). He has to appear gay, valiant, and heedless in one scene, to make love in another; and, not for the first time by many, he does all to perfection. The music, for the most part, if not always, lies easily for his voice—exhibiting without fatiguing it. Thus we have,' concluded Davison, 'the union of fine acting with a vocal expression not surpassed.'

Grisi and Patti appeared together in *Don Giovanni* on Saturday 6 July, when the former sang Donna Anna and the latter, Zerlina. According to the *Musical World*, at the end of the first act, when Grisi was called before the curtain alone after all the artists had been applauded, 'she would not appear without Mlle. Patti, the Zerlina of the evening, whom accordingly she led on amid the most enthusiastic cheers from all parts of the house. This most graceful act will assuredly not be forgotten.' Grisi could afford this gesture to a singer more than 30 years her junior and never exhibited the slightest jealousy towards Patti either professionally or personally, although Mario became the younger soprano's stage partner in a great many operas.

It would be satisfying to record that Mario sang Don Ottavio in the *Don Giovanni* that united Grisi and Patti, but in fact it was Tamberlik who took the part. Mario first sang with Patti on Saturday 13 July in *Martha*. According to the *Musical World*, the young prima donna displayed remarkable ability, vocal and histrionic; she sang the music with great brilliancy and was encored in 'The Last Rose of Summer'. Mario's Lionel was in 'every way incomparable, and though the great tenor was not in his best voice on Saturday night, his singing was so inimitable and his acting so graceful, natural and passionate when required, that the audience was delighted throughout.'

'M'appari', Lionel's aria, 'which no one sings with such profound sentiment as Signor Mario, who lends an additional beauty to the music of M. Flotow,' was also encored.

Finally, on Wednesday 24 July, Grisi took her farewell of the London opera public in a benefit performance comprising Act I of *Norma* and Acts I and III of *Les Huguenots*. It was a sad and moving occasion. Since 1834 Grisi had sung every season but one (1842) in London, first at Her Majesty's, then at the old Covent Garden theatre, the Lyceum and, since 1858, at the new Covent Garden. Only the very senior members of the audience could remember a time when Giulia Grisi was not the reigning prima donna.

Chorley, having written his tribute to her in 1854, when her retirement was first announced, refused to add anything to the compliments he had paid the singer then. In *The Times* Davison, after praising her versatility, continued: 'Perhaps of the two performances last night, that of *Norma* was the most thoroughly enjoyed—doubtless because it was most congenial to the nature and idiosyncrasy of the artist. We shall not attempt to describe the reception that greeted the Norma of Normas when she stepped forth from among the priest-esses, sickle in hand, to rebuke the murmuring crowd. "Sediziose voci" (rebel voices) they were not, but the voices of hearty admiration and allegiance, that now for the last time bade her welcome on the stage she has done so much to elevate and refine.'

Grisi's voice apparently betrayed her emotion in the slow section of 'Casta diva' but the 'eloquent dialogue in which Norma listened with an interest that no one has ever been able to assume like Grisi to the story of Adalgisa,' and the trio in which the two women are joined by Pollione (Tamberlik), 'conspicuous in the midst of which were, as of old, the two declamatory passages, "O non tremare, o perfido" and "O di qual sei tu vittima" (the first encored, the second applauded with rapture)—one and all enthralled the audience.'

Turning to the excerpts from *Les Huguenots*, Davison asked 'what need be said? Suffice it that Mario was Raoul, and that, although labouring under a slight hoarseness, the great Italian tenor threw all the passion of which he is so complete a master into the delineation of his part. It was nearly an hour past midnight when Raoul had leapt through the window, and Valentine uttered the scream of despair which accompanies the abrupt departure of her lover. Not a soul, however that quitted the theatre. All remained to do honour to Grisi.'

Grisi took three curtain calls—a gratifying number in those days; on the first she was accompanied by Mario, 'without whose assistance one half of the magnificent bouquets flung from the most prominent boxes must have been abandoned; and twice alone, when—why suppress the truth?—her face was suffused in tears and she seemed to have hardly strength to express her grateful recognition of the sympathy she had elicited.'

The following Wednesday 31 July, there was a concert at the Crystal Palace for Grisi's benefit; the season at Covent Garden ended on 3 August, but Mario and Grisi were not able to leave London till a week later, as one of their daughters was ill. The family set off for Italy on 10 August, for a brief visit to their home in Florence before Grisi's farewell tour of the British provinces, promoted by Willert Beale.

Some time in September Frederick Gye, who was enjoying a well-earned rest in Exmouth, received a letter from a Mr Potter, Collector of Government Taxes in Fulham: 'Sir, I was the bearer of a note sometime ago from Madam Grisi to you respecting Income Tax and Taxes on Mulgrave House amounting to £153-3-1 which as I was informed by Madam that you would pay me on receiving her note. Would you please reply to that note at your earliest convenience and oblige, your most obliging servant, M. Potter.'

Gye replied that Grisi was announced to sing at Exeter shortly, and no doubt would be in England in a few days, but that he did not know where she was at that moment. He asked Potter to send him the particulars of each sum due from Mario and Grisi, promising to pay rather than allow the singers' goods to be seized.

Potter replied that Mario owed £78-2-6 personal Income Tax; Grisi owed £61-2-6; and that the combined House duty, Land Tax, Servants and Arms Tax came to £13-18-1.

On 10 October Gye, now back in London, answered: 'Sir, if I understand your letter received this day rightly, it is your intention to seize Madame Grisi's and Signor Mario's goods at Mulgrave House unless the taxes are paid. I have no doubt whatever if you could have waited the arrival of either Madame Grisi or Signor Mario, they would have immediately paid you. However under the circumstances I will advance the money and enclose you a cheque for M. Mario for £92-0-7 and another for Mme. Grisi for £61-2-6.'

Mario, meanwhile, was in Paris preparing for the season at the Théâtre-Italien. He first appeared on Sunday 13 October in *Il barbiere* and the same opera was given for his benefit on 28 March 1862. During the intervening months he sang in *Un ballo in maschera*, *Il trovatore*, *Martha*, *Rigoletto* and *Don Giovanni* (as Ottavio).

The house being built in the rue des Bassins was still not ready, so one was rented in the rue Pamquet. Judith Gautier, daughter of Théophile Gautier and of Giulia Grisi's cousin Ernesta, was taken as a girl of sixteen to dine at the house in the rue Pamquet. Judith described the visit: 'Giulia Grisi is still beautiful—she does not seem to allow time to overcome her. Perhaps she is not now quite the perfect statue that inspired my father to write an enthusiastic ode to Beauty when, for the first time, he saw her in her box at the Salle Favart, during a performance of *Mosé*, and wished he had not abandoned the paint-brush for the pen.'

The Diva, continued Judith, 'is a little stout, her features have fattened, and the destructive finger of time has drawn the corners of her mouth; but the whole is noble and superb. The pose of the head, the warm colouring, the soft blue eyes under the heavy bands of black hair, have still an extreme charm.'

Judith Gautier was even more struck with the appearance of her host: 'Mario is a type of remarkable beauty, a favourite with dowagers and absolutely fatal to young hearts. This dominion he does not renounce, but still holds with a graceful hand.' Judith also commended Mario's manner. 'He has none of the customary conceit of tenors and shows supreme distinction. With his sparse beard that appears never to have been cut, his lightly curling hair and his beautiful dark eyes, so soft under their long fringe of eyelashes, he reminds me of Raphael Sanzio.'

During the evening Judith whispered to Mario that a school friend of hers was in love with him and wanted a signed photograph of the tenor.

'She saw you at the Italiens as Almaviva,' explained Judith, 'and found you so beautiful that now she thinks only of you. She keeps your picture in her pocket to look at all day.'

'Is she pretty, your friend?' enquired Mario.

'Oh yes, she's tall and elegant and at least twenty years old,' came the reply. 'She wears a crinoline—a real grown-up lady. I don't know why she's still a student.'

'You have that photograph?'

'Of course!' answered Judith. 'My friend made me swear at least ten times that I would bring it for you to sign.'

Judith produced the photograph from her pocket and gave it to Mario.

'What a beautiful man,' remarked the tenor. 'I'm not surprised that he still turns the head of schoolgirls.' He wrote a few words on the back of the photograph, sighing as he did so, 'Poor girl!'

Before Christmas Gye wrote to Mario confirming his engagement for the 1862 season, as set out in the contract of the previous year. Gye added: 'I had intended to visit Paris this week, and to have the pleasure of seeing you, but we have had the misfortune to lose a relative the day after the death of the poor Prince, and from the same illness.' The Prince Consort had died on 14 December, of typhoid. The Queen mourned her beloved Albert for many years in seclusion but did not forget, as will later become apparent, the innumerable evenings she had spent at the opera in the Prince's company.

Mario did not answer Gye's letter immediately and on 26 December Gye sent the tenor a telegram demanding an early reply. An amicable arrangement was agreed upon and Mario made his first appearance of the 1862 season at Covent Garden on Tuesday 6 May in *Un ballo in maschera*. The following Saturday he sang in *Il barbiere* with Patti and a week later, on 17 May, appeared as the Duke of Mantua in *Rigoletto*. 'The first honours fell to Signor Mario, whose freshness and power of voice this year are incomprehensible,' wrote Chorley; 'not so his grace and elegance of stage presentation—because these are things which never die, save with life, in those to whom they innately belong.'

The Mario-Patti partnership, which was to last a decade, had by now become fully established. Patti was in every possible way the antithesis of Grisi as an artist. Though she developed into a competent if careful actress, the younger singer had none of the impulsiveness of the elder, she never allowed herself to be carried away by the emotion of a part or a performance. Nevertheless, she apparently got on extremely well with the famous tenor more than 30 years her senior. Perhaps Mario, as he grew older, found the self-containment of Patti soothing after the demands, exciting but also fatiguing, made on her stage partners by Giulia Grisi. Whatever the reason, the success of the new association undoubtedly prolonged Mario's career by several years.

Gye received a letter from Mario on 24 June, in which the tenor expressed surprise at being sent a notice of rehearsals for *Don Pasquale*, as Ernesto 'is one of the roles I gave up long ago, firstly because I am now rather old for the part, but chiefly because it is too high for me, and cannot be transposed because the tessitura is always so elevated that it would need lowering so much the others could not manage it. The role is not so important that it must be taken by me . . . all it needs is to be well sung, and I would sing it badly because I cannot reach it.'

Mario suggested two tenors, Italo Gardoni and Neri-Baraldi, who could well make a good impression as Ernesto. 'I will come and see you later,' he ended his letter, 'to arrange about this—today is a family celebration.'

The family celebration was Mario's Saint's Day, 24 June being dedicated to St John the Baptist. It was a day on which his children gave him small presents they had made themselves and acted a little play or sang for him.

Gye replied to Mario's letter the same afternoon: 'I beseech you to sing the role of Ernesto in *Don Pasquale*, if only for one or two performances. Not having the slightest idea that you would object to singing the part, I have already announced it several days ago.'

Mario eventually agreed. A few days later Gye sent him tickets for *Lucia di Lammermoor*, so that Mario and Grisi could hear the new tenor, Theodor Wachtel, who was singing Edgardo opposite Patti's Lucia.

Don Pasquale was performed, for the first time for seven years, on Saturday 12 July, with Patti, Mario, the baritone Enrico delle Sedie and the bass Giuseppe Ciampi. The opera proved very successful. 'Not at the time of its birth did the music sound more welcome for its elegance and gaiety than it does in these days,' wrote Chorley, 'but the merit belongs to Donizetti, and not to the singers now at Covent Garden. Their performances (Signor Mario's excepted), as compared with that of the original artists reminded us of a pale and diminished water-colour of a forcible oil painting.'

Chorley found Ciampi and Delle Sedie in no respect adequate substitutes for Lablache and Tamburini, but owing to Patti's great popularity and 'to Signor Mario's "Com' è gentil" (which he still sings with unrivalled lover-like elegance) *Don Pasquale* may probably draw a few great houses.'

In fact there were only two performances of *Don Pasquale* that year, and three more the following season, when Ronconi replaced Delle Sedie as Doctor Malatesta. Mario sang Ernesto in Paris during February 1864 and for three performances during the 1865 season at Covent Garden; those were the last occasions when a member of the original cast of Donizetti's comic masterpiece took part in *Don Pasquale*, 22 years after the Paris première. Mario continued to sing 'Come è gentil' at concerts until the end of his career.

Another favourite concert piece was 'Raggio d'amore' from Donizetti's *Il furioso all'isola di San Domingo*, which Mario sang at Chesham House on Wednesday 9 July, 1862 when, according to the faithful Lady Geraldine, he 'sang like the dear angel that he is, and what else can one say. His singing is heavenly, and that indeed is the only word for it.'

A week later both Mario and Grisi sang at Henry Greville's concert. 'Mario sang,' chronicled Lady Geraldine, '*c'est tout dire!!!*' His main contribution on this occasion was 'Nel furor' from Bellini's *Il pirata*, with 'O donna amata', a song by Ciro Pinsuti, as an encore. Henry Greville gave two musical parties that summer at his house, 19 Queen Street, in Mayfair; the second was on Tuesday 22 July and in the opinion of the host, both Mario and Grisi 'sang as well as in their best days.'

The final opera of the 1862 season at Covent Garden was *Masaniello*, with Mario back in the title role. In *The Times* of Monday 18 August, Davison wrote that 'the season terminated on Saturday with the fifth performance of Auber's *Masaniello*, on the whole one of the best since the revival.' The house was crowded, not always the case when the season extended to mid-August.

'Signor Mario,' continued Davison, 'was in splendid voice; and his vocal declamation alone might have been a lesson to those who are capable of profiting by good examples. Thus the musical was not—as it sometimes is—thrust into the shade by the histrionic part of the performance.' Davison considered the spectacular production of this *Masaniello* 'one of the most remarkable in the annals of Covent Garden, and scene after scene, situation after situation, raised the sympathy and applause of the audience.'

At the end of August Mario, as he wrote at the end of a business letter to Gye, went 'to stun the ears of the provinces, after having deafened London.' After a short visit with his family to Florence, he then returned to Paris.

That autumn the Paris Opéra was also planning to revive Auber's *Masaniello* under its original French title of *La Muette de Portici*. Michot, the tenor originally engaged for the role of Masaniello, was found ill-suited to the part. It was now early in November and as no other suitable tenor could be found, Mario was asked to sing Masaniello. Rehearsals continued, then on 15 November there was a terrible accident of the kind only too frequent in the days of gas lighting. Emma Livry, the dancer taking the part of the dumb girl Fenella, was waiting in the wings for her entrance when she approached too near a naked gas jet and her costume caught fire. Panic stricken she rushed across the stage; a fireman managed to seize her in his arms and smother the flames, but not before the dancer was horribly burnt.

The unlucky production of Auber's opera was again postponed, while another dancer was rehearsed in the part of Fenella. Meanwhile, to give the Italian tenor under contract something to do, Mario appeared in *Les Huguenots* on Monday 24 November. It was well over twenty years since he had last sung at the Opéra. Though he knew the part of Raoul de Nangis so well in Italian, his command of the French style and language was less than perfect. In the uncharacteristically kind words of Berlioz in the *Journal des Débats*, 'Luck did not second his efforts.' In short, the performance was a fiasco and Mario resigned from the Opéra the same night.

La Muette de Portici was not produced until January 1863, when the tenor Guémard, known as the 'Atlas of the Opéra', sang Masaniello and Mlle. Vernon danced the role of Fenella. Emma Livry ultimately died of her injuries, and the whole episode left Mario with an indelible dislike of Masaniello, which he sang only once more during the rest of his career.

Less than a week after the disastrous performance of *Les Huguenots* at the Opéra, Mario reappeared at the Théâtre-Italien in *Il barbiere di Siviglia*, with Patti as Rosina and Delle Sedie as Figaro. 'When the Almaviva appeared on the stage where for so long he has enraptured the public,' wrote Délécluze in the *Journal des Débats*, 'he was received with salvos of applause which lasted for seven or eight minutes, and a shower of bouquets which quite surrounded him. After he had recovered from the sweet emotion aroused by this ovation, the celebrated singer performed his role with all his accustomed grace and skill.'

That winter Mario and Grisi with their daughters finally moved into their new home in Paris, 19 rue des Bassins (now the rue August-Vacquerie) in the sixteenth arrondissement. The street runs between the Avenue Joséphine (now the Avenue Marceau) and the Avenue du Roi de Rome (now the Avenue Kléber). It was conveniently near the Bois de Boulogne, where Grisi could walk with the children. One day the Tsar Alexander, driving in his carriage, is reputed to have stopped to speak to Grisi.

'Are those your little grisettes?' he asked, pointing to the three girls.

'No Sire,' answered Grisi, 'they are my marionettes.'

In the middle of April 1863 the entire household was transported across the channel to London and settled down at Mulgrave House for the summer. Gye sent Mario a telegram on Thursday 30 April, asking him if he would sing Alfredo in *La traviata* the following Tuesday. Mario replied: 'Unfortunately I was not woken when your telegram arrived, or I would have wired my answer—which is negative, as it is a century since I have sung in *Traviata*, not since the days of poor Bosio, and then I think only a few times, as well as in Paris with Piccolomini, therefore I don't remember the part.'

Mario offered to open in *Un ballo in maschera*, *Rigoletto*, *Il trovatore* or *Il barbiere*, 'in short in an opera of my current repertoire. Tomorrow I will come and see you, and we will talk of this. Excuse my scrawl, but

I have only just been given your message, and must make do with what pen I can find.' Mario's handwriting, never very easy to decipher, is barely legible in this letter, which looks as if a spider or some other insect had dipped its legs in the ink and wandered across the paper.

The tenor Emilio Naudin sang in *La traviata* and Mario made his first appearance of the season in *Il barbiere*, with Patti and Ronconi, on Saturday 9 May. Just under three weeks later, on 28 May, Mario sang Manrico in *Il trovatore*, a role he had not taken in London for four years. Patti sang her first Leonora and Graziani was Di Luna. The opera scored a great success, while the singers were much applauded—according to *The Times* Mario's 'Di quella pira' created 'a sensation almost without parallel'—and *Il trovatore* was billed to be repeated on the following Tuesday.

However, on Friday, the day after the first performance of the revival, Gye wrote to Mario:

The rehearsals of *La gazza ladra* are so behindhand that it will be impossible to give *Trovatore* on Tuesday as Patti cannot rehearse the same day that she is singing such a heavy role. Unfortunately Tamberlik, Fioretti and Battu [two sopranos] have gone to Liverpool, and the only thing I can give on Tuesday is *Norma*, but I would strengthen the performance with a little concert. Will you sing 'Goodbye Sweetheart' and will you also give me the name of a duet you could sing with Carlotta Patti [sister of Adelina]. May I compliment you heartily on yesterday's performance.

Mario replied the same day:

Your letter upset me very much, above all because it wrongs Mlle. Patti not to give the second *Trovatore* when it has already been announced; I think it would be much better to postpone *La gazza* rather than harm an opera newly in Mlle. Patti's repertoire, that it is to your advantage to support. As for Tuesday the change is hardly flattering to the subscribers, and I think that *Norma* followed by a ballet would make a better evening. I don't know what duet you mean, and I find that sort of a concert in a theatre like yours unworthy of its standards; it is like admitting to the public that the performance is bad. You also have Naudin who could sing the last scene from *Lucia* as well as the ballet.

The tenor's good sense appeared to have prevailed, because *Il trovatore* did receive its second performance on Tuesday 2 June, while *La gazza ladra* was postponed until 6 June.

At the beginning of July Mario received another 'final demand' from the Income Tax Commissioners, threatening that unless the sum of £121 was paid without further delay, a warrant would be issued against his person. Gye paid the Tax as he had done before. Perhaps as a result of the Tax Collector's persistence, Mario had a bad bilious attack on 8 June and wrote to Gye that he was unable to rehearse *Don Pasquale*; but he was sufficiently recovered the next evening to sing in the opera. He appeared in *Les Huguenots* on 18 July, when Valentine was sung by Pauline Lucca, a Viennese soprano making her London début. Lucca was just twenty-two years old, another pocket prima donna destined to sing a great deal with Mario during the next few years. Her vocal technique was no match for Patti's, but she was very good looking and possessed plenty of temperament.

Chapter 14

SINCE GRISI'S RETIREMENT from the stage, she and Mario and their children had managed to make longer and more frequent visits to their villa in Florence. Of all the houses that at different periods they owned or rented, the Villa Salviati was the one they preferred and the one on which they lavished the most care and money. A large, four-storey building dating originally from the eleventh century, it stood—indeed still stands—on the road to Bologna, with a magnificent view over the city of Florence, the river Arno and the hills to the south. Behind the villa rises the still higher hill on which the village of Fiesole is perched.

The fortified castle, as it then was, came into the possession of the Salviati family in 1450. It was partially destroyed during a siege in 1529 and rebuilt in substantially its present form. The Salviati were a large and powerful family; a Jacopo Salviati married Lucrezia Medici, daughter of Lorenzo the Magnificent, and Jacopo's daughter Maria became the mother of Cosimo Medici, first Grand Duke of Tuscany.

In the early seventeenth century, another Jacopo Salviati married the notorious Veronica Cybo who, according to contemporary accounts, was 'endowed with but small beauty and hath a most violent and imperious temper.' After ten years of marriage to the tempestuous Veronica, Jacopo fell in love with Caterina Canucci, the beautiful young wife of the seventy-year-old Giustino Canucci.

Bartolomeo Canucci, Giustino's son by a former wife, made dishonourable advances to his step-mother and when she repulsed him, he told Veronica Salviati of her husband's affair with Caterina. Veronica then goaded Bartolomeo into having his step-mother murdered. The murder was carried out on 31 December 1638 and Veronica had Caterina's head, wrapped in linen and placed in a basket, delivered to Jacopo as a New Year's gift. Veronica escaped from Florence, but Bartolomeo was executed for the crime. The Villa Salviati was supposed to be haunted by the ghost of a woman and during the alterations made by Mario after he bought the villa, some workmen discovered the walled-up corpse of a female, which disintegrated to dust and bones on exposure to the air.

The many rooms of the villa were crammed with furniture, objects, books and paintings bought by Mario in London, Paris or any other city he happened to visit in the course of his career. Some of the things were of great value, while some had a purely sentimental worth. Mario could not pass an antique shop or second-hand bookseller without going in and buying something. There were also his own sketches, paintings and clay models. The courtyard of the villa contained the statue of a siren rising from a large shell, sculpted by Mario, in which he had copied Grisi's arms and neck, Rita's ear, Cecilia's nose and Clelia's eyes.

When the singers were in residence, the gates stood permanently open and a procession of visitors, Italian, English and French, drove up the hill from Florence. On Sundays there was a standing invitation to their friends for lunch and dinner, while impromptu musical evenings frequently took place. On these occasions, both Mario and Grisi would sing.

In 1864 Florence temporarily became the capital of Italy, and diplomats from many countries enlarged the rather narrow Anglo-Italian society of the city. As they were not legally married, Mario and Grisi were not invited to official functions, but their own circle of acquaintance was so wide that this can have mattered little to them. Essentially domestic in their way of life, they were perfectly content to share the peace of the Tuscan countryside with their family and friends.

Early in January 1864, Mario had to return to Paris for what turned out to be his final season at the Théâtre-Italien. He appeared for the first time on Tuesday 26 January in *Il barbiere*, with Patti as Rosina; during February he sang in *Don Pasquale* and *Martha*, also with Patti, who was as immensely popular in Paris as she was in London.

At the beginning of March Mario gave some performances of *Il trovatore* and on the evening of Wednesday 9 March, Frederick Gye, who was in Paris on business, attended the performance. He visited Mario in his dressing room during the opera and next day, 10 March, had a long talk with Bagier, manager of the Italiens. The result of this conversation was an almost incredible series of misunderstandings between the tenor and the two managers.

Mario had a contract with Gye to sing at Covent Garden from 29 March 1864, for four months at £2,500 for the season. Bagier, owing to Patti's success, wished to prolong his own season during April; he arranged with Gye at their meeting on 10 March to keep Mario at the Théâtre-Italien for a further four weeks, until 24 April, and to pay him 15,000 francs. Gye wrote Mario a note to this effect, giving it to Bagier to hand on to the tenor and then himself returned to London.

Bagier wrote to Mario on 11 March, saying he had a letter for him from Gye and would the tenor please call for it at the theatre the following day, Mario came to Bagier's office as requested, read Gye's letter and left without taking it with him. He did not answer until 17 March, when he wrote to Gye, now back in London, that 'Bagier gave me your letter, in which you consent to my staying here in Paris until 24 April—you should have consulted me beforehand, but as you did not, I tell you now that I do not accept this new arrangement, that I hold by my original contract and that I shall leave for London on the 28th or 29th [of March] at the latest.'

Bagier also wrote to Gye, saying that 'Mario tells me that it does not suit him to use this permission, and that he insists on going to London at the time previously agreed on, so our plan is null and void, my dear colleague.'

Gye received both letters on 19 March, and answered them immediately. To Mario he wrote:

Your letter of the 17th only [sic] arrived this morning. Need I tell you of my astonishment? You yourself asked me to let you stay in Paris during April, and I said you could remain for the first 3 weeks. I gave you written permission in my letter of 10 March. Now I have made all my arrangements and it would be very inconvenient to start your engagement before 25 April. I hope you will not make any difficulties, but will stay with Bagier.

To Bagier, Gye wrote:

I learn with astonishment from your letter as well as one from Mario that he refuses to stay in Paris during April as agreed. You are a witness that Mario himself asked me for permission to stay, saying I already had enough artists without him. He began the conversation by asking if you had already spoken to me on the subject. I replied that he could stay for the first 3 weeks of April. I gave him written permission on 10 March, and he keeps this letter for 9 days before he changes his mind.

The same day, Gye wrote yet another letter, to Maurice Strakosch, Patti's manager and brother-in-law. Mario, he explained, 'refuses to stay in Paris in April. I suppose he has had some row with Bagier. Please be so kind as to write to me by tomorrow's post and tell me *what is the matter*.'

Mario received and answered Gye's letter the following day,

Sunday 20 March—the post was astoundingly quick and reliable in those days:

> I do not understand your astonishment. I never asked you verbally or in writing to prolong my season in Paris. If, before arranging matters with Bagier, you had consulted me, there could have been no mistake possible. When you and Bagier came into my dressing-room, I asked if you were in agreement. You replied that it was only possible for some weeks, and then the conversation turned to something else. I imagined it was Naudin who was under discussion, as the day before Bagier had mentioned him; I am very upset by this misunderstanding, but it is not my fault and I hold positively to our contract, and will be in London by 1 April.

Strakosch also replied to Gye on 20 March, writing in somewhat eccentric English—the rest of the correspondence was in French. 'Immidiatly [sic] after having received your favour of yesterday,' he wrote, 'I called on Bagier, having told him the contents of your letter he informed me that Mario had said to him, that he never promised you definitably [sic] that he would stay here, and he was determined to leave Paris the 28th.'

Strakosch added that, in Bagier's opinion, the reason why Mario was so determined to leave Paris was the arrival in the French capital of the Italian tenor Gaetano Fraschini. Strakosch continued: 'I do not think that you will be able to change Mario's mind. Last night [during a performance of *Martha*] Adelina insisted greatly with Mario to stay here and do *Traviata* with her, but she did not succeed in persuading him . . . Her success in *Traviata* was by *far* the greatest she has ever had in Paris.'

Bagier wrote again to Gye on 21 March, repeating that Mario had always firmly stated his intention of leaving Paris after his engagement, and had advised Bagier to ask for Naudin instead. 'As for being a witness,' he continued, 'that Mario himself asked to be allowed to stay, this is a definite misunderstanding on your part, as I never heard him say anything of the sort, and I suppose you thought he was speaking of himself, when he meant Naudin. I am very sorry that our plan came to nothing, and must now seek another way out of my difficulties.'

Gye wrote to Mario again on 22 March:

> It grieves me very much there should be a misunderstanding between us. The evening Bagier and I came to your dressing-room,

you said to me that I should have so many artists during April, I should have no need of *you*; I answered it had been arranged so that you could stay in Paris the first three weeks [of April]. Next day I gave you written permission. If you had no intention of staying, why did you make those remarks? When I said you could stay, why did you not tell me then, you did not wish to? Above all, why did you leave my letter of 10 March unanswered for 9 days? Consider these questions I beg of you.'

Mario answered Gye by return of post with a letter in which his habitual good humour had deserted him.

Before pointing out the inaccuracies in your letter, and the way in which you continue to distort the facts, I state once again that the contract between us obliging me to sing at your Theatre gives you no right whatsoever to force me to sing on any other stage, and any contract with a third party for that purpose is null and void. I repeat my astonishment that you could have thought such an arrangement with Bagier would be binding, without my consent. Concerning the conversation that took place between you, Bagier and I where you attribute to me the remarks applicable to Naudin, I will only confirm what Bagier told you in his letter of 22 March, which must have convinced you of your mistake in making these allegations. I reply to your letter, therefore, as I replied to the previous one, and state that I shall be in London, as agreed on 1 April.

Before replying to Mario, Gye wrote once more to Bagier, dating his letter 24 March. 'It is possible we should differ so much in our recollections of this affair over Mario?' he asked. 'When we signed our little contract, you mentioned Mario's consent, and I reminded you that the evening before he had himself asked for permission to stay. You did not then tell me I was mistaken, on the contrary, you agreed. I do not see how it is possible to bring Naudin into the affair. It is not at all likely that I should talk to Mario about a contract for Naudin, and certainly he (Mario) would not have bothered himself about a matter that concerned Naudin.' At the end of his letter, Gye added rather despairingly: 'I have now arranged the repertoire for the first 3 weeks without Mario, and shall not know what to do with both him and Naudin.'

Bagier, on receipt of this plaintive demand for understanding and co-operation, fired a withering broadside back at the unfortunate Gye. He wrote:

We differ, no doubt, on the events which preceded, accompanied and followed the exchange of our signatures, but that is because you interpret these events wrongly, instead of seeing them as they are. You say that when we exchanged signatures and I mentioned that Mario's consent must be obtained, you *reminded* me that he had himself asked for this permission. One can only be *reminded* of something one knows already, and I declare that in front of me, Mario asked for no such *permission*, and I feared he would not avail himself of that you were offering him.

Abandoning the heavy irony of his opening paragraph, Bagier continued in even plainer terms. 'By ceding me this artist without authority, you have aggravated my difficulties in finding a tenor, and caused me to lose valuable time in seeking for a way out of my embarrassment, which is very damaging to me, and of which you are the cause. I cannot refrain from expressing my extreme annoyance.'

Gye, outflanked on both sides, capitulated and on 26 March wrote to Mario: 'I know perfectly well that I have no right to cede you to anyone else, but I know too that I did not say a single word to you about Naudin. I do not see how you could have thought I meant Naudin when I said that I had arranged the repertoire so that you could stay in Paris for the first 3 weeks of April. Certainly it is *possible* that you misunderstood me, but in that case why did you leave my letter of 10 March unanswered for 9 days?'

Well used to Italian singers and their eccentricities, Gye ended his letter philosophically. 'Keep your opinion and I shall keep mine. You and I are too old friends to have serious disputes. Let it be as you wish, and your engagement can begin on 29 March as in our original contract.'

Mario sang in a performance of *Martha* on 27 March, the last occasion on which he appeared at the Théâtre-Italien, and then immediately left Paris for London. Gye and Bagier exchanged a further letter each on the subject of the tenor's engagement. Gye ended his letter: 'I have my own considered opinion on this affair, my dear Bagier, and it is useless to continue the discussion. In the future I will endeavour not to put myself in such a position again.'

Bagier was less polite; his letter, dated 4 April, concluded the correspondence: 'In future I too, my dear Gye, will do my very best not to find myself in a similar situation, and when I need an artist, I shall discover well in advance if the person who cedes him to me has the right to do so. Because of this irregularity on your part, I am in grave difficulties, having only one tenor. Think what would happen if Fraschini became indiposed—it is too frightful to imagine!'

Mario made his first appearance of the season at Covent Garden on Tuesday 5 April, in the title role of *Masaniello*. 'It was one of his good nights,' wrote Chorley in the *Athenaeum*, 'we have never heard him so subtle and watchful in using every device of art to make his hearers forget the devastations wrought by the old sorcerer with scythe and glass. Every part of his performance was exquisitely finished, and if not animated with the old power, was throughout instinct with the old charm.'

Despite the evident success of the performance, Mario never sang the part of Masaniello again. During April he appeared in *La favorita* and *Un ballo in maschera*.

Garibaldi was in London on an official visit and on 16 April he was presented with an address of welcome and a sword of honour at the Crystal Palace. The ceremony was followed by a concert of Italian music, conducted by Luigi Arditi. All the Italian singers in London took part and the huge audience joined soloists and chorus in singing Arditi's song 'O Garibaldi nostro salvator'—'O Garibaldi, our saviour'. The composer-conductor became very excited during the performance and unwittingly brought his baton down rather hard on the head of Mario, who was standing beside him. Mario, according to Arditi himself, behaved most admirably and without uttering a word of reproach, laughed the matter off, as though nothing untoward had happened.

Meanwhile the tenor was preparing a new part, one that was to bring him the greatest success of the final decade of his career and which he was to repeat 50 times during the next five seasons at Covent Garden—the title role of *Faust*. Gounod's opera had first been produced by the Royal Italian Opera the previous year, with Tamberlik as Faust and Marie Miolan-Carvalho as Marguerite, the role she had created at the Théâtre-Lyrique, Paris in 1859. '*Faust e Margherita*' immediately became tremendously popular with London audiences, but Tamberlik, fine singer though he was, did not find the role of Faust wholly suited to his talents. Mario, on the other hand, found the part utterly congenial from the start.

He sang Faust for the first time on Thursday 19 May, with a cast that included Lucca as Marguerite, Faure as Mephistopheles and Graziani as Valentine. A week later Chorley wrote in the *Athenaeum*: 'Such a Faust has not been seen or heard before. The miracle of the play (without strain or hyperbole, be it said) might have been wrought in the renewed personal youth of the artist, whose appearance was exquisitely picturesque—a figure that had walked out of some old German picture. The music suits his voice to a wish, and this granted who need be told of the effect produced by him.'

As usual, Mario had designed his own costumes and had largely rewritten the appalling Italian translation of the text. 'There is no such love-music as the garden duett,' stated Chorley, 'and no singer of love-music to be compared with Signor Mario.'

Pauline Lucca's Marguerite received no such critical praise; her interpretation was considered far too bold, and most of the critics were as shocked as Chorley at her performance. Lucca left London suddenly at the beginning of June, writing to Gye from Calais that she was ill and must go to Germany to take a cure. As a result of Lucca's unannounced departure, it was Patti who sang the role of Marguerite at the performance of *Faust* on Tuesday 6 June. 'Every note of the music,' commented Chorley, 'every word of the text, every change of the situation, had been thought over, and felt by the artist.'

Mario's Faust came in for further praise from Chorley. 'What a life does Signor Mario give to the part, by his grace of bearing (a gift that time has nothing to do against), and by that exquisite beauty and abandonment to the passion of the moment of his expression.' After praising Faure's Mephistopheles and commending the orchestra, chorus and scenery, Chorley remarked that thus cast and thus played, *Faust* could run for years and years.

In fact there were thirteen performances of Gounod's opera that season, which ended on 30 July, after a final week that was, in Chorley's phrase, 'an astounding trot for the avenue.' There were three performances of Meyerbeer's *L'Étoile du nord*, with Miolan-Carvalho and Naudin; one performance of *Faust* with Mario and yet another new Marguerite, Désirée Artôt; one performance of *Martha* (the only one that year) with Patti and Mario; and a final benefit night, when Grisi sang in the first act of *Norma*, with Artôt as Adalgisa, to be followed by Patti and Mario in two acts of *Faust*.

It was 'a week the like of which is not in our recollection,' commented Chorley. 'In no other capital than ours would such a feat be possible. *Faust* has been the greatest attraction of the season, and has renewed the lease of Signor Mario's youth in a manner little short of magical.'

Grisi had appeared in public once already that summer, in Signor Ciabatta's concert on 2 July. She sang in nine items and was apparently in excellent voice.

Grisi had also sung at Henry Greville's musical party, held that year on Friday 27 May. Lady Geraldine was of course there, with her employer the Duchess of Cambridge, and wrote afterwards in her diary: 'Henry Greville's concert, oh the perfection!! It was beyond all words. And such a good selection. Grisi sang gloriously, her Semiramide, divine, and Mario!!!!!! oh Mario—the *Raggio d'amor*!! The latter half of the concert I sat between Grisi and dear Princess Augusta [the Grand Duchess of Mecklenburg-Strelitz and elder daughter of the Duchess of Cambridge] who was charming, and I had a great deal of conversation with Grisi and with dear Mario, Grisi in such pretty English.'

The love duet from *Faust* figured on the programme of a concert at Leeds Town Hall on Saturday 29 October, when it was sung by Mario and Grisi during their autumn tour of the English provinces. Mario also sang 'M'appari' from *Martha* and Hatton's ever-popular 'Goodbye Sweetheart', while Grisi contributed Elvira's Mad scene from *I puritani*, 'The Last Rose of Summer' (in Italian) and 'The Minstrel Boy' (in English).

That summer, Mario and his family had moved from Mulgrave House, remembered in later years with such affection and nostalgia by Arditi, Willert Beale and others, and immortalized by Caldesi in the photograph he took of Mario and Grisi, the former dressed as Manrico, serenading his Leonora (in her everyday clothes) on the steps of the verandah. During the 1864 season they lived at Fairfax House, Putney, and the following year rented a furnished house, Gothic Lodge, in Queen's Road, Clapham Park.

In January 1865 Gye, who was in Berlin, received a request for a reference, and was asked if he thought Mario a 'desirable and careful tenant and such an one as you would not hesitate to entrust with a well-furnished house of your own.' Gye replied: 'I beg to say that M. Mario has two houses of his own, one of which I have seen [presumably the house in Paris] and which is most *luxuriously* furnished, and the other is I believe filled with works of art. I should therefore think he knows well how to take care of such a house and furniture as he is likely to hire in London.'

Mario spent the winter of 1864/65 in Madrid, where Bagier was presenting a season of Italian opera at the Teatro Real. *Rigoletto*, the first opera produced, was a fair success, but after that nothing the French impresario put on met with the approval of the Madrid public; singers, sets, productions and orchestra were all adversely criticized. Even *Faust* was only partially successful, firstly because the work had already been performed in the Spanish capital at another theatre the previous autumn (with Tamberlik as Faust); and secondly because Bagier had announced the appearance of Patti as well as Mario in

Gounod's opera and she was detained in Paris, where, in the words of Herman Klein, 'so overwhelming was the demand to hear her that all Spain, with *Faust* and Mario, was impatiently awaiting her advent in Madrid.'

As it turned out, Patti did not arrive in Madrid until the last week of March and by then Mario had had to return to London for the opening of the Royal Italian Opera season at Covent Garden. This took place on Tuesday 28 March, 1865, with a performance of *Faust*. The tenor was obviously in his finest form.

'As for Signor Mario,' wrote Chorley, 'we should hardly expect distant persons to believe us did we tell *how* marvellously he played and sang the part [of Faust] on Tuesday. It is obviously now one of his first favourites, and is more perfect, we think, as an impersonation than even his Raoul or his Gennaro.' The Marguerite on that occasion was a soprano named Berini, but later in the season both Lucca and Patti sang with Mario in *Faust*, which was given twelve times.

For the first time for several years, Mario sang the title role of *Le Prophète*, on Tuesday 11 April. Jean of Leyden had always been a heavy part for him, and at the present stage of his career cannot have been an easy undertaking, but he seems to have tackled it with more than usual energy, and to have made up dramatically for any diminution of vocal power. 'His appearance and action in the Cathedral scene are of themselves worth a visit to the theatre,' was Chorley's opinion.

Patti arrived back in London at the beginning of May and appeared with Mario in *Il barbiere* on 13 May. There were also the three performances of *Don Pasquale* mentioned earlier, the last sung by Mario, the only member of the original cast still active in the theatre. Lucca, her differences with Gye made up, had also returned to London, and sang with Mario in *Les Huguenots* as well as in *Faust*.

Gye wanted another role for Lucca and chose that of Zerlina in Auber's *Fra Diavolo*, asking Mario to sing the title role. By 19 June the opera was already in rehearsal and Gye wrote to Mario to enquire on what day the following week he would be ready to sing his new part, and beseeching him not to miss the rehearsal next day. Mario attended the rehearsal and then went to see Gye in his office. The scene that ensued clearly offended Mario's tender susceptibilities and the following day, 21 June, the tenor wrote to Gye in plaintive mood:

I think the feminine impatience and lack of tact of the persons who surrounded you in your office yesterday have forced you into an action you would not have taken if you had reflected on what you were doing in giving the order to send me a *Maestro* and to *pay for his Cab*.

   I am very poor it is true and also very stupid, but I still have friends who are capable of teaching me my roles when necessary, so that I need not be treated like a I-don't-know-what. As you have someone who knows all the best roles in my repertoire, and I know has sung that of Fra Diavolo elsewhere, you can enlarge your repertoire and please both feminine impatience and myself in giving it to him.

This was a reference to the tenor Pasquale Brignoli, who sang Lionel in *Martha* and Fernando in *La favorita* that season, while the 'feminine impatience' was undoubtedly Lucca's.

   'As I know that my good friend Licalzi has had his cab paid for him,' continued Mario, 'I am giving him the score of *Fra Diavolo* to return to you.' But the unfortunate Licalzi had already dismissed his cab, and Mario had to send score and letter by the hand of his own servant. Gye did not receive the letter until three o'clock the following afternoon and replied at once: 'We have been together and friends for too long a time to quarrel, and therefore I will not reply to the accusations in your letter. Besides I am sure that you wrote under a false impression. I am sending you back the score of *Fra Diavolo* as I am sure that you will not force me to break my word to the public yet again. I sent you Licalzi because I thought you had agreed to accept his help. If you no longer need him, would you kindly let me know.'

   Mario, however, was adamant in refusing to sing *Fra Diavolo* either that or any other year. Auber's opera was not produced at Covent Garden until the following season, when Naudin sang the title role with Lucca as Zerlina. Mario, even without this addition to his repertory, sang in 44 performances of eight operas during the four months of his 1865 engagement, more often than he had done for many years.

   Patti gave a concert at St James's Hall on 4 July; Mario took part, as well as Lucca, Brignoli and other singers. Gye had asked Grisi to sing, but she refused, saying she had to go to Paris at the end of June.

   The season ended on 30 July and immediately Gye and Mario began a correspondence on the renewal of the tenor's contract for the following year. It had been rumoured that Gye was planning to sell the theatre to a company, so that he would no longer be personally liable for the huge expenses, as he had been in the past. Mario claimed that if this came about, it would mean his contract with Gye became null and void. Gye, for his part, insisted that as he would remain manager of the Royal Italian Opera, as hitherto, Mario's contract for the next three seasons remained binding.

Mario left London about 10 August with the dispute still unresolved. Gye's latest letter had been delivered to Gothic Lodge by hand, and the messenger, who signed himself H. Nelson, wrote to Gye on 9 August: 'Sir, I delivered your letter into Signor Mario's hands last night at about a quarter past eight. He read it, but said there was no answer. Not being well I did not return to the theatre last evening, but had I known you would not have been here today, I would have come to Springfield [Gye's own house in Wandsworth] to let you know the result. From what I saw in the passage I would conclude that in a day or two Signor Mario will leave London.'

MARIO ESCORTED HIS family to Florence, but was himself able to stay only a few days at the Villa Salviati, as he had been engaged by J. H. Mapleson for the autumn tour of the company from Her Majesty's Theatre. Antonio Giuglini, the company's usual tenor, had begun to show signs of insanity earlier in the year and was put into an asylum, where he died in October.

Mario's engagement gave him the opportunity of singing with Therese Tietjens, the soprano who, more than any other, could be said to have inherited the mantle of Giulia Grisi. Gye's two pocket prime donne, Patti and Lucca, were phenomenally gifted, but neither had the range of Tietjens, who excelled in roles as disparate as Norma, Semiramide, Lucrezia Borgia, Donna Anna and Valentine (*Les Huguenots*), all once sung by Grisi.

The tour began in Manchester on Saturday 9 September, with a performance of *Il trovatore* in which Tietjens sang Leonora, Mario was Manrico and the baritone, Charles Santley, played the Count di Luna. Mario was not in good voice; he suffered from hoarseness after his hurried journey from Italy, and this indisposition had so increased by 11 September that he was unable to sing in that evening's performance of *Faust*. His place was taken by Roberto Stagno, the then 25-year-old Sicilian tenor who would, many years later, create the role of Turiddu in Mascagni's *Cavalleria rusticana*.

By Wednesday Mario had recovered and as the Duke in *Rigoletto* exhibited, according to the *Manchester Guardian* critic, 'a marked improvement over his performance of Saturday night, much of the power and sweetness of voice being regained.'

The following day, Thursday 14 September, Santley sang the title role of *Don Giovanni* for the first time in his career. 'As usual I had one rehearsal the morning of the day of performance,' he wrote in his book of memoirs, *Student and Singer*. 'Mario, who was always a late riser, did not come in until we were half-way through the rehearsal; the others who, except Tietjens, had like myself never played in *Don Giovanni* before, were all present throughout. Mario, who had played the Don himself, gave me several valuable hints.'

Santley, though he did not exactly look the irresistible seducer, sang Mozart's music admirably; Tietjens was a superb Donna Anna while Mario, though as usual he cut 'Dalla sua pace,' sang 'Il mio tesoro' with his accustomed skill. On Friday, for her benefit, Tietjens chose Act I of *Fidelio*, Act III of Cherubini's *Medea* and Act II of *Un ballo in maschera*, in which last excerpt she was joined by Mario, his best voice now recovered.

By 18 September the company was in Dublin, where the first opera performed was *Faust*. 'A feature of the present engagement,' wrote the *Irish Times* critic, 'is the re-appearance of Signor Mario, the only representative of the great school of Italian artists who still retains after a public service of thirty years the power to charm an audience.'

Dublin opera-goers and music-lovers of the older generation, who had heard Mario in his hey-day, 'attended the performance not without some feeling of anxiety but also in the full confidence that so accomplished an artist must always be worth listening to. More than any singer who ever appeared on the lyric stage within the memory of the present generation, Signor Mario associates the qualities of great histrionic genius with the attractions of vocal talent.

'It would be vain to deny,' continued the *Irish Times*, that 'his voice is not what it was in the zenith of his career, but "Salve dimora" was sung with exquisite grace and finish, though freely transposed.'

Dublin was a place of many happy memories for Mario and he usually sang his best there. During this three-week season he appeared four times each week, singing, as well as Faust, the Duke of Mantua, Don Ottavio, Manrico, Lionel and Riccardo. During a performance of *Il trovatore* there occurred an incident, related by Arditi, the conductor for the tour. 'The orchestra,' he wrote, 'was not of course to be compared with that of Her Majesty's Theatre, and we had on that occasion, as on many others, been obliged to engage a scratch lot of musicians. On the night in question we had reached the last act, in which Manrico upbraids Leonora for her infidelity, when Mario suddenly smiled at the men in the orchestra and sang the words, "Ah, quest'infame, infame orchestra," substituting the word orchestra for donna, in his most passionate style.'

The Dublin season ended on 6 October with a Grand Morning Concert, at which Mario sang 'La donna è mobile' and the inevitable 'Goodbye Sweetheart'.

The Mapleson tour, as well as offering Mario the chance to sing with Tietjens, brought him a very good friend in the person of Santley. The two singers had, of course, been acquainted for several years, since the English baritone first sang in London during 1858.

Santley was nearly a quarter of a century younger than Mario, but the two men grew to feel genuine affection for each other.

'When we were together on operatic tours,' wrote Santley in *Student and Singer*, 'we generally lived together in the same hotel, and always occupied the same dressing-room in the theatre, where he smoked incessantly, leaving his cigar in his dresser's hands as he went on the stage, and taking it up immediately as he came off.' According to Santley, Mario smoked from 25 to 30 ordinary-sized cigars a day, and in Italy, where real Havanas were difficult to obtain, he used to get through 100 of the small Cavours a day.

Mario's besetting sin, laziness, is illustrated in another of Santley's anecdotes. 'I tried all in my power to induce him to rise at a decent hour—it was generally mid-day or later before he left his bedroom—but I only succeeded on one occasion.' Santley had been telling Mario about the beauty of the scenery in the vicinity of Bolton Abbey and of the picturesque state of the ruined Abbey itself. Mario became very interested and decided he would like to visit the ruins himself, but 'then came the question of starting in time. We were in Hull, and had to return to Leeds to take a train to Skipton, from which we were to take a carriage to the Abbey. The train started at half-past eight a.m. What was to be done?'

Santley arranged to pull Mario out of bed in time to catch the train. When, next morning, he found the tenor peacefully asleep, Santley was at first inclined to leave him to his slumbers, but thinking that Mario might later be disappointed to have missed the expedition, 'I pulled down the bed-clothes and literally hauled him out. I must admit,' continued Santley, 'he was much more good-natured than I should have been myself. I went into the station, took the tickets, and stood watching the clock until the finger pointed to two minutes before starting time. I told the guard of my anxiety about my friend, and as he knew me he promised to delay the train two minutes. I had given up all hope, when I descried Mario, hat in hand, rushing frantically towards the ticket-office.'

Santley pursued the tenor, grabbing him by the collar and steering him to the train for Leeds, which promptly departed. Mario at once fell asleep and Santley left him in peace until they arrived in Leeds and had to change trains. There was another moment of panic while Mario retrieved his hat, which he had left behind in the train from Hull, but Santley again craved the indulgence of the guard and the tenor, his hat safely on his head, was installed in the train to Skipton.

'We ultimately arrived all safe and sound at the Abbey, and when we returned to Leeds in the evening he told me he had never enjoyed a day so much in his life. "But I should not have gone," he said, "if you had not pulled me out of bed."'

At the end of the Mapleson tour, Mario rejoined his family in Paris. By mid-January 1866 both Mario and Grisi had returned to England for another extended concert tour of the provinces. The conductor was again Arditi, who thought that Grisi had emerged from retirement because of her extreme reluctance to give up her career while she still had any voice left at all.

No doubt that was one reason, and a powerful one, but a contributing factor was certainly the necessity of earning some money. For five years Mario alone had supported the family and he neither sang so much as before, nor did he command the enormous fees that he had earned during the early years of his career. The establishments in Paris, Florence and London, the apartment rented in Brighton for the children and their governess, all consumed vast amounts of money.

Mapleson wrote in his *Memoirs* that he paid Grisi nothing at all for her appearances, but engaged Mario at £300 a week, so that Grisi would not have to pay her husband de Melcy the percentage of her earnings to which he was still legally entitled.

The tour began at Nottingham and covered many towns in the Midlands and the North of England. On Wednesday 17 January, for instance, there was a Grand Concert at the Town Hall, Leeds. Mario and Grisi sang a duet, 'One night in Venice', by Arditi (again the conductor); Mario offered the popular 'Raggio d'amore' from Donizetti's *Il furioso*, while Grisi obliged with 'Casta diva' by request. 'The Minstrel Boy' and 'Goodbye Sweetheart' took their accustomed places in the second half, while the concert ended with the Spinning quartet from *Martha*.

A rather grander occasion was the Grand Morning Concert given on Saturday 17 February at the New Town Hall, Newcastle; the promoter, Mr Hare, announced with justifiable pride that he had 'at a large outlay engaged the services of the following Eminent Artists, it being the ONLY occasion on which such an array of talent can be brought together.' The Eminent Artists included Tietjens as well as Grisi and Stagno as well as Mario. The first half of the concert consisted of a recital from Gounod's *Faust*, and the second of a miscellaneous selection of arias and ensembles. Top price for admission was five shillings for reserved and numbered seats, while the Gallery cost only one shilling, which was surely very good value, even a century ago.

Gye, meanwhile, was still trying to get Mario to sign his engagement. He wrote on 1 February:

I learnt a few days ago that you were in England. Having been away you probably have not seen several paragraphs which have appeared in the newspapers, stating more or less positively that 'M. Mario will sing at Her Majesty's Theatre next season.' I do not want to write to the newspapers myself to deny this rumour, as I do not think my contradiction would have the same force as yours. I ask you therefore kindly to write a few lines to the newspapers which have published this false statement, or if you would prefer, to have the kindness to *write me* a note that I can send to the newspapers, which might be less bother for you.

At our last meeting, you mentioned firstly, the company who wanted to buy the theatre from me, and secondly, your contract and the clause in it which gives me the right to renew your engagement for 1866, 1867 and 1868, saying that you did not think it fair that *you* were tied to me, while I was not tied to you. As to the first point, I regret to tell you that the company have not fulfilled their obligations, so the deal is off, and the theatre is my responsibility as before.

As to the second point, Gye was willing to acknowledge that the tenor was partly justified in his objection. He offered to make the contract with Mario obligatory on both sides for the three following seasons and, 'to set your mind at rest, I ask you to accept this letter as notification that I require your services at my theatre for those years, according to our contract dated 30 July 1864. Please acknowledge this letter,' ended the manager, 'which I dare to hope you will find acceptable.'

Two days after the concert in Newcastle, the Mapleson company began a nine-day season at the Theatre Royal in Edinburgh. The season opened on Monday 19 February with *Faust*, with Tietjens and Mario. The latter was in admirable voice and, according to the *Scotsman*, he 'sang throughout like a true artist. His great air "Salve dimora" was given with an intensity of feeling positively delicious.'

The occupants of the gallery, mainly students, behaved rather badly during this performance and when Tietjens appeared before the curtain at the end of the opera, someone threw an orange at her.

The following night Grisi sang in *Norma*, with Stagno as Pollione, and on Wednesday *Il trovatore* was given, with Tietjens and Mario. Grisi sang again the next evening, in *Lucrezia Borgia*, and the *Scotsman* found her Lucrezia 'still an impersonation to which we cannot listen without admiration.' The week ended with *Don Giovanni*, in which

Mario sang Don Ottavio and Tietjens was the Donna Anna; then, after a repeat of *Faust*, the season closed on Wednesday 27 February with a benefit performance for Tietjens. This entertainment comprised Act II of *Der Freischütz*; Act I of *Norma*, with Grisi in much better voice than at the complete performance the previous week; Act III of *Don Pasquale*, in which Mario had as usual to repeat 'Com' è gentil'; and Act I of *La traviata*.

The company then moved to Glasgow, where the same operas were performed. Grisi sang in *Norma*, *Lucrezia Borgia* and *Don Giovanni*, and the state of her voice was such that Mapleson engaged her for his summer season at Her Majesty's Theatre in London. Since Grisi's retirement from Covent Garden, the five years stipulated by Gye, during which she was not to sing at any other London theatre than his, had now gone by. It was twenty years since Grisi and the other members of the *vieille garde* had abandoned Her Majesty's and when Mapleson announced that he 'had prevailed upon Mme. Grisi to revisit the scene of her early triumphs, and again to appear at the Theatre, her previous connection with which formed one of the most brilliant epochs in operatic history,' the interest aroused was naturally very great.

Grisi's first appearance was to be on Saturday 5 May in *Lucrezia Borgia*. According to Mapleson she showed signs of nervousness and had been visited by misgivings before the performance began. 'I had done my best,' he wrote, 'to reassure her, and was under the impression, judging from the apparent result, that I had succeeded. But her hands, I remember, just as she was going on, were extremely cold. I took them in my own, and found that they were like stone.'

An eye-witness account of the performance was provided by Lady Geraldine who, although she was certainly prejudiced in favour of Grisi, was also a shrewd and truthful observer. 'We went to the nasty Her Majesty's to see the rentrée of poor dear Grisi,' she wrote. 'She appeared in *Lucrezia Borgia* with [the tenor Pietro] Mongini, was gloriously beautiful, her acting as superb as ever and really sang the whole 1st act divinely, but it was such a vile cold audience, ignorant fools, incapable of judging for themselves, unknowing of music, *not having been told by a newspaper*, whether they were to applaud her, they sat like lumps of flesh and except Blanche's [the Countess of Kinnoul, Lady Geraldine's sister] and mine scarce a hand in the house moved, it was too chilling and depressing, and told tremendously on her. She was already very nervous, but in such really fine voice, a little encouraged she would have carried all before her, instead of which she was chilled, mortified and one felt it was an effort. Yet she was so fine in the trio, and the end, her acting her gestes, glorious. Blanche and I were miserable.'

The performance was almost certainly not the fiasco it has sometimes been made out, but Grisi's confidence in herself was badly shaken and she did not sing again at Her Majesty's, though *Norma* had been announced for Monday 7 May. The following day Lady Geraldine went in the afternoon to her sister Blanche's house in Belgrave Square to meet Grisi and her three daughters. Almost immediately after her arrival, Lady Geraldine received a telegram with news that her mother was ill, so she had to leave again at once. 'Met Grisi on the doorstep as I went out,' she noted in her Diary, 'just spoke to her, and she told me she was very displeased at her reception on Saturday, as well she might be.'

The Royal Italian Opera season at Covent Garden had opened on 3 April with Mario in *Un ballo in maschera*. Two days later, he sang in *Il trovatore*, in excellent voice and a week after that, on Thursday 11 April, in *Le Prophète*. As Davison wrote in *The Times*, 'none can witness Signor Mario's Jean of Leyden at the present time . . . without admitting that, in his way, Signor Mario is a phenomenon.'

At the end of the month the tenor appeared as Fernando in *La favorita*, thus regaining one of the roles of which he had complained of being deprived the previous season. Chorley praised 'the charming, spontaneous, and withal thoroughly noble, and chivalresque, vocal and dramatic art, which Signor Mario sets forth, and which he will set forth till Time strikes on the clock and warns the singer to be still.'

Mario was not singing on Saturday 5 May, so presumably he was present at the performance of *Lucrezia Borgia* at Her Majesty's. Four weeks later, on 2 June, he himself appeared in Donizetti's opera, for the first time for six years at Covent Garden. 'Signor Mario's Gennaro is wonderful for the beauty and semblance of youth still thrown into it by him,' wrote Chorley. 'As a piece of operatic acting nothing can exceed it.'

Mario also sang in two performances of *L'elisir d'amore*, with Patti, Faure and Ronconi, which were his last appearances in the role of Nemorino; and there were nine performances of *Faust* with Mario and Lucca. Mario also sang the Garden scene with Patti at her benefit on Wednesday 25 July and the season ended three days later.

That autumn Mario was again invited to join Mapleson's operatic tour. Grisi and the children were installed in Florence at the Villa Salviati, while the Paris house in the rue des Bassins was let to Patti, whose entourage included her father, Maurice Strakosch her manager and brother-in-law, and her companion, Karolyn Baumeister.

Mapleson's tour opened in Dublin on Monday 17 September with *Faust*; the cast included Tietjens, Mario and Santley. Two days later Mario sang in *Martha*. He was in particularly fine voice and sang 'M'appari' in the original key of F, reaching a perfect final B flat. The piece was naturally encored and when he had repeated it—and the B flat—the tenor was wildly applauded. *Il trovatore* was added to the repertory on Saturday and this time it was Manrico's 'Di quella pira' which brought the audience cheering to its feet.

Les Huguenots, *Rigoletto* (with an encore for 'La donna è mobile') and *Don Giovanni* followed in the second week of the season. During the third week the same operas were repeated and the season ended on Saturday 6 October with the usual Grand Morning Concert, at which Mario sang 'Goodbye Sweetheart' and, as an encore, 'Com'è gentil'. He also took part in the quintet from *Un ballo in maschera* and the Spinning quartet from *Martha*.

From Dublin the company went to Leeds and then to Hull. By Monday 15 October they were in Liverpool for 'the Grand Inauguration and opening of the New Prince of Wales Theatre with a season of 12 nights of Italian Opera,' as the *Liverpool Daily Post* announced. The first performance began with the National Anthem; Tietjens and Santley sang a verse each. This was followed by *Faust*, with the same cast as in Dublin.

'The Faust of Mario was an immense surprise,' wrote the *Daily Post* critic, 'and it really seemed as though the interference of Mephistopheles had revived the singer's powers with marvellous effect. To say that Mario is what he was would be absurd; but that he should have the vocal energy, the command of his upper notes, and so much of the excellence of the past, is simply astonishing.' As usual it was 'Salve dimora' and the duet with Marguerite at the end of the Garden scene that received most praise.

Don Giovanni followed on Tuesday night and then on Thursday, *Il trovatore*. Mario apparently saved his voice during the first two acts, but in the third he gave a polished account of 'Ah si ben mio' and once more astonished the *Liverpool Daily Post* critic by the vigour of his singing and the steadiness and fulness of tone with which he took the upper notes in 'Di quella pira'.

The *Daily Post* expressed reservations, though, about the performance of *Les Huguenots* on Monday 22 October: 'Tietjens, admirable as we are bound to admit her, is neither Grisi nor Viardot, and Mario unfortunately is not so young as he was; but,' continued the critic, 'his every phrase is a study, his method is so perfect, his stage business so finished, and despite of impaired power, his voice is so good at times that we are simply astonished as well as delighted. There were places where the old fire was as bright as ever, like some old war horse hearing the trumpet sounding the charge, and rushing to the front to do or die.'

Whether or not Mario appreciated being likened to an old war horse, he was certainly in fine voice that autumn and had no intention of dying, in any sense, for quite some time yet. *Martha*, introduced to the new theatre on Wednesday 24 October, was considered the best all-round performance of the short season. After a repeat of *Faust* on Friday, the Grand Inauguration finished with a concert on Saturday 27 October. Mario and Tietjens sang the last-act duet from *Don Pasquale* and 'by popular request' Mario obliged with 'Goodbye Sweetheart'. The Mapleson tour had to end in Liverpool as both Tietjens and Santley were expected in Norwich the following week, to sing in Handel's *Israel in Egypt*.

Mario joined his family in Florence at the beginning of November. In December Garibaldi honoured the tenor with a special visit to the Villa Salviati to thank him for all the help he had given the cause for a free and united Italy over the past 25 years.

Mario drove Garibaldi and his son and daughter from Florence in his own carriage. Grisi, together with her eldest daughter, Rita, and all the servants and peasants from the estate, waited on the terrace of the Villa Salviati. Those of the tenants who had been followers of the General wore their red shirts. Cecilia, Mario's second daughter, described the arrival of Garibaldi: 'By degrees a crowd of men, women and children collected in the avenue, and presently the sound of cheering and cries of "Viva Garibaldi! Viva Garibaldi!" gave notice to those on the terrace of the guest's approach. Then came the carriage followed by a cheering crowd of people. Mario was the first to alight, followed immediately by Garibaldi, who kissed the Diva's hand repeatedly. Grisi was so moved that her tears flowed unrestrainedly.'

After Garibaldi's daughter had been presented to Grisi and her daughter Rita to Garibaldi, the latter thanked his hosts for their kind welcome. Then, continued Cecilia, 'Mario spoke a few words of warm welcome, and in his pure ringing voice started the Garibaldian hymn, in which Grisi joined and, finally, all the people crowding round.'

Cecilia herself and her younger sister Clelia were waiting inside the villa to be presented to Garibaldi, who kissed them and promised to send them a signed photograph of himself—a promise that, according to Cecilia, he kept. After refreshments had been served, Garibaldi recounted some of his experiences in the long battle to free and unite Italy. When he left, again escorted by Mario, he was 'as enthusi-astically cheered on his departure as he had been on his arrival, the peasants crowding round the carriage to shake his hand or touch him.'

This visit must have given enormous pleasure to Mario, who was now vindicated in the eyes of the world for his actions 30 years previously when he had been forced to desert from his regiment and abandon his family and country. Cavour, the friend and inspiration of Mario's youth, was dead, while Mazzini had refused to acknowledge the monarchy under which Italy had been united. Only Garibaldi, therefore, of the three chief architects of free Italy, remained to express the gratitude owed to the many patriots and exiles who had helped the cause. In Mario's case, this gratitude was shown in the most public and gratifying way imaginable.

At the end of February 1867 Mario had to return to England, or rather to Scotland, in order to join Mapleson's spring tour. After appearing in Glasgow, the company arrived in Edinburgh on Monday 18 March for a two-week season, opening as usual with *Faust*. Mario next sang on Wednesday, in *Martha*, and the *Scotsman* found his Lionel 'a wonderfully fine performance . . . All through he sang and acted as still the greatest tenor of the lyric stage.'

Il trovatore and *Don Giovanni* followed on Thursday and Saturday respectively, then the second week began with a performance of *Les Huguenots* in which Tietjens and Mario were much applauded in the great duet. Mario's final appearance was to have been in *Martha* on Thursday 28 March, as he then had to leave for London. Another tenor had been engaged for the final two performances in Edinburgh, but on Saturday, the last night, when *Les Huguenots* was repeated for Tietjens's benefit, a 'Signor Tasca was to have impersonated Raoul, but his continued indisposition rendered this impossible, and Signor Mario kindly delayed his departure in order that the public might not be disappointed by any change in the opera.'

The theatre was full that night and the audience, according to the *Scotsman*, 'testified by frequent and hearty applause [its] thorough appreciation of the performance.' Mario left for London immediately afterwards. In his *Memoirs* Mapleson claims that he, too, travelled overnight from Edinburgh to London, in order to attend the opening night of the Royal Italian Opera season at Covent Garden on Tuesday 2 April, when he professes to have heard Mario in *Un ballo in maschera*. In fact, as Harold Rosenthal has pointed out in his edition of Maple-son's *Memoirs*, the 1867 season opened with *Norma*, and *Un ballo in maschera* did not enter the repertory until 23 April. The previous season, however, *did* open with Mario in *Un ballo in maschera* (on 3

April 1866) and Mapleson, always cavalier in his treatment of dates, was probably confusing the two years.

In 1867 Mario made his first appearance of the season at Covent Garden on the second night, Thursday 4 April, in *Faust*.

During May, Mario went to Paris, to hear Gounod's new opera, *Roméo et Juliette*, which had had its première at the Théâtre-Lyrique on 27 April and which was already in preparation at Covent Garden. *Don Giovanni*, which had been announced for 23 May, was postponed owing to Patti's indisposition and finally given on Friday 31 May, when Mario sang Don Ottavio, a part he had not sung in London for ten years, since the season before his attempt at the title role of Mozart's opera. Although suffering from a cold caught on his recent visit to Paris, Mario sang again the following night, in *Faust* with Lucca, and on Monday 3 June in *Il barbiere* with Patti.

Both of Gye's pocket prime donne then succumbed to indisposition, and the manager wrote to Mario on Wednesday to ask if he could sing *Un ballo in maschera* the following night. Mario replied at once:

> A veritable thunderbolt has fallen on my head. You say that two have already fallen on you from Patti and Lucca, but my God, I am not very well either, and on Friday I have to sing Don Ottavio again. If you could give *Masaniello* or something else, or *Ballo in maschera* with Fancelli, it would be a great kindness to me, especially as I have arranged to go to the theatre at 2 o'clock to study my Romeo with Licalzi—you know it means I am really ill if I say I cannot.
>
> If there is no other solution, and if I am better than today, then your will and that of Heaven will no doubt be done. I am to be pitied, you are to be pitied, send me a ray of hope tomorrow, I entreat you.

Gye did not wait until the next day, but wrote again to Mario at 10.15 the same evening:

> I am in despair, *Ballo in maschera* will be announced in tomorrow morning's newspapers, and it is now too late to alter the announcement. Unluckily I have to go to Ascot tomorrow morning, and I dine with the Duke of Sutherland at his house, where the Prince of Wales will be a guest. I hope you will be well enough to sing, because it would be terrible to change the opera tomorrow yet again. I do not think that Fancelli knows the role [of Riccardo]. In

any case I will send Harris to you tomorrow morning. I must apologise for having announced you like this, but I was so upset I quite forgot you were singing Don Ottavio the following day.

Mario was well enough to sing Riccardo in *Un ballo in maschera* on 6 June as well as in *Don Giovanni* on 7 June; by the following week, both Patti and Lucca were recovered.

Mario's Romeo, the last new role he was to take on, though not quite so popular as his Faust, was nevertheless greatly admired during the remaining years of his career. The first London performance of Gounod's operatic version of Shakespeare's tragedy took place at Covent Garden on Thursday 11 July, with Patti as Juliette and Mario as 'a picturesque Romeo. His is the bearing,' wrote Chorley in the *Athenaeum*, 'which befits the son of a noble house. The stage has had no such lover as he. As a personation his Romeo will presently pair off with his Raoul, since on his first taking up a part he is habitually apt to be uncertain in his effects; but the indication of the real character is throughout evident and in the great scenes he is intense yet delicate to a wish, without a shade of extravagance.'

The second performance of *Roméo et Juliette* was announced for Saturday 13 July. Mario had a relaxed throat and asked Gye to make an apology for his indisposition—'the thirteenth is always fatal for me,' he wrote—but Davison in *The Times* considered him the ideal Romeo, whatever his state of health. At the first performance Mario had worn a blond wig, but he thought it made him look ridiculous and at subsequent performances he merely added extra curls to his own dark hair.

Playing opposite a Juliet of twenty-four, the 57-year-old tenor could still look convincing as a young lover on stage. The enormous care he took over his costumes also helped the illusion. A few days before the first performance of *Roméo*, Mario had sent Gye the unpaid bill for his costumes in *Faust*, bought three years previously in Paris. The bill amounted to £57-6-1 and Gye paid it without comment.

Roméo et Juliette was repeated three times the following week and twice the week after that, when the Royal Italian Opera season ended on Saturday 27 July with the seventh performance of Gounod's opera.

Chapter 16

MARIO HAD NO engagement for the winter of 1867/68 and after the usual autumn visit to Florence, spent the winter months in Paris with Grisi and the children. The weather was exceptionally cold, with heavy snowfalls and the girls enjoyed sleighing in the Bois de Boulogne, where the Emperor Napoleon III, an acquaintance of Mario's since the 1830s, would sometimes drive them in his own sleigh. It was the last winter that Mario and his family spent in the house in the rue des Bassins, as the following year the house was sold to a Russian Princess.

By the beginning of April 1868 the move to London was accomplished and the family settled at Arlington House, Turnham Green. That season Mario sang in eleven different operas at Covent Garden, including two, *I puritani* and *Lucia di Lammermoor*, in which he had not appeared for many years. But it was in the Gounod operas that he sang most frequently, eight times as Faust and four times as Romeo, the 55th and 56th roles of his long career.

Cecilia de Candia, now fifteen years old, began to keep a diary. The first entry was dated Wednesday 24 June, 1868.

San Giovanni, dear papa's saint day, and we kept it as his birthday; we all gave him presents. In the morning several friends came to see him, and remained to dinner, and we three girls were allowed to sit up for the occasion. Papa made me make a speech in Italian to his honour. I thought I should have died with fright. After dinner we did some tableaux vivants, and Clelia and I acted the last act of *Il trovatore* with great success. We wound up with dancing the Tarantella, and had great fun.

Patti's benefit was taken on the penultimate evening of the season, Thursday 23 July. For once all three of Mario's daughters were allowed to attend the opera, 'which was an exciting event for Clelia and me,' wrote Cecilia.

Papa does not at all like our going, and he says he is always more nervous if he knows we are there. Adelina Patti and papa sang the first act of *Romeo and Giulietta* . . . His costume was lovely, prune de monsieur satin, with jet trimmings. He sketched out his dress himself, and was most particular, even to the gloves, and looked admirable. Then came the third act of *Faust*, which I know by heart, as he has often made Clelia play it over to see if the words which he wrote for himself went well with the music. Then we had the last act of the *Figlia del reggimento*, the nun scene from *Robert le diable*, and finally God Save the Queen. The house was crammed, and papa enthusiastically received, and Patti covered with flowers.

This was the last performance given by Patti before her marriage to the Marquis de Caux. Apparently she had never been confirmed, and asked Giulia Grisi to be her sponsor.

Cecilia's diary continues:

Monday, July 27. A warm bright day. Mamma has gone to the confirmation of Adelina Patti, and papa has given her as a cadeau the coral earrings of the Queen of Naples, and mamma gives her a diamond locket.

Wednesday, July 29. We were up at seven, and dressed in new white dresses. Rita is bridesmaid to Adelina. There was a great commotion, as breakfast was not ready, and papa not up. So mamma, Rita and I went first to Adelina's. There were many people there, and she has received some lovely presents. She was dressed in a gown from Worth's sent from Paris. It was of white satin, and fitted like a glove. She was pale and sad. The Marquis de Caux also seemed out of sorts; he has lost the diamond out of the ring which Adelina gave him as a wedding-gift, and he is suspicious of bad luck in consequence. The little Roman Catholic church was crammed, and she was given away by her father, who is a very old man, and seemed very nervous.

Salvatore Patti was in fact only in his late sixties and about ten years older than Mario. He died the following year.

Mario must have arrived in time for the ceremony, as while Patti and the Marquis de Caux were exchanging their vows, he whispered to his neighbour in the pew, H. Sutherland Edwards, '*he* may be marrying her, but *I* have made love to her many more times.'

There was a wedding breakfast at the Pattis' house in Clapham, followed by speeches and toasts. The entire party was photographed in the garden. Almost immediately after the wedding, Mario, Grisi and the three girls left London for Scarborough, where they were to spend the month of August.

Mario's three-year contract with Gye expired at the end of the 1868 season. At the beginning of August Gye sent the tenor a new contract, offering him an engagement for 1869 for three months at a salary of £700 a month. Mario returned the contract unsigned, demanding £800 a month and an additional clause to the effect that he need not sing at private parties or concerts, not more than three times a week in the theatre and never on two nights running. He then left London for Scarborough.

Gye sent the contract back to Mario on 30 August, with a letter in which he wrote:

I heard by accident last night that you were in London, and leaving today. I have added the clauses you demanded to the contract, that is to say those dealing with private concerts and the number of performances a week. It was your own suggestion you should come for three months, and when I saw you at Arlington House, it was clearly understood that you had accepted the conditions of three months at £700 a month.

I must tell you that it is *very possible* that next year I will not be *alone* in the direction of my theatre, and that I shall not be able to do exactly as I wish. So please let me persuade you to sign the contract as it stands. This is the advice of a friend.

Mario did not take notice of this advice and returned the contract, still unsigned, to Gye the same evening. In an accompanying letter he argued:

If you give me a season of four months, I will leave the salary at £700, but if you only engage me for three months from 27 April, I must insist on receiving £800 a month—the expenses will be the same, and you will have saved four hundred pounds, which with the £113 you have kept back this season, is five hundred pounds less that I shall have earned.

I have done many favours for your administration, and have been of some help to your theatre, without ever demanding any extra compensation—I have made many sacrifices to help establish Covent Garden, and am only too happy to have done so, but please excuse me for reminding you, that after that it is unworthy of you to bargain over the last notes of my career. I know that you are manager of a theatre, but I thought you were also a *gentleman* and a friend. I leave for the continent this evening and send you my best wishes.

Every word that Mario wrote was true, but he would have done much better to take notice of Gye's genuinely friendly warning. Gye, as he hinted in his letter, was already making plans for a joint season with Mapleson, whose theatre, Her Majesty's, had burned down the previous December. Mapleson found a temporary home at Drury Lane, but already in June 1868 he had received a letter from Gye, suggesting that their companies should join forces the following year. Mapleson rented Covent Garden from Gye for his autumn season and negotiations were able to continue in secret.

Meanwhile, after a few days at the Bath Hotel in Piccadilly (which stood where the Ritz now stands), Mario and his family set off for Venice, which they were to visit before returning to Florence. They journeyed by way of Brussels, Cologne and Frankfurt, from where they drove to Bad Homburg, where Patti and the Marquis of Caux were staying. From Frankfurt they travelled to Munich, taking seventeen hours in intense heat. All the hotels in Munich were full, as the wedding between Princess Sophie (once engaged to King Ludwig II) and the Duke of Alençon was to take place the following Sunday. So Mario and his party continued to Verona, where they stayed for 24 hours at the Hotel de la Tour de Londres. From Verona Grisi and Cecilia travelled to Venice, while Mario and the other two girls followed a day or two later. The whole party then journeyed to Florence, arriving on 16 September. For the first time since Mario had bought the Villa Salviati, they were able to go the whole way by train to Florence. The railway line between Bologna and Florence was only completed that year, and previously they had had to take the diligence, a carriage that held six people comfortably, for the last stage of the journey. The diligence was usually escorted by mounted carabinieri, as the mountain roads between Bologna and Florence were still infested by bandits and Grisi, who had been stopped by brigands once when she was a girl, always insisted on a double escort.

In September 1868 Mario and the family found their own carriage waiting for them at the station in Florence, as well as the girls' pony-carriage.

'We found the villa and garden looking beautiful,' wrote Cecilia in her diary, 'and the weather is divine, so soft and mild, and the perfume of the flowers completely pervades the place. Clelia and I drove to the

villa in our little pony-carriage with the two little black Sardinian
ponies that papa has given us; they are very rare, and are like tiny little
horses. We have them harnessed in the Russian manner, and they are
much admired. Clelia and I take it in turns to drive them.'

The week after their arrival in Florence, there was a severe thunder-
storm and the Villa Salviati was struck by lightning, which caused a
considerable amount of damage. A monk from the monastery at
Fiesole was sent for the next morning to put up a lightning-conductor.

It had now become imperative for Mario, the indulgent papa who
could deny his children nothing and gave them rare Sardinian ponies
to drive in their pony-carriage, to earn some money. On 8 November he set off for St Petersburg, where he had a five-month
engagement. Grisi and the girls remained at the villa. The following Saturday, 14 November, Grisi and Rita went to the Pergola
Theatre in Florence, but returned almost immediately, as they had
heard the news of Rossini's death the previous day in Paris. Cecilia
wrote:

Mamma felt it deeply. She had known him from a child, and had
been in the habit of visiting him continually when in Paris, and
taking us children with her. I fancy I see the great composer now,
sitting at a long table covered with manuscript music, paper, pens
and ink, and in the centre of the table four bonnet-stands, with four
different wigs on them—curly, frizzled, cropped short hair, or long
and wavy. Our delight was to ask him to put these wigs on
alternately, and he did so, much to our amusement.

We used to sing to him, and he was very pleased with my
rendering of the *Inflammatus* [from Rossini's own *Stabat Mater*]
when I was but eight years old. He gave us each a new silver 50
centime piece, saying, 'Je paye toujours mes artistes.' He also gave
me his photograph, which I have now, and written on by himself,
'A ma vaillante interprète, Cecilia de Candia—G. Rossini, 4 Mai
1867.'

The date on the photograph reveals that Cecilia was fourteen, not
eight, at the time of this episode. On the day of Rossini's funeral in
Paris, Saturday 21 November, memorial services and performances of
his music were held throughout Italy. In Florence the *Stabat Mater* was
performed at Santa Croce. Grisi sang, making what was to be her very
last public appearance, but not Mario, as Cecilia erroneously states; he
was already in St Petersburg.

During his long absence that winter, Mario was greatly missed by

Grisi and his daughters, who wrote to him every day. Because of Grisi's invidious position, she was not invited to official or semi-official functions. Lady Paget, wife of the British Ambassador, left an evocative if slightly malicious description of the ex-Diva at this period.

> Grisi had left off singing, but not spending money. She never drove to Florence with her three little Grisettes, as her daughters had been wittily nicknamed, without spending seven or eight hundred francs at the jewellers . . . The whole of Florence used to drive to the villa on Grisi's day, when the most delightful music was performed, but nobody ever dreamt of asking her to their house because Grisi was not married to Mario, her husband being still alive. Grisi even then had a fine head, but she was very stout. The three girls, Rita, Cecilia and Clelia, were all pretty and rather like her, but on a smaller scale.

Grisi, according to Lady Paget, never returned a card. 'It was the eldest girl who left it with *Rita de Candia* on it and above it was written, in pencil, *et Madame*, a very clever way of getting out of the difficulty.'

At the request of a mutual friend, Lady Paget invited Grisi and her three daughters to a ball she gave in the embassy. 'People stared prodigiously at first, but whether with horror at the innovation or at Grisi's world-famous black pearls, I did not try to find out, but after this Florence opened its arms to them.'

On his return from Russia, Mario went to thank Lady Paget. 'His hair and beard were already snow-white, but he looked so fresh and clean, with his pink cheeks and bright brown eyes, wearing a white waistcoat, a lavender-coloured-batiste tie and lemon-coloured kid gloves.'

Mario almost certainly dyed his hair and beard to their original shade of dark brown until he retired altogether from the theatre. Lady Paget, who saw him frequently in Rome a few years later, when his hair was indeed snow-white, may have recollected wrongly in this account, written over 50 years later.

The winter passed, and at last on Friday 9 April, 1869 a telegram arrived from Mario, announcing his arrival in Florence that evening. The whole family drove to the railway-station to meet him, the children so excited they were unable to keep still. As the train appeared and Mario was glimpsed leaning out of a carriage window, they burst into a cheer, crying out 'There he is!'

The next morning the presents that Mario had brought Grisi and the girls from St Petersburg were unpacked. 'He gave us each a Greek cross in gold set with turquoises, and a fan and bracelet,' chronicled Cecilia, 'also to each a *baslik* in red and gold.' These hoods, worn over one's hat and covering the shoulders as well, were made in dark colours for day-wear, 'but for evening wear they are made of very costly material. For dear mother he brought a white one, richly embroidered in gold thread. To mother he also gave the ring which the Emperor had presented him on the occasion of his benefit—a large ruby surrounded by eight large diamonds; also a pin with a large single black pearl.'

His adoring public had presented the tenor with a beautiful tea service; on the lid of the box containing it was written: 'Au plus grand des artistes, Mario, de ses admirateurs de son talent sublime.' The tea service was in gold, with views of Moscow on the pieces. 'He also received a splendid gold and vermeil vase, inscribed "au Roi des chanteurs" and the titles of all the operas in which he sang are engraved upon the vase.'

As Mario was not singing in London, for the first time for 30 years, that spring he took his family on a tour of Tuscany, visiting Siena, Pisa, Bagni di Lucca and other cities. During July and August the family went to Wiesbaden, to provide a change of air and to teach the girls German.

Mario was already in communication with Gye and Mapleson, whose first joint season had been a considerable success. They offered the tenor a contract for three months, to begin on 25 April 1870, at £700 a month, to sing only in London or at the Crystal Palace. Mario insisted again on the clause 'only three times a week, and never two nights running,' to avoid, as he wrote to Gye, 'the farce of the previous season, when hardly had I arrived back from the Crystal Palace, and without dining, I had to sing Faust in the evening.' Otherwise he agreed to the contract, which Gye signed on 25 August and immediately sent to Mario in Wiesbaden for his signature.

Mario and Grisi, meanwhile, were receiving visitors in Wiesbaden. Grisi's son Frederick Ormsby, now a Captain in the Second Dragoon Guards, was there during August, and also Colonel Walker, a friend from Berlin. Lady Geraldine Somerset, who was staying at Rumpenheim, near Frankfurt, with Princess Augusta, Grand-Duchess of Mecklenburg-Strelitz, the Duchess of Cambridge's elder daughter, came over to Wiesbaden for the day on Saturday 7 August. She was accompanied by her niece, Lady Constance Dupplin, the daughter of Lady Geraldine's sister Blanche, the Countess of Kinnoul. Lady Geraldine wrote:

Cecilia, Clelia, Rita came to meet us, and took us to their room, where immediately Grisi came; we sat and talked a minute or two and then Grisi said 'I'll fetch him' . . . in came Mario with Capt. Ormsby and Colonel Walker of Strelitz and Berlin, who was just paying them a visit. We all sat together ½ an hour and talked of Wiesbaden, Prussia and Prussians, Petersburg, etc. When Sissy [Lady Constance] and I got up and said good-bye, Mario having rung the bell gave us his arm, and we went downstairs together to the door and there parted.

In the afternoon Lady Geraldine and her niece were on the promenade listening to the band when they met Grisi and the girls again, 'and we walked about the rest of the time with them.' Grisi went back to their house to see if Mario would not join them, then Rita went to fetch Grisi, 'then we all walked about again together. At length at 20 to 6 our pleasant day came to an end and we were obliged to take leave of them all, so sorry to part, have *so* enjoyed it, everything has gone well.'

A month later Lady Geraldine was staying in Bad Homburg with her sister Lady Kinnoul. On Saturday 11 September she wrote in her diary that 'about ¼ to 11 I started with Sissy for Wiesbaden, which we reached at 1 and went to the Kursaal to secure seats for the concert on Monday; then up to 4 Sonnenbergerstrasse and called on Grisi, who asked us to luncheon and we had a charming luncheon with her, Mario and their 3 daughters, rice, poached eggs, cold beef, cold chicken, cheese and grapes, then coffee—a great deal of talk.' Having arranged to go to Monday's concert with Grisi and her family, Lady Geraldine and her niece returned to Homburg by train.

The following Monday Lady Geraldine, together with her sister and niece, left Homburg at three in the afternoon, reaching Frankfurt at five o'clock. They dined at the Hotel de la Rose and just before seven walked up to 4 Sonnenbergerstrasse. Lady Geraldine wrote:

Grisi met us at the foot of her stairs. They offered us tea but we all agreed it would be better to have it after the concert, so we sat and talked with her and Mario and the 3 girls till 7.20, and then all walked together down to the Kursaal to the concert—Lucca and Delle Sedie sang, Vieuxtemps on the violin, Brassin a Belgian on the piano. When it was over we went again to their house, and had a *very* merry gay tea, and after much fun and greatly enjoying it, at 10.25 taking a very cordial leave, we started [back to Homburg].

Mario, Grisi and the girls left Wiesbaden on Thursday 16 September. They stayed that night at the Hotel d'Angleterre in Frankfurt and next morning Grisi and Clelia were shopping when they met Lady Geraldine, who was now back at Rumpenheim. Later in the day they all met again. This time Grisi and Clelia were accompanied by Mario, who jumped out of a fiacre to greet Lady Geraldine, exclaiming: 'Charmé de pouvoir encore une fois vous dire adieu!' The following day Mario, Grisi and the girls left Frankfurt for Munich and thence to Florence and the Villa Salviati. They were accompanied by the girls' former governess, Fräulein Gutermann.

Less than a month later the whole family set off once more, for this winter Grisi and the girls were to accompany Mario to St Petersburg. Grisi was not well; she had been suffering from toothache and a carbuncle on her neck behind the ear. When the party left Florence on 25 October, Grisi seems to have had a premonition that she would not see the Villa Salviati again. The girls were thrilled at the idea of visiting Russia.

The party travelled by slow stages, stopping in Munich so that Grisi could receive treatment for her neck. On the way to Berlin their train was involved in an accident. The engine ran off the line down a steep embankment, and the coach in which the three girls and Fräulein Gutermann were travelling was dragged after it. Cecilia was hit in the spine by a heavy box which fell from the luggage rack, otherwise they were not hurt, beyond a severe shaking. The coach in which Mario and Grisi were travelling did not leave the line, but they, too, were badly shaken.

It was now November, the weather was very cold with snow lying on the ground. During the long wait before their journey could be continued, Mario caught a bad cold. At last they arrived in Berlin, where Grisi and the girls were to stay at the Hotel du Nord, Unter den Linden, while Mario continued to St Petersburg to arrange for their accommodation.

'When we reached the hotel,' wrote Cecilia, 'mother's condition was very sad. She complained of a sense of suffocation, and frequently expressed her conviction that she was doomed to die at the hotel. My dear father did his utmost to calm her and assure her that she was upset with the long journey, and eventually he succeeded in persuading her to lie down and take some repose.'

Mario started for St Petersburg the next evening and after Grisi had said goodbye to him at the door of the hotel, she turned to her daughters, saying: 'Je ne le verrai plus.' Weeping bitterly she hurried to their rooms and 'after this she never left the apartments to take her customary long walks and her unwillingness in this respect, and her increasing weakness, began to make us very nervous about her.'

Grisi was also suffering from severe dysentery and inflammation of the bowel, while the doctor who was called in said he ought to operate on the carbuncle, but Grisi would not give her consent. On 24 November she had an apoplectic stroke, and her condition was obviously serious. That night Cecilia slept in her room—the girls took it in turns to do so—and was kept awake by her mother's feverish and rambling speech. Towards morning Grisi fell asleep.

'The sun appearing through the blinds,' wrote Cecilia, 'I looked out of the window to see the military band pass, playing the march from *Le Prophète*, and turned round to observe if it had awakened her. I saw her sitting up, her eyes apparently fixed on something in front of her. "Mamma, do you want anything?" I asked. "Bella, la mia Bella!" she said, in a faint, low voice, and her expression of face told me she was dying.'

Cecilia rushed into the next room to waken her sisters and a maid was sent to fetch the doctor. 'We all crowded round her,' continued Cecilia, 'I on my knees to get near her, and Clelia, with a bunch of violets (her favourite flowers), which we put under her cheek as she lay on the pillow. She seemed to see and hear us, and fixed her eyes alternately on each of our faces, as if she wished to, but could not speak.'

Towards midday Grisi, who had been unconscious for some time, opened her eyes. 'She then looked round her and upwards with a smile. We heard a gasping, gurgling noise in her throat, which frightened us, and we cried "Mamma, Mamma." A deep sigh was the only answer to our cry, and our beloved, kind mother was gone.'

Colonel Walker took charge of all the arrangements and telegraphed to Mario in St Petersburg. He also telegraphed to Lady Geraldine, who was at Strelitz with the Duchess of Cambridge, staying with Princess Augusta. The Court dined at five o'clock. Lady Geraldine wrote:

Just as we sat down they brought me a telegram from Colonel Walker—Grisi *died* today at noon! oh the horror, just at that moment, in the paraphernalia of court dinner!! too terrible! Thank heaven I had nice dear little Lühe [the Grand Duke's equerry] next to me, kind, sympathetic, and sensible; *nice* little man, so helpful and kind.

Poor, poor children, all alone, helpless, how terrible! My first longing was to go to them and sat on tenter-hooks through the

interminable dinner, which lasted so long it was too late for me to
take tonight's diligence, before I could ask the Duchess [of Cam-
bridge]. Told her and P[rincess] A[ugusta] at once after dinner,
settled with them I should go tomorrow early, then got away to my
room. No, it's *too* terrible, thus *alone* in an Hotel, far from her
home, far from *him*. Oh it is beyond all words sad, poor children!

Lady Geraldine obviously wrote up her diary that night, while still
suffering from the shock of the news. But she was practical as well as
highly emotional, and next morning, Friday 26 November, she left
Strelitz at a quarter to eight, in cold, foggy weather. She caught the
train at Brandentorg, and had to change trains twice, at Pasewalk and
Angermunde, an enormously long detour on the map, but there was
no direct line from Sterlitz to Berlin at that time.

'Got to Berlin a little before 4,' wrote Lady Geraldine. 'Col.
Walker met me at the station, told me they could not allow her poor
body to remain the night at the Hotel, so had to have her placed at once
by 7 o'clock last night in her coffin and removed to the mortuary
chapel of the Dorotheen Kirche, where she can remain till Mario
decides what he wishes. I went of course straight to the Hotel du
Nord, and at once to the children.'

The girls poured out the details of their mother's death to the
sympathetic ears of Lady Geraldine, who gave them what comfort she
could.

Poor, *poor* thing! so melancholy and depressed Grisi was all the 3
weeks they were at Villa Salviati, and most terribly so on the
journey. Before leaving the Villa she said to Frl Gutermann, "Je ne
retournerai jamais ici!" and all the last weeks was always talking of
dying.

Rita is wonderfully calm, darling Clelia *too touching* in her deep
grief, and poor little Ceci too. We all dined together at 5. Soon after
dinner Col Walker came in, in thick great coat, packed for travelling, having just received a telegram; his mother—*or his wife*—
dangerously ill and he had to start at once.

Colonel Walker gave Grisi's money, her letters of credit and the key
of her jewel box to Lady Geraldine, who promised to stay with the
children until Mario arrived. The girls were sent early to bed, and
Fräulein Gutermann gave Lady Geraldine the '*saddest, saddest* details' of
Grisi's death.

The following day, Saturday 27 November, Frederick Ormsby

arrived in Berlin, too late to see his mother alive. He had been staying in Ireland with Lord Powerscourt (Lady Londonderry's son by her first marriage) and on the Wednesday, the day before her death, when Grisi had repeatedly asked for him in her delirium, he had been sent for by telegram.

About one o'clock Lady Geraldine went with the girls to the Dorotheen Kirche to see the body of Grisi. 'She is in a coffin, all the length of the top of which is plate glass,' described Lady Geraldine. 'Oh! what pain to see her thus, how vividly I see her, that day at Rumpenheim!! Our *happy* days at Wiesbaden! Our charming tea with her!! and the last day I ever saw her, at Frankfurt the 17 September.'

Cecilia and Clelia threw themselves on their mother's coffin, weeping bitterly. Rita was more contained and after the two younger girls had returned to the hotel, asked Lady Geraldine to take her to thank the Countess Virginia Hacke, who had shown the children much kindness during their mother's illness. Already many telegrams of condolence had arrived from all over Europe.

Mario arrived in Berlin at five o'clock on Sunday morning. He had left St Petersburg about noon on Friday, having persuaded himself that the children had been frightened by a *schier Tod*, as Lady Geraldine put it, or false death, and that Grisi was not really dead.

'He arrived with full *conviction* he should find her alive!!' wrote Lady Geraldine, 'Captain Ormsby met him at the station and brought him to the hotel. Frl Gutermann was up, he fell forward with the most *terrible gasp, too, too, too* sad, she told me, it was to see him. He would have no coffee, no anything, but would only go at once, *at once* to the vault. He went, and saw her. Then he came back to the hotel and went to his children's bedside.'

'He sank down on the sofa in the drawing-room and wept like a child,' wrote Cecilia. 'We three were sleeping in the room adjoining and his sobs woke us up. We called him to come and embrace us, and we mingled our tears with his. His agony of mind seemed to be increased by the reflection that, after more than thirty years passed by her side, he had not been with her during her last moments.'

Later in the day Mario, with Cecilia and Clelia, went to see Lady Geraldine, to thank her for her care and support. She wrote:

Never did I see anything so *touching* as him in his deep grief, having seen him always gay, bright, merry, joyous, malin and full of fun, to see him thus, grave and earnest and bowed with brief, too sad, too *touching*; what touched me most, was the tone of his voice, totally changed, not his own at all, hoarse, broken, deep in his chest.

He kissed my hand, thanked me for having come; talked of her, told me, same as they had, how melancholy she was all the time in Italy, and on the journey, 'd'une tristesse accablante', but how he had no dream of anxiety when he left her, thought only a little anxiously of Clelia who had so horrible a cold.

Lady Geraldine gave Mario Grisi's letters of credit and other papers, then he politely asked about her own plans and enquired after her brother, the Duke of Beaufort, and his sons, whom he had known since they were small children. 'That's how I know that I'm getting old,' he added with a sigh.

Leaving the children with Fräulein Gutermann in Berlin, Mario accompanied Grisi's coffin to Paris, where she was buried on Thursday 2 December in Père Lachaise cemetery, with her three small daughters, as she had always wished. Immediately afterwards Mario returned to Berlin, where he collected his daughters, and they continued on to St Petersburg, arriving there on 8 December.

In spite of his grief, Mario had to fulfil his engagement. On Saturday 18 December he sang in *Un ballo in maschera*. This was not an opera in any way associated with Grisi, but even so his emotion on the first stage appearance he had made since her death, deepened by the sympathetic applause of the audience, threatened to overwhelm him. But after a career of 31 years Mario was nothing if not professional, and sang to the best of his ability.

Chapter 17

MARIO HAD HAD no time to arrange an apartment for himself and his daughters in St Petersburg, so the four remaining members of the family were at first separated, offered hospitality by kind Russian friends. Mario himself stayed with Baron and Baroness Kuster at the Hermitage in the Winter Palace. Rita and Fräulein Gutermann went to Colonel and Madame Stahovitch; Clelia was taken in by the Countess Hendrikov, while Cecilia was welcomed by a lady with a fine house looking on to the Neva. Clelia soon joined her sister and they went every day to visit Mario and the Kusters at the Hermitage.

The children were given permission to wander freely through the apartments in the Palace, but were forbidden to pass through a large folding door at the end of a corridor. Clelia one day disobeyed this order, and peeped round the door, only to find herself in the presence of the Tsar himself. When there were receptions at the Palace, the two girls were allowed to watch the guests assemble, from the vantage point of a high gallery. They had a magnificent view of the arrival of Tsar Alexander and the Tsarina themselves, as well as the large number of official guests.

On another occasion they witnessed a Court ball from an interior window in a corridor. The royal family, headed by the Tsar and Tsarina, promenaded round the ballroom before the dancing began. Cecilia kept her diary as usual all through the visit to St Petersburg, but when she left Russia that particular volume was unaccountably missing, removed, perhaps, by the police.

Mario and his daughters spent their Christmas, the first since Grisi's death, very quietly alone together. Twelve days later the Russians celebrated their Christmas with 'an endless va et vient, most people,' according to Cecilia, 'drunk in the streets and many too merry in society!' But everyone was endlessly kind to Mario and his children, showering them with expensive gifts.

Mario was entertained to dinner by a hundred friends and admirers at the end of February and presented with a large crown of laurel leaves tied with white silk ribbon. His farewell performance in St Petersburg was on Saturday 5 March, 1870, as Raoul in *Les Huguenots*. His reception, even by generous Russian standards, was wildly enthusiastic and after the performance he was presented with another laurel wreath, gold this time, from Russian musicians and artists, as well as an enormous bouquet on the ribbon of which was inscribed 'The setting sun still eclipses all the stars in the firmament.' The applause was tremendous, and a large part of the audience invaded the stage, to divide up his gloves, his handkerchief and various other wreaths and bouquets given to him, as souvenirs of the evening.

Mario, as usual, gave all the gifts, the jewellery, the flowers and the laurel wreaths to his daughters. When they left St Petersburg, a large, cheering crowd saw them off at the station.

In Paris, where they stayed at the Hotel Heldor, as the house in the rue des Bassins had been sold the previous year, Mario took the girls to Père Lachaise to visit their mother's grave, which they covered in flowers.

Mario's contract with Covent Garden began on Monday 25 April, and he had planned to arrive in London on the Saturday before, so as to be ready to sing on 26 April. However, on Friday he sent a telegram to Gye asking if he could stay another day in Paris to attend to an urgent business matter. Gye, as it happened, was himself in Paris and received the re-directed telegram there on Saturday.

Mario travelled to London on Sunday, and next day he wrote to Gye from the Bath Hotel: 'I am very sorry and annoyed to begin with a letter of excuse, but where I could have caught such a bad cold I do not know. I cough like a consumptive, my right cheek is swollen and I have earache, so I must stay in the hotel to try and cure myself. I have been in this state for two days and hope to be better soon, but meanwhile I haven't even a hope of being able to sing tomorrow.'

Frederick Gye was still in Paris and this letter, or a copy of it, was forwarded to him there. On 26 April he sent a telegram to his son Ernest at Covent Garden, which read: 'Letter received, Mapleson should try to force Mario to sing *Pasquale* or *Ballo* and announce his name unless he agrees that his engagement begins on 5 May. His object is to debut in *Barbiere*. I hear his voice is deplorable . . . You could have rehearsal of *Pasquale* tomorrow evening, I shall be home tomorrow night.'

Gye returned to London on the Wednesday night as planned and the following Tuesday he wrote to Mario: 'I have just received a telegram from the Marquis de Caux in which he says that Adelina cannot sing before Saturday. We are giving *Don Pasquale* on Thursday. I hope you will sing Ernesto on that day, but if you prefer to start with *Il barbiere* on Saturday, I will ask Naudin to sing in *Don Pasquale*.'

Mario replied the same day: 'Oh, yes please ask Naudin to sing in *Don Pasquale*, I have no clothes for it, and will wait till Saturday with pleasure, or whenever it suits you best.'

Mario therefore made his first appearance for two years at Covent Garden on Saturday 7 May as Almaviva in *Il barbiere*. He was given an immensely warm welcome by the audience, which crammed the theatre from pit to gallery and demonstrated in no uncertain terms how pleased it was to have its favourite tenor back again.

'His phrasing was perfect,' wrote the critic of the *Morning Post*, 'and his vocalisation generally was a model to all who call themselves singers.' Mario's daughters waited up for him at the Bath Hotel, to hear how the performance had gone, and he told them that he had been so greatly moved at the enthusiastic reception that, at first, he could hardly utter a sound. 'I had tears in my eyes, and my voice trembled,' he said, 'I always feel at home on the English stage, they greet their old artists with true affection—it does one's heart good to hear them.'

Three days later, on Tuesday 10 May, Mario appeared in *Faust*, with Pauline Lucca and on 13 May in *La favorita*, also with Lucca. During the great scene at the end of Act III, when Fernando breaks his sword and throws it contemptuously at the King's feet, Mario's acting 'was most magnificent and excited the audience to a simultaneous shout of applause,' while at the end of the opera, when Mario appeared before the curtain, he 'received a perfect ovation from every part of the house.'

Mario continued singing in the same three operas twice a week throughout May. Meanwhile he had moved with his daughters from the Bath Hotel to Fernleigh, a house in Leigh Court Road, Streatham, and by the end of the month was urgently in need of money. He wrote to Gye on 31 May to ask him to advance his monthly cheque.

Gye replied next day: 'I was not in the theatre last night, and only received your letter this morning. Mr Mapleson told me that, when I was in Paris, it was arranged between you and him that your appointment would not begin until 5 May instead of on 25 April, and you will remember that when we (you and I) talked about this at the Bath Hotel, the 5th was changed to the 7th. That is agreed is it not? I enclose a cheque for £500.'

Mario acknowledged the five hundred pounds, then continued:

I am thunderstruck at what you write about an agreement between Mr Mapleson and myself at the Bath Hotel that my engagement should begin on 5 May instead of 25 April—in the first place, my dear friend, I have nothing to do with Mr Mapleson as my contract is with you. It was only a question of which day I should make my first appearance, and on your return from Paris you suggested the 7th instead of the 5th; I believed that this arrangement was as convenient to you as to me, and also that it was a kindness on your part, which after more than twenty years in your theatre was quite usual.

You cannot be serious, [continued the tenor in handwriting that grew more and more distraught] the engagement started as agreed, it is written in the contract, on the 25th, and on the 24th I was at the Bath Hotel. Please write and reassure me, as I am too much in need of money to give in lightly over this matter.

Mapleson and Gye certainly appear to have behaved in an unscrupulous manner towards Mario in this case, and one would like to think it was the former's influence that caused Gye to treat an ageing singer and, as Mario wrote, a friend of more than twenty years standing, in such a fashion.

During June there were performances of *Don Giovanni* with Graziani in the title-role, Mario as Don Ottavio, Tietjens as Donna Anna and Patti as Zerlina. At a later date, Lucca replaced Patti. Mario also sang in *Les Huguenots* with Lucca and in *Un ballo in maschera* with Tietjens. His last performance of the season was on Thursday 21 July, when *Faust* was given for Patti's benefit.

Willert Beale had arranged a farewell tour for Mario through the British provinces, to begin in September 1870. Mario spent August with his daughters at Eastbourne, then took a house for them and Fräulein Gutermann in Brighton. The tour began at Bath in the first week of September, and covered every city of consequence in the British Isles.

As often as he could, Mario returned to Brighton to spend a day with his daughters; consequently he passed a great deal of his time in the train. At the beginning of October the party was in Harrogate, and Mario, who had spent the previous Sunday in Scarborough with Willert Beale, caught a bad cold. He sang at the Harrogate concert notwithstanding, but afterwards, being so hoarse that he could not speak, returned to Brighton, where he was forced to remain for nearly a fortnight.

October 17th was Mario's sixtieth birthday. The next day he wrote to Gye from Brighton to ask for 'a yes or a no for next season.' By 19 October he was well enough to continue the tour and travelled, via London, to Cheltenham, where he sang on the 20th. The next morning he left for Gloucester, and on the evening of Sunday 23

October took the train to Preston. From there he went to Liverpool and Huddersfield and on 29 October, passing through London again, he met Gye and they settled their arrangements for the tenor's final season at Covent Garden. After spending 24 hours with his daughters in Brighton, Mario resumed his travels on 31 October.

Before the tour started, Mario had asked Willert Beale for a free week at the end of November, so that he might visit Grisi's grave on the first anniversary of her death. The fact that the Prussian Army was at that moment besieging Paris did not deter him in the slightest. According to Beale, Mario had already written to the Prussian High Command for permission to cross the lines and enter the city. Beale, who attended to all the tenor's correspondence and business affairs during the tour, managed to persuade Mario that it would be too dangerous to go to Paris, and that he should spend the week with his children. Mario arrived in Brighton on 20 November and left again on the 28th. The final concert took place in Brighton, on 17 December.

Mario's final season at Covent Garden, 1871, was marred by none of the painful incidents that had so upset him the year before. Gye was once more in sole control of his theatre and seems to have done everything he could to make the tenor's last appearances as successful as possible.

Mario had spent the winter in Brighton with his daughters. Consequently he was rested and in good voice when, at the end of April, the family moved to London, taking a house in Larkhall Rise, Clapham. His first appearance was in *Il barbiere* on Saturday 22 April and a week later he sang in *La favorita*. *Faust* was announced for 8 May, but both Mario and Faure were ill and *Rigoletto* had to be substituted at the last moment. Mario had caught a bad cold and as the weather was most un-springlike, it took him ten days to shake it off. He was well enough to appear in *Don Giovanni* by Saturday 20 May, when he sang his last Don Ottavio.

Faust, with Mario, Lucca and Faure, was given on 26 May; *Un ballo in maschera*, announced for Saturday 3 June, was postponed for a week until 10 June, when Mario sang Riccardo for the last time. The following Saturday, 17 June, there was a performance of *Martha*, the occasion for Mario's last Lionel. *Les Huguenots* was presented on Friday 30 June, with Mario and Lucca. The following Monday, Mario sang in *Il trovatore* with Patti; three nights later, at a performance of *Il barbiere di Siviglia*, Mario sang the role of Count Almaviva for the 102nd and last time in London. Patti was his Rosina, as she had been on some 60 occasions during the last decade.

Rigoletto was announced for 11 July, but changed at short notice to *Faust*. This was Mario's last appearance in the title role of Gounod's opera; Miolan-Carvalho sang Marguerite and Faure was Mephistopheles. Two nights later an extra performance of *Il trovatore* was given 'by public request', with Patti as Leonora to accompany Mario's final Manrico.

At a matinée concert in the Floral Hall on Saturday 15 July, Mario sang 'Adieu', attributed to Schubert but in fact by Heinrich von Weyrauch, in the first half, and Hatton's 'Goodbye Sweetheart', accompanied by the composer, in the second.

His final Raoul, a part he had sung nearly 120 times at Covent Garden alone, followed on Monday 17 July, when Patti sang Valentine, the first time she had appeared in *Les Huguenots* in London.

Finally, on 19 July, 1871, Mario took his benefit and his farewell of the stage, in a performance of *La favorita*. 'Such a leave taking as that of Signor Mario last night is without precedent,' wrote Davison in *The Times*. 'The opera selected for the final appearance of the greatest Italian singer and the most universally popular lyric comedian who ever trod the Italian boards, was *La favorita*.

'It was a happy chance,' continued Davison, 'that the incomparable artist who last night bade adieu to a public which had recognised him from the beginning, followed his career with ever increasing interest, given him full credit for absolute supremacy at his prime, and watched those years of more arduous and painful exertion which showed that even Mario, though becoming greater and greater as an actor, must at no distant period bid adieu to the lyric stage, should be in full possession of his powers.

'Never, we may say without hesitation, did Signor Mario more emphatically prove himself the Fernando of Fernandos, the singer of singers, the actor of actors, than on the occasion under notice . . . We repeat that we have never witnessed such a leave-taking; and with even more satisfaction, we may add that it was in honour of one whom we have for a long time considered and upheld as the greatest, most versatile, and in all respects, thoroughly accomplished lyric artist of his day.'

The Cambridge contingent was present in full force, with the Duchess, her two daughters, Princess Augusta and Princess Mary Adelaide, and their respective husbands, the Grand Duke of Mecklenburg-Strelitz and the Duke of Teck, accompanied, of course, by Lady Geraldine, who described the reaction of the Covent Garden audience to Mario's final performance: 'The scene of enthusiasm is difficult to describe, he was in glorious voice and acted quite magnificently. They gave him a tremendous reception, and at the end of the fine 3rd act, the ovation was beyond anything I ever saw, *the whole house rose* to receive him, waving handkerchiefs and hats, *shouting* showering wreaths and flowers upon him. P[rincess] A[ugusta]'s wreath was the first thrown and she threw it beautifully. HRH [the Duchess of Cambridge] threw him her bouquet and he *caught it in his hand* in the air as it reached him, so prettily that there was a roar of applause at it. P[rincess] M[ary Adelaide] caught up my bouquet round the corner of the box and threw it to him! again and again and again he had to come forward, five or six times.'

Between the second and third acts the Grand Duke went to see Mario in his dressing-room, to convey the compliments of the Cambridge party to the tenor. After the last act there was a second ovation, even greater than the previous one. Lady Geraldine could hardly believe 'an *English* audience capable of giving [such a one], a really delirious excitement, the *whole* house standing—quite a choking sight! He was quite pale and really overcome.'

After Mario had been called out eight or nine times, and the footlights had already been turned down, 'the public were determined to see yet again!! and called and shouted so he was forced to come on, in his dressing gown and stood all ému, only able to press his hand to his lips to express his emotion.'

Next day Lady Geraldine heard from Mario's daughters that the scene as he left the theatre 'was *wonderful*!! they could hardly reach their carriage the people pressed and crowded so and of all the immense quantity thrown to him he only succeeded in bringing home 7 wreaths and 3 bouquets, *so* they snatched them from him to keep as mementos, and all seized his hand to kiss it, and with greatest difficulty he got through. They cheered and shouted like madmen racing along the street after his carriage.'

On his retirement Mario received many gifts from admirers, among them an ivory and gold cigar-case, on which was inscribed a quotation from Dante, which read, in translation, 'The compassionate gods said for once let the earth hear the music of heaven, and they touched the lips of . . . Mario.' This present came from the novelist Ouida (Louise de la Ramée), who had conceived a passion for the 61-year-old tenor, nearly 30 years her senior. In her villa in Florence, where she went to live in 1874, two years after Mario had sold the Villa Salviati, Ouida displayed a full-length portrait of the tenor, though there is no evidence at all that she ever actually met him.

Mario—or his portrait—did, however, inspire one of Ouida's best novels, *Moths*, in which Mario figures as Raphael Corrèze, le beau

Corrèze, whose voice was 'pure as a lark's, rich as an organ's swell, tender as love's first embrace, marvellously melodious, in a word . . . a perfectly beautiful tenor voice.'

Two days after his farewell performance, Mario dined at the Dowager Lady Kinnoul's house, accompanied by his three daughters. Lady Geraldine sat next to Mario, 'who was charming and *most* agreeable. Ceci and Cle were to have sung but there was confusion and muddle about their music, which did not turn up and unfortunately included also Mario's.'

Later in the evening, however, Mario 'most amiably and kindly sang by heart "Allons au près ma belle reine" and "Raggio d'amor" accompanied by Alary, and "O donna amata" accompanied by Pinsuti.'

Mario remained in England for the autumn of 1871, then after Christmas he went to Florence to arrange the sale of the Villa Salviati. He had not been to Florence since Grisi's death, and the villa must have reminded him unbearably of his loss, the pain of which did not lessen with the years. But he was desperately short of money. His daughters were growing up and needed dowries or other provision for their future lives.

Cecilia was married on 29 February 1872 at St Paul's Church, Wilton Place, London, to Godfrey Pearse. The witnesses included Rita and Clelia de Candia and Fräulein Gutermann. After the wedding, Rita went to stay in Germany with Fräulein Gutermann, while Clelia travelled to Florence to help her father. In Paris, where she broke her journey, she was approached by Maurice Strakosch, who suggested that Mario might accompany him, Carlotta Patti and other artists, on a concert tour of North America.

Clelia carried the offer to her father and Mario accepted—he was in no position to refuse. Having sold the Villa Salviati, together with all its contents, to Herr Hagermann, a Swedish gentleman, Mario returned to England. On 25 August 1872 he sailed from Liverpool, bound for New York, where the concert party assembled. The tour lasted for more than six months and covered most of the United States. It must have been an exhausting experience, but the tenor bore it with his usual cheerfulness, and did not complain of the incessant train travel and whistle-stop visits to innumerable towns and cities. Occasionally an episode such as his meeting with the poet Longfellow at Cambridge, Massachusetts, brought an unusual interest to the tour. Longfellow gave Mario his photograph as a souvenir of their meeting.

Mario arrived back in England in April 1873 and joined Rita and

Clelia in Surbiton, where they had been living during his absence. It was time for him to decide where he wished to spend his retirement. Though he had always liked England, Italy called to him irresistibly. In November he escorted Rita, Clelia and Fräulein Gutermann to Frankfurt, and then himself continued on to Rome, where he found an apartment on the Corso, at the corner of the Piazza del Popolo. As soon as he had settled in, his two unmarried daughters joined him.

Rome, at long last the capital of a genuinely united Italy, was the ideal place for Mario's retirement. It held no former connection with either the De Candia family or with Giulia Grisi to remind him of the painful past, the city was full of wonderful museums, each one overflowing with great works of art; fascinating excavations were being made of historical sites; the climate suited him—he liked the heat; and Rome contained a great many friends, old and new. Adelaide Sartoris was an example of the first, Prince Ladislas Odescalchi of the second category.

Mario returned to England in 1875 for the marriage of his youngest daughter Clelia to Powys Vaughan; the following year he returned once more, to see his first grandchild, Clelia's daughter. Meanwhile both his health and his financial position had been deteriorating. In 1877 Frances Kemble, then in London, received a letter from her sister Mrs Sartoris, who was living in Rome. 'They are settled,' wrote Frances Kemble in *Further Records*, 'but by no means comfortably; for, out of a charitable desire to serve her old friend Mario, she has taken his apartment, which is in the Corso, instead of one of the higher and sunnier situations. It is dark, and small and inconvenient; and she is suffering much from cold in it. Mario, who lives in the same house, is constantly with them and by all accounts his principal contribution to the general conversation is a set of stories, more improper and indecent, the one than the other.

'I have not much sympathy for Mario's ruin,' continued Frances Kemble. 'A man who stood for years literally in a shower of gold has no right, in my opinion, to be much pitied for not having saved at least enough for a subsistence in his old age. One thing I do pity him for, with all my heart, and was much shocked to hear it, that he has become blind. Moreover his unmarried daughter is not comfortable to him; for these afflictions in his impoverished old age I have indeed infinite compassion.'

Mario was not blind. His sight was affected when, not being able to afford the cigars he had so long enjoyed, he took to smoking cigarettes. When he changed to a pipe, his eyes improved. Luckily for him, Adelaide Sartoris did not share her sister's puritanical

disapproval of Mario's spendthrift way. She set about raising a sub-
scription for him at Coutts Bank in London, and also wrote to Santley,
Sims Reeves and other singers and musicians to arrange a concert for
Mario's benefit.

Another old friend who had not forgotten the pleasure she used to
derive from Mario's singing was Princess Mary Adelaide, Duchess of
Teck. Hearing of his circumstances she lost no time in using her
influence to obtain a grant from the Royal Bounty. Her efforts were
successful, as in March 1878 she wrote to Lord Beaconsfield, then
Prime Minister, to thank him for 'so kindly taking poor Mario's case
into consideration and obtaining the Queen's sanction to so generous
and munificent a grant from the Royal Bounty.'

With the aid of the concert, the Duchess of Teck hoped to make up
the £2,000 needed to purchase an annuity for Mario.

Mario was particularly grateful to the Duchess, herself in frequent
financial trouble, for the efforts she had made, and on his last visit to
England went to White Lodge, Richmond to thank her personally.

Meanwhile Santley had consulted Arthur Chappell, and a concert
was arranged. Patrons of the Mario Testimonial Fund included the
Princess of Wales as well as the Duchess of Cambridge and Princess
Mary Adelaide. On the Committee were Sir Julius Benedict, Sims
Reeves, Santley, John Woodford (a friend of Mario's of very long
standing) and Arthur Chappell, who acted as Treasurer.

The concert took place on 29 May 1878. The programme included
an aria from Rossini's *Tancredi*, sung by Zélia Trebelli, the French
mezzo-soprano who had appeared with Mario at Covent Garden
during his last seasons there; The Jewel Song from *Faust*, sung by the
famous Swedish soprano Christine Nilsson and billed as 'her only
appearance in public this season'; 'I would I were a King', a new song
by Arthur Sullivan sung by Santley; and a duet from *Semiramide* in
which Nilsson and Trebelli joined forces. At the last moment Sims
Reeves was unable to appear, but, according to Santley, he 'sent a
most liberal donation to add to the receipts of the concert, in the shape
of a cheque for £100.'

The net receipts of the concert amounted to £1,500, while the
private subscription raised by Mario's old friends and admirers
amounted to £2,500. 'The proceeds of the two funds,' wrote Santley,
'were together invested in an annuity, which provided our old friend
and comrade with sufficient means to make him comfortable for the
remainder of his life.'

Owing to the kindness of people like Princess Mary Adelaide,
Santley and Adelaide Sartoris, the last five years of Mario's life were

free from financial worry. He moved from the Corso to rooms on the second floor of 176 via di Ripetta, overlooking the river Tiber. Books in several languages on every aspect of the visual arts lined the walls of these lodgings. Tubes of colour, paint brushes, palettes, varnishes, modelling and wood-working tools littered the tables and chairs.

Mario had many acquaintances among the artists and musicians who thronged the cafés of Rome, and frequently dined at the Café Morteo on the Corso with them. Otherwise he went out very little. At Palo, the castle on the coast near Civitavecchia belonging to Prince Ladislas Odescalchi, he was an ever-welcome guest and at Palo he renewed acquaintance with Sir Augustus and Lady Paget.

'With snow-white hair and beard,' wrote Lady Paget, 'and the complexion of a girl of sixteen, he also retained the fire of his dark eyes. His dress was superlatively neat and fresh looking, and even when he dined with us quite alone he wore white waistcoat and gloves, things unknown to his countrymen of that day.'

Mario, in Lady Paget's opinion, 'was a most agreeable talker, and the extreme freshness and naivety of his mind was an additional charm, besides his wide experience and his wonderful knowledge in art and science.'

In 1881 Prince Odescalchi took Mario on a surprise visit to England, when he saw his daughters Cecilia (Mrs Pearse) and Clelia (Mrs Vaughan) and his two grandchildren, Mrs Vaughan's little girls, for the last time. Rita de Candia, who did not marry, lived in Berlin. The following year Mario collapsed while staying at Palo and caught pneumonia. He also suffered from angina pectoris.

Despite warnings from his doctor to avoid extremes of temperature, he went as usual to the Café Morteo one evening in December 1883 when the weather was particularly cold. Next day he was ill with bronchitis and on 10 December he had another sharp attack of angina.

W. G. Cusins (later Sir William), Master of the Music to Queen Victoria, called on Mario the following day, not having heard of his illness. Cusins found the old man conscious, but very weak and obviously dying. He stayed only a few minutes and left at half past five on that afternoon of Tuesday 11 December. By seven o'clock the same evening, Mario was dead.

Cusins at once telegraphed the news to the Queen at Windsor and received the reply: 'Her Majesty with sincere regret has heard of Signor Mario's death and wishes you if possible to assist at the funeral, and to place a wreath upon his grave in the Queen's name.'

The funeral took place on 13 December, in the Church of San Rocco, which was almost opposite Mario's lodgings in the via di

Ripetta. The coffin was temporarily placed in the vaults of the church as the De Candia family, as soon as they heard of Giovanni's death, had asked for the body to be sent to Cagliari, for burial in the family tomb.

Mario himself would surely have wished to be buried in Père Lachaise cemetery in Paris, next to Giulia Grisi and their three little girls. But after some months' delay his family's request was granted and during the week before Easter 1884, his body was taken to Cagliari in an Italian warship. After lying in state for 24 hours in the Church of San Francesco di Paolo, the coffin was re-interred in the De Candia tomb.

The remains of Giovanni de Candia may lie in Cagliari, but the spirit of Mario lives on in other cities: in Paris, where 'Mario' was born and where the woman he loved so unreservedly is buried; in Florence, where the Villa Salviati still looks across the city and the river Arno to the Tuscan hills beyond—the home in which they spent their happiest hours together; above all in London, where Mario sang for 32 seasons, where together with Grisi he inaugurated the present Covent Garden theatre with *Les Huguenots*.

The widowed Queen Victoria wrote in her diary for 15 December 1883:

> Much grieved to hear of poor Mario's death, which occurred on the 13th [the funeral was on the 13th]. He was 73. He was the greatest tenor that ever existed, and had a most heavenly, rich, full voice, without, excepting for some particular very high notes, any 'voce di testa' [head voice], and sang with such feeling. He was so handsome and acted so beautifully.
>
> Who could ever forget him as Gennaro in *Lucrezia Borgia*, or as the Prophète, in which he looked so magnificent in the Coronation scene. But above all his rendering of Raoul in the *Huguenots*. That duet with Valentine, given by him and poor Grisi (she also gone), was the finest thing possible. His "tu m'ami" was touching and exquisite. We used to go again and again to the Opera, only for that scene.

The last time that Queen Victoria had heard Mario sing was in 1871, the year of his retirement from the stage, when he took part in the opening ceremony of the Albert Hall. 'Dearest Albert's composition the "Incoronazione all'Armonia" was performed under the direction of Costa. Mario's voice, which my beloved one so admired, sang his solo beautifully though he is now 61'.

In the *Morning Post* of 20 July 1871, there appeared a long and generous encomium of the tenor who had taken his leave of the theatre the previous day. 'Signor Mario's exit from the stage has been a suitable termination in the splendour of its *éclat* to his entire professional career. For more than a quarter of a century he has been continuously before the public eye; and the history of his life is the history of a nearly unbroken series of conspicuous and richly merited triumphs. Genius and industry—or shall we say genius, which is but another form of the most elevated and indefatigable industry—have secured for Signor Mario a position second to none of those occupied by the past demi-gods of song.

'He will be remembered,' continued the *Morning Post* critic, 'with a like gratitude by composer and by audience; to the works of the former he has given a more complete expression, histrionic as well as vocal, than any actor or singer within our memory; to the latter he has afforded a richer measure of the highest and purest enjoyment—and it is no exaggeration to speak in these terms of music—which humanity knows, than any artist of the century.

'The star of Mario has never paled. It has been his good fortune to retain with unparalleled uniformity the rank which so soon after his first appearance the verdict of the public awarded him . . . New candidates for popular favour have in turn made their début, and many have reaped no disproportionate share of laurels. But if Signor Mario has seen those who would fain be his rivals, he has at no time had anything to fear from the competition. His position has been unrivalled.'

Let that be Mario's epitaph.

Bibliography

Arditi, Luigi: *My Reminiscences*, London, 1896
Barrett, William Arthur: *Balfe: His Life and Work*, London 1882
Beale, Willert: *The Light of Other Days*, London, 1890
Blaze, François Castile: *Théâtres Lyriques de Paris: L'Académie Imperiale de Musique*, Paris, 1855; *L'Opéra-Italien*, Paris, 1856
Budden, Julian: *The Operas of Verdi*, vol I, London, 1973
Chorley, Henry F.: *Thirty Years' Musical Recollections*, London, 1862
Clayton, Ellen Creathorne: *Queens of Song*, London, 1865
Cooke, Sir C. Kinloch: *Princess Mary Adelaide, Duchess of Teck, a Memoir*, London, 1900
Cox, The Rev. T. C.: *Musical Recollections of the last Half Century*, London, 1872
Davison, J. W.: *From Mendelssohn to Wagner*, London, 1912
Edwards, H. Sutherland: *The Prima Donna*, London, 1886
Enfield, Viscountess (editor): *Leaves from the Diary of Henry Greville*, London, 1883-1905
Engel, Louis: *From Mozart to Mario*, London, 1886
Éscudier, Léon: *Littérature musicale*, Paris, 1863; *Mes Souvenirs*, Paris, 1868
Éscudier, Marie: *Études Bibliographiques sur les Chanteurs contemporains*, Paris, 1840; *Vies et Aventures des Cantatrices célèbres*, Paris, 1856
Esher, Viscount (editor): *The Girlhood of Queen Victoria*, London, 1912
Fitzlyon, April: *The Price of Genius*, London, 1964
Fouque, O.: *Histoire du Théâtre Ventadour*, Paris, 1881
Gatti, Carlo: *Il Teatro alla Scala nella storie e nell'arte*, Milan, 1964
Gautier, Judith: *Le second Rang du Collier*, Paris, 1903
Gautier, Théophile: *L'Histoire de l'Art dramatique en France depuis 25 Ans*, Paris, 1858-59
Giulini, Maria Ferranti: *Giuditta Pasta e i suoi tempi*, Milan, 1935
Gronow, Rees Howell: *Reminiscences and Recollections*, London, 1964
Hedley, Arthur (editor): *Selected Correspondence of Fryderyk Chopin*, London, 1962
Hugo, Victor: *Journal 1830-1848*, Paris, 1954
Kemble, Frances Anne: *Further Records*, London, 1890
Kenney, Charles Lamb: *A Memoir of Michael William Balfe*, London, 1875
Klein, Herman: *The Reign of Patti*, London, 1920
Kuhe, Wilhelm: *My Musical Recollections*, London, 1896
Lumley, Benjamin: *Reminiscences of the Opera*, London, 1864

Maurois, André: *Lélia, ou la Vie de George Sand*, Paris, 1952

Millingen, J. C.: *The History of Duelling*, London, 1841

Ouida (Louise de la Ramée): *Moths*, London, 1880

Paget, Walburga Lady: *Scenes and Memories*, London, 1912; *Embassies of Other Days*, London, 1923; *The Linings of Life*, London, 1928

Pearse, Mrs Godfrey and Hird, Frank: *The Romance of a Great Singer*, London, 1910

Pearse, Mrs Godfrey: *The Enchanted Past*, London, 1926

Pougin, Arthur: *Acteurs et Actrices d'autrefois*, Paris, 1896; *Giuseppina Grassini*, Paris, 1920; *Marietta Alboni*, Paris, 1912

Rosenthal, Harold: *Two Centuries of Opera at Covent Garden*, London, 1958

Rosenthal, Harold (editor): *The Mapleson Memoirs*, London, 1966

Santley, Sir Charles: *Student and Singer*, London, 1893; *Reminiscences of my Life*, London, 1909

Soubies, A.: *Le Théâtre-Italien de 1801 à 1913*, Paris, 1913

Steinmetz, Andrew: *The Romance of Duelling*, London 1868

Strakosch, Maurice: *Souvenirs d'un Imprésario*, Paris, 1887

Véron, Louis: *Mémoirs d'un Bourgeois de Paris*, Paris, 1853–55

Weinstock, Herbert: *Donizetti and the World of Opera*, New York, 1963; *Rossini, a Biography*, London, 1968; *Vincenzo Bellini, his Life and his Operas*, New York, 1971

Whitehouse, H. R.: *A Revolutionary Princess, Christina Belgiojoso-Trivulzio, her Life and Times*, London, 1906

Unpublished Sources:

Queen Victoria's Journal, Royal Archives, Windsor Castle

Lady Geraldine Somerset's Diary, Royal Archives, Windsor Castle

Letters and Documents in the Archives of the Royal Opera House, Covent Garden

Periodicals and Newspapers consulted:

The *Times*	The *Liverpool Daily Post*
The *Morning Post*	The *Irish Times*
The *Illustrated London News*	The *Dublin Evening Mail*
The *Athenaeum*	The *New York Courier Enquirer*
The *Musical World*	*Opera News*
The *Strand Magazine*	*Le Journal des Débats*
The *Scotsman*	*Le Journal de Saint-Petersbourg*
The *Manchester Guardian*	*Museo Universal*, Madrid

Index

Accursi, Michele 70
Alary, Giulio 78–9, 144–6, 210
   Sardanapale 117
Albert of Saxe-Coburg-Gotha,
   Prince 32–3, 44–5, 47, 56, 72,
   88–9, 111, 113, 127, 160
   'Incoronazione all'Armonia' 214
Albertazzi, Emma (Howson) 40, 54, 55
Alboni, Marietta 88–9, 90, 93, 95–9,
   101, 103, 124, 125, 136, 138, 140–1,
   151
Angri, Mlle 103
Arditi, Luigi 133–4, 147, 149, 155,
   172, 174, 179, 181
Artôt, Désirée 173
Auber, Daniel 55, 83, 86
   L'Enfant prodigue 115
   Fra Diavolo 175–6
   Gustave III 15
   La Muette de Portici (*Masaniello*) 102,
   110, 117, 127, 162–3, 172, 188

Bagier, J. 167–71, 174
Balfe, Michael William 23, 34, 55, 131
   Elfrida 55
   Falstaff 40, 55
   Keolanthe 55
   The Maid of Artois 33
Barroilhet, Paul 46
Battu, Marie 164
Baucardé, Carlo 114
Beale, Frederick 50, 51, 57, 80, 94
Beale, Willert 52, 94, 124, 131, 134,
   138, 140–1, 142, 147, 158, 174,
   206–7
Beethoven, Ludwig van 45
   'Adelaide' 45, 71
   'Busslied' ('La Pénitence') 45, 98
   Fidelio 32, 86, 179
   Symphony No 4 102
Bellini, Mme 66
Bellini, Vincenzo 15, 24–5, 30, 32, 34,
   84, 85–7, 95

Beatrice di Tenda 19, 47, 55
I Capuleti e i Montecchi 23, 24, 26
Norma 24, 25, 30–2, 35, 41–3, 46–8,
   50, 51, 54–7, 61, 65, 67–70, 74, 79,
   87, 91, 98, 100, 101, 108, 110, 121,
   126, 129, 130, 132–4, 136, 138,
   140–2, 147, 149, 154, 157, 164, 173,
   178, 181–4, 187
Il pirata 45, 68, 72, 74, 96, 161
I puritani 28–30, 32, 37, 40, 43, 44,
   47, 50–3, 57, 59, 62, 63, 65, 70,
   73–5, 96, 101, 108, 110, 116, 117,
   120, 121, 124–6, 133, 134, 142, 148,
   174, 190
La sonnambula 24, 28, 37, 40, 44, 48,
   50–3, 57, 58, 61, 63, 70, 71, 87, 89,
   95, 97, 101, 124, 125, 133, 138, 154
La straniera 13, 26, 49
Benedetti, Nicola 141
Benedict, (Sir) Julius 30, 37, 49, 62,
   78, 101, 127, 128, 212
   The Crusaders 76
Bériot, Charles de 26, 33
Berlioz, Hector 19, 20, 43, 163
Blumenthal, Jacques 148
Boigne, Charles de 59
Bologna
   Teatro Comunale 22, 23
Borghi-Mamo, Adelaide 135, 136
Bosio, Angiolina 123, 126, 128, 136,
   137, 139, 144–6, 148, 163
Bottesini, Giovanni
   L'assedio di Firenze 136
Brambilla, Giuseppina 77
Brambila, Marietta 59, 64, 71, 73, 77
Brignoli, Pasquale 176
Bull, Ole 32, 33
Bunn, Alfred 34, 43

Calzado, Torribio 136, 150
Cambridge, Duchess of 57, 122, 123,
   128, 140, 155, 174, 199, 200, 208–9,
   212

Cambridge, Duke of 57, 122
Castellan, Jeanne 70–2, 77–9, 97, 99,
 111, 113, 116
Castlereagh, Viscount (later Marquess
 of Londonderry) 37–9, 42, 44, 45,
 48, 50, 55, 72, 87
Cavour, Count Camille 12, 187
Celli, Filippo
 Ezio 23
Cherubini, Luigi
 Medée 179
Chopin, Frédéric 15, 96, 98, 101
Chorley, Henry 28, 31, 35, 40, 41, 49,
 61–7, 73, 75–9, 84, 88–92, 97–9,
 102–6, 109–111, 113, 118, 121, 123,
 126, 137–9, 143, 146, 148, 150, 154,
 156–7, 160–1, 172–3, 175, 184, 189
Ciampi, Giuseppe 161
Cimarosa, Domenico
 Il matrimonio segreto 38, 65–6, 76, 77,
 79, 104
 Gli Orazi e i Curiazi 47
Clesinger, Solange 96
Coccia, Carlo
 Enrico di Montfort 24
Coletti, Filippo 44, 80, 95
Corbari, Mlle 90, 108
Cordella, Giacomo
 Lo sposo di provincia 23
Costa, (Sir) Michael 34, 35, 42, 44, 50,
 71, 79, 80, 88, 90, 91, 97, 99, 113,
 115, 129, 136, 143, 144–5, 150,
 214
 Don Carlos 66
 Malek Adhel 35, 37, 76
Cox, Reverend T. C. 27, 28, 30, 100,
 105, 111
Cruvelli, Sophie 98, 125, 126
Curioni, Alberico 27, 30
Cusins, Sir William G. 213

Damcke, B. 116–7, 118
Davison, J. W. 121–2, 154–7, 162,
 184, 189, 208
De Candia, Bella Maria 135–6, 146,
 151–2
De Candia, Donna Caterina
 (b. Grixoni) 12, 13, 15, 17, 101
De Candia, Cecilia 146, 153, 167, 186,
 190–1, 193–203, 210–1, 213
De Candia, Clelia 125, 146, 153, 167,
 186, 190–1, 193–5, 197–9, 200–3,
 210–1, 213

De Candia, Marchese Don
 Stefano 11–15, 101
De Candia, Giovanni Matteo (Mario,
 Giovanni) *passim*
De Candia, Giulia 57, 65
De Candia, Maria Augusta 114, 124
De Candia, Rita 101–3, 105–6, 108,
 146, 153, 167, 186, 191, 194–5, 197,
 200–1, 203, 210–1, 213
De Candia, Serafino 104
De Candia, Teresa 14, 15
Delle Sedie, Enrico 161, 163, 197
Delafield, Edward 94, 96, 97, 100,
 102, 103, 105
Donizetti, Gaetano 19, 30, 32, 55, 56,
 70, 74, 83–7, 95
 Anna Bolena 13, 24–8, 33, 37, 57,
 63, 65, 77, 93, 98, 129, 154
 *L'ajo nell'imbarazzo, o Don
 Gregorio* 78
 Belisario 64
 Don Pasquale 59, 60, 62, 63, 65, 70,
 74, 75, 98, 101, 126, 128, 134, 135,
 137, 138, 142, 160–1, 165, 167, 175,
 183, 185, 186, 204–5
 L'elisir d'amore 41, 43, 45, 53, 56, 67,
 82, 113, 124, 129, 184
 Fausta 49, 78
 La Favorite 97–8, 115, 122, 123, 126,
 128–130, 133, 150, 172, 176, 184,
 205, 207, 208
 La Fille du régiment 87, 90, 191
 Il furioso all'isola di San Domingo 161, 181
 Gemma di Vergy 74
 Linda di Chamounix 58, 62, 68, 109
 Lucia di Lammermoor 36, 37, 43, 46,
 47, 53, 56, 58, 70, 71, 95, 108, 116,
 133, 134, 161, 190
 Lucrezia Borgia (La rinegata) 20, 23,
 41, 45, 46, 54, 55, 58, 67, 69, 77,
 89–90, 98, 101, 103, 109, 110,
 120–4, 126, 128, 129, 132–4, 136,
 138, 141, 148, 149, 154–5, 175, 178,
 182, 183, 184, 214
 Maria di Rohan 64, 65
 Marin Faliero 28, 29, 33, 49, 62
 Parisina 36, 37, 39
 Pia de' Tolomei 55
 Roberto Devereux 19, 40, 49, 73
 Torquato Tasso 46, 47
 Ugo, conte di Parigi 25
Donzelli, Domenico 24, 60
Dorus-Gras, Julie 19, 49, 103

Mario and Grisi

221

Dublin
  Theatre Royal 50, 101, 141, 147
Duponchel, Charles 11, 16, 17
Duprez, Gilbert 11, 18, 43, 47, 98, 99, 105

Edinburgh
  Theatre Royal 182
Elssler, Fanny 90, 102

Fancelli, Giuseppe 188
Faure, Jean-Baptiste 150, 151, 172–3, 184, 207–8
Fioraventi, Valentino 29
Fioretti, Mme 164
Flavio, Signor 97
Florence
  Teatro della Pergola 22–4
Flotow, Friedrich von
  Martha 142, 144–9, 151, 156, 158, 167, 169, 171, 173, 174, 176, 179, 181, 185–7, 207
Formes, Karl 112, 116, 117, 144
Fornasari, Luciano 61–4, 66, 70–3, 75, 79
Fraschini, Gaetano 92, 169, 172
Frezzolini, Erminia 108, 114, 124

Galetti, Signor 79, 84
Garcia, Manuel 26, 60, 144
Gardoni, Italo 90, 95, 136, 160
Gautier, Judith 36, 159
Gautier, Théophile 11, 18, 36, 37, 40, 46, 47, 53, 54, 59, 60, 61, 64, 68, 69, 74, 83, 159
Giles, Miss 131, 133, 134, 141, 151
Giuglini, Antonio 178
Glinka, Mikhail 25
Gnecco, Francesco
  La prova d'un opera seria 129
Gounod, Charles 86
  Faust 172–3, 174–5, 178–9, 181–191, 196, 205–8
  Roméo et Juliette 188–9, 190–1
Grassini, Josephina 22, 25
Graziani, Francesco 125, 136–8, 145, 147, 148, 150, 151, 164, 172, 206
Grétry, André 55
Greville, Henry 16, 17, 101, 107, 123, 125, 128, 140, 142, 146, 155, 161–2, 173–4
Grisi, Carlotta 22, 36, 73
Grisi, Ernesta 22, 36, 49, 50
Grisi, Gaetano 22, 95

Grisi, Giovanna (b. Grassini) 22
Grisi, Giuditta 22, 24–6
Grisi, Giulia passim
Guasco, Carlo 56, 79
Guémard, Louis 163
Gye, Ernest 204
Gye, Frederick 94, 100, 103, 110, 112, 115, 123, 125, 126, 128, 130, 136–8, 140, 143–6, 150, 152, 158–68, 170–1, 173–7, 181–3, 188–9, 192–3, 196, 204–7

Hackett, James H. 130, 131
Halévy, Fromental
  Le Drapier 43
  La Juive 112–3, 146
Handel, George Frideric 45
  Acis and Galatea 39
  Israel in Egypt 186
  Messiah 30
Harris, Augustus 127–8, 129, 189
Hatton, John
  'Goodbye Sweetheart' 146, 174, 179, 181, 185–6, 208
Haydn, Joseph
  The Seasons 34
Hugo, Victor 69, 82–3
  Angelo, tyran de Padoue 148

Ivanov, Nikolay 27, 29, 34

Kean, Charles 141, 146
Kemble, Adelaide (Mrs Sartoris) 98, 107, 211–2
Klein, Herman 175
Kuhe, Wilhelm 98

Lablache, Frederick 49, 50, 52, 54, 57, 58, 61, 62, 76
Lablache, Luigi 28, 29, 31, 33, 34, 37–41, 43–5, 47, 49–59, 61–3, 66, 70–2, 74–80, 82, 83, 90, 93, 95, 98, 104, 113, 125–7, 129, 135, 136, 142, 161
Lanari, Alessandro 23–5
Laporte, Pierre 34, 39, 43, 44, 48, 66
Levasseur, Nicholas 19
Licalzi, Signor 176, 188
Lind, Jenny 72, 86–7, 88–91, 98, 99, 101, 110, 113
Liszt, Franz 15, 49
Liverpool
  New Prince of Wales Theatre 185–6

Loewe, Sophie 49
London
  Covent Garden, Royal Italian
    Opera 28, 34, 49, 79, 80, 83–91,
    93–4, 96–106, 109, 110, 112,
    115–8, 120–2, 126–7, 135–7,
    143–4, 148–50, 154–5, 157–8,
    160–2, 167, 172, 175–7, 183–4,
    187–90, 193, 204, 207–8, 214
  King's Theatre, later Her Majesty's
    Theatre 20, 25–44, 47, 49, 50, 55,
    61–2, 64–5, 67, 70–2, 75–7, 79–80,
    84–92, 98, 103–4, 136, 138, 140,
    149, 157, 178–9, 182–4, 193
  Lyceum 55, 136–9, 155, 157
  Princess's Theatre 141, 146
  Theatre Royal, Drury Lane 28,
    32–4, 39, 138, 193
Lucca, Pauline 165, 172–3, 175–6,
  178, 184, 188–9, 197, 205–7
Lumley, Benjamin 44, 56, 61, 64,
  65–7, 72, 73, 75–80, 88, 114, 136,
  138, 140

Madrid
  Teatro Oriente 149
  Teatro Real 174
Malibran, Maria 26–30, 32, 33, 36, 37,
  41, 58, 72, 93
Mapleson, J. H. 155, 178–9, 181–8,
  193, 196, 204, 205–6
Maralti, Enrico 112
Maretzek, Max 78
Marini, Ignazio 99, 101, 103
Mario, Giovanni see De Candia,
  Giovanni Matteo
Marliani, Count Marco Aurelio 24–6,
  35, 101
  Il bravo 26
  Il degonda 35, 37
Mary Adelaide, Princess (later Duchess
  of Teck) 122–3, 126, 128–30, 139,
  140, 143, 208–9, 212
Mascagni, Pietro
  Cavalleria rusticana 178
Mayr, Simon
  Medea 35
Mazzini, Giuseppe 12, 14, 114, 146, 187
Melcy, Vicomte Gérard de 31, 32,
  37–9, 42, 45, 55, 58, 65, 72, 102,
  135, 181
Mendelssohn, Felix
  Athalie 102

Elijah 107
Piano Concerto in G minor 127
Mercadante, Saverio 55
  Andronico 32, 33
  I briganti 31, 32
  Il giuramento 73, 148
  La Vestale 54
Méric, Mlle de 109, 110, 150
Méric-Lalande, Henriette 109
Meyerbeer, Giacomo 11, 16–19, 86–7,
  99, 111, 113, 137, 143
  Il crociato in Egitto 17, 76
  Dinorah, ou le Pardon de Ploërmel 15
  L'Étoile du nord 173
  Les Huguenots (*Gli ugonotti*) (*Les
    Guelfes et les Gibelins*) 16, 46, 47,
    56, 72, 85, 87, 99–101, 103, 105,
    109, 111–3, 115, 117–8, 121–2,
    124, 126, 128, 130, 141, 143–5, 149,
    151, 154–5, 157, 162–3, 165, 175,
    178, 185, 187, 203, 206–8, 214
  Le Prophète (*Il profeta*) (*Le Siège de
    Gand*) 87, 100, 103, 105–6,
    111–3, 115–6, 118, 122, 175, 184,
    199, 214
  Robert le diable 11, 17–19, 42, 49,
    86–7, 89, 110–1, 112, 115, 191
Milan
  Teatro alla Scala 23–5, 56, 88
  Teatro Carcano 24
Miolan-Carvalho, Marie 172–3, 208
Mirate, Raffaele 46
Moltini, Adelaide 56
Mongini, Pietro 183
Monnier, Étienne 69
Moriani, Napoleone 70–1, 73, 79
Mozart, Wolfgang Amadeus 45, 83–6
  Così fan tutte 56, 73, 85
  Don Giovanni 26, 27, 33, 36, 43, 62,
    72, 75, 79, 85, 88, 90–1, 95, 97–8,
    103, 106, 124–6, 134, 137–8, 141,
    144–8, 151–2, 156, 158, 178–9,
    182, 183, 185, 187–9, 206, 207
  Idomeneo 56
  Laudate Dominum 30
  Le nozze di Figaro 37, 39, 40, 43, 49,
    55, 85, 98
  Die Zauberflöte (*Il flauto magico*) 85,
    115, 118

Nantier-Didiée, Constance 145, 150
Naudin, Emilio 164, 169–71, 173,
  176, 204–5

Neri-Baraldi, Pietro 160
New York
 Academy of Music 133
 Castle Garden 131–3
 Metropolitan Theatre 134
Ney, Jenny 136
Nilsson, Christine 212
Nourrit, Adolphe 11, 18–9, 47, 99,
 102, 144

Ormsby, George Frederick 42, 140–1,
 196–7, 200–1
Ouida (Louise de la Ramée) 209

Pacini, Giovanni 29, 34, 96
 Amazila 110
 Il corsaro 25
 La fidanzata corsa 80
Paisiello, Giovanni
 Il barbiere di Siviglia 56
Palermo
 Real Teatro Carolino 23
Paris
 Opéra (L'Académie Royale de
 Musique) 11, 17, 18, 20, 40,
 42–3, 54–7, 97, 99, 103, 105, 110,
 162
 Opéra-Comique 150
 Théâtre-Italien 20, 23, 25–6, 28, 31,
 35, 36, 40, 42–3, 47, 53–61, 64–5,
 67, 69–70, 74–5, 80, 82–3, 87,
 95–6, 108, 114, 124, 125, 135–6,
 138, 142, 147, 150–1, 156, 158, 163,
 167, 171
 Théâtre-Lyrique 172, 188
 Tuileries 82
Pasta, Giuditta 24–6, 30–1, 35–6, 72,
 123, 154
Patti, Adelina 154, 156, 160, 163–4,
 167, 169, 173–6, 178, 184, 188–91,
 193, 204, 206–8
Patti, Carlotta 164, 210
Pedrazzi, Francesco 23
Penco, Rosa 135, 148, 151, 156
Persiani, Giuseppe 79, 94
 Il fantasma 64–5
 Irene 29
Piccolomini, Marietta 138, 163
Pillet, Léon 46
Pinsuti, Ciro
 'O donna amata' 162, 210

Poniatowski, Prince Josef 80–1
 Don Desiderio 142, 147
Pyne, Louisa 140

Reeves, Sims 129, 212
Ricci, Federico
 Corrado d'Altamura 65–6
Robert, Édouard 26, 36, 42
Rode, J.P.J.
 Variations on an Air 52
Roger, Gustave 100, 105–6
Romani, Felice 69
Ronconi, Giorgio 56–7, 64–5, 74, 80,
 82–3, 92, 113–5, 117–8, 121–2,
 126, 128, 137, 144–6, 148, 161, 164,
 184
Roppa, Giacomo 80
Rosa, Lina 55
Rosenthal, Harold 187
Rossini, Giacomo 15, 26, 30, 32, 34,
 36, 83–7, 95–6, 142, 194
 L'assedio di Corinto 28–9, 33
 Il barbiere di Siviglia 23, 26, 28, 33–4,
 49, 52, 54, 61–2, 65, 70, 71, 74, 95,
 117–8, 121, 124–6, 133, 135–6,
 138, 142, 145, 147, 150–1, 154, 158,
 160, 163–4, 167, 175, 188, 204–5,
 207
 Bianca e Faliero 22
 La Cenerentola 63–4, 97, 101, 119,
 124
 Le Comte Ory 19–20, 42, 57
 La donna del lago 26, 28–30, 43, 45,
 85, 93, 95–6, 110, 125
 La gazza ladra 26–7, 30–1, 33–4, 62,
 93, 96, 101, 150, 164–5
 Guillaume Tell 29, 46–7, 54, 129
 L'Italiana in Algeri 19, 62, 111
 Matilda di Shabran 37–8
 Mosé (Pietro l'eremita) (Zora) 49, 52,
 76, 127, 159
 Otello 24, 26–7, 33, 35, 37–8, 40–1,
 43–4, 47–8, 60–1, 65–6, 69, 74, 96,
 122, 125–6, 129, 142, 146,
 149
 Riccardo e Zoraide 23
 Semiramide 24, 26, 47–8, 53, 58, 65,
 69, 71, 77, 79–80, 88–9, 98, 103,
 108, 133–4, 136, 141, 150, 154, 174,
 178, 212
 Stabat Mater 54, 57, 97, 125, 127,
 137, 194
 Tancredi 23, 96, 212

Rossini, Giacomo – *cont.*
  Torvaldo e Dorliska 23
  Zelmira 23
Rubini, Giovanni 26–9, 31, 34–5,
  37–8, 40, 43–7, 49–50, 53, 56–7,
  60, 62–4, 68, 73, 76–8, 87, 89, 97,
  104, 108–10, 116, 120–1

Salvi, Lorenzo 102
St Petersburg
  Italian Opera at Bolshoi
    Theatre 108–9, 114–9
Sand, George 15, 48, 96
Santley, (Sir) Charles 146, 178–80,
  185–6, 212
Schiller, Friedrich von
  Don Carlos 66
  Die Räuber 31
Schira, Francesco 49
Schubert, Franz 71
  'Ave Maria' 71
  'Lob der Thränen'
    ('La douce peine') 117
Scribe, Eugène 18, 86, 109
Severini, Carlo 26, 36
Shaw, Mrs Alfred 33
Sheridan, Richard B.
  The School for Scandal 71
Smith, E. T. 138
Somerset, Lady Geraldine 139–40,
  144, 146, 155, 161, 173, 183–4,
  196–202, 208–10
Sontag, Henriette 93
Stagno, Roberto 178, 181, 182
Staudigl, Joseph 57, 72
Stephan, Petit 75
Strakosch, Maurice 168–9, 184,
  210
Strepponi, Feliciano
  Ulla di Bassora 24
Strauss, Johann 152
Sullivan, Arthur
  'I would I were a King' 212
Sutherland Edwards, H. 191

Tacchinardi-Persiani, Fanny 36–8,
  40–1, 43, 45–7, 49, 53, 55–6,
  58–9, 62, 64–6, 68, 70, 72, 76, 79,
  80, 82–3, 89–90, 95, 97–8,
  104
Tadolini, Eugenia 98
Tadolini, Giovanni 96

Tagliafico, Joseph 82, 99, 101, 104,
  127, 136
Taglioni, Paolo 38, 45
Taglioni, Marie 18, 37–8, 73, 75
Tamberlik, Enrico 110–1, 115, 122,
  128–9, 136–7, 144, 146, 155–7,
  164, 172, 174
Tamburini, Antonio 26–9, 31, 33–4,
  37, 39–41, 43–5, 47–9, 52–6, 58–9,
  61–3, 74, 76, 80, 88–90, 93, 97–9,
  101, 104, 113, 125–6, 135, 142, 145,
  161
Tasca, Signor 187
Tietjens, Therese 155–6, 178–9,
  181–3, 185–7, 206
Trebelli, Zélia 212

Vaccai, Nicola
  Giulietta e Romeo 23
Venice
  Teatro la Fenice 23
Vatel, Monsieur 74
Vera, Mdlle 101
Verdi, Giuseppe 24, 75, 80–2, 84–7,
  91–3
  Un ballo in maschera 151, 155, 158,
    160, 163, 172, 179, 184–5, 187–9,
    202, 204, 206–7
  I due Foscari 80–2, 91–3, 122
  Ernani (Il proscritto) 71, 74, 76, 78,
    128, 149
  I Lombardi alla prima crociata 76,
    78–9, 81
  Macbeth 88, 147–8
  I masnadieri 31, 86, 91–2
  Nabucco (Nino) 56, 74–6, 78–9
  Otello 84
  Rigoletto 84, 120, 122, 125–6, 137–9,
    141, 145, 147–8, 151, 158, 160, 163,
    174, 178–9, 185, 207–8
  La traviata 84, 121, 136, 138–9, 141,
    149, 163, 169, 183
  Il trovatore 76, 84, 87, 135–9, 141–2,
    147, 149, 151, 158, 163–4, 167, 174,
    178–9, 182, 184–5, 187, 190,
    207–8
Véron, Dr 18
Viardot, Louis 42
Viardot-Garcia, Pauline 41–3, 47–9,
  58, 72, 76, 87, 88, 97–100, 103, 105,
  111–3, 115, 118–9, 127–9, 147–8,
  185

Victoria, Princess (later Queen) 27,
29–33, 35, 37, 39, 41–2, 44–5,
47–9, 56–7, 62, 70–3, 88–91, 98–9,
102, 111, 113, 115, 117–8, 122, 127,
138, 160, 214
Vieuxtemps, Jules J. E. 49, 197
von Weyrauch, Heinrich
'Adieu' 208

Wachtel, Theodor 161
Weber, Carl Maria von
Der Freischütz 86, 102, 183
Oberon 127
White, Richard Grant 132–3
Woodford, John 146, 212

Zelger, Signor 112